P9-ASN-695

GIL VICENTE

Farces and Festival Plays

Gil Vicente
Farces and Festival Plays

Auto da Índia

Quem Tem Farelos?

Frágua de Amor

Cortes de Júpiter

O Triunfo do Inverno

Edited by

THOMAS R. HART

UNIVERSITY OF OREGON
EUGENE, OREGON

Preface

Perhaps no other European writer—certainly none in Hispanic literature—has suffered so much as Gil Vicente from our practice of dividing up the academic study of literature along national and linguistic lines. Because three-quarters of his plays are wholly or partly in Portuguese, it is hard to find a place for him in our classes in Spanish literature. Though we often ask our students to read one of his Castilian plays—the *Auto de la Sibila Cassandra,* perhaps, or the *Tragicomedia de Don Duardos*—we seldom venture to suggest that they also read a bilingual work like the delightful farce *Quem Tem Farelos?* or the moving *Comédia de Rubena.* Yet the linguistic difficulties are not insuperable. Learning to read a classical Portuguese text is a very different task from learning to speak Portuguese. More than a dozen years of classroom experience have convinced me that English-speaking students of Spanish can read and enjoy at least some of Vicente's Portuguese and bilingual plays without previous training in Portuguese.

We do both Vicente and ourselves a grave disservice if we read only his Castilian works. We cut ourselves off from the court entertainments, like the *Cortes de Júpiter* and the *Triunfo do Inverno,* which belong to a rich international tradition, with no other real counterpart in the Hispanic literature of the first half of the sixteenth century. Worse still, we cut ourselves off from Vicente's farces, perhaps his most enduring contribution to the Hispanic theater. Vicente is a far more solemn figure when he writes in Castilian than when he writes in Portuguese, perhaps in part, as I have suggested elsewhere, because he did not feel at ease with rustic and popular Spanish. The present edition aims to provide reliable texts of these two types of plays, chosen both for their intrinsic interest as works of literature and as representative examples of Vicente's achievements as a writer of farces and of court entertainments; with one exception, I have selected only plays which are not accessible in satisfactory modern editions.[1]

I have transcribed the texts from the facsimile edition of the *Copilaçam* of 1562 published by the Biblioteca Nacional in Lisbon in 1928. A facsimile is, however, not a wholly satisfactory basis for such work since it necessarily reproduces, not the original edition, but only one particular copy of it, or an arbitrary combination of several copies. The reasons have been succinctly set forth by Professor Fredson Bowers: "In early books, well into the eighteenth century in some cases, special proofs were not usually pulled for authorial review and correction before printing. Instead, after only cursory examination the type-pages would be placed on the press and printing started. An early pull would usually be read by some printing-house functionary, who would then stop the press for corrections. As a result, the text of each sheet in early books may exist in two or more states that reflect different stages of the proofreading."[2] In fact, as Professor Stephen Reckert has recently shown, no two of the half-dozen surviving copies of the *Copilaçam* of 1562 are exactly alike; the facsimile of 1928 is not a faithful reproduction of any one of them.[3] I have incorporated Professor Reckert's corrections to the text of the facsimile in my transcription wherever they affect the words of the text;

[1] The exception is Ernesto de Campos de Andrada's edition of *Quem Tem Farelos?*

[2] "Textual Criticism," p. 33.

[3] "El verdadero texto de la *Copilaçam* vicentina de 1562."

most of them, however, deal with differences in punctuation and, therefore, do not directly affect my work, since, for reasons to be set forth in a moment, I have chosen to modernize the punctuation throughout.

We can, then, compensate for the deficiencies of the facsimile; but we can do nothing about those of the *Copilaçam* itself. They are too well known to need repeating here, thanks in large measure to the painstaking studies of I. S. Révah; for a brief summary of the problems, see my edition of Vicente's *Obras dramáticas castellanas,* pp. xlviii-l. We can be quite certain that the *Copilaçam* does not offer us the text of our five plays as Vicente wrote it, but there is very little we can do to correct it. None of our plays appeared in a printed edition during Vicente's lifetime, nor, indeed, so far as we know, at any time before the publication of the *Copilaçam;* no manuscript versions of any of them are known to exist.[4] Even the correction of mistakes in scansion or rhyming which we might undertake with confidence in dealing with other sixteenth-century writers is largely forbidden to us by the special qualities of Vicente's versification and, in particular, by his use of both Castilian and Portuguese in the same play, often, indeed, within the limits of a single line of verse.[5] My aim has been the modest one of providing a readable text of the plays; I make no claim

[4] The text of these plays in the *Copilaçam* of 1586 is simply a reprinting of that of '1562,' not, as in the case of the *Tragicomedia de Don Duardos,* one which incorporates passages from a different version of the text, which may be the work of Vicente himself. The few differences between the texts of our five plays in '1562' and '1586' are conveniently set forth by Braamcamp Freire, pp. 446-449. Most of the changes, including the omission of two fairly extensive passages in the *Frágua de Amor,* may safely be attributed to the censorship imposed by the Inquisition.

[5] Paul Teyssier declares that "une édition critique de Gil Vicente ne devra donc jamais essayer de restituer une forme ou un mot . . . sous le seul prétexte que la rime l'exige" (*La Langue de Gil Vicente,* p. 323). Exactly the same thing might be said of emendations based on metrical irregularities; mistakes in scansion, moreover, can often be "corrected" in more than one way. See Celso Cunha, "Regularidade e irregularidade na versificação do primeiro *Auto das Barcas.*"

that my text reproduces the plays precisely in the form in which they left Vicente's hands.

Both the punctuation and the spelling of the *Copilaçam* are, in general, far more likely to reflect the preferences of the printer, or perhaps those of Vicente's son Luís, who prepared the text for publication, than those of the playwright himself.[6] I have felt free to modernize completely the punctuation of my texts, the more so as the norms of sixteenth-century punctuation were quite different from our own; to keep the old punctuation, even if it were demonstrably Vicente's, would cause many passages to become misleading, and sometimes even unintelligible, to a modern reader.[7] I have been unwilling, however, to modernize spelling in the same way. The juxtaposition of Spanish and Portuguese in Vicente's plays, even the occasional insertion of a word in one language in a line written in the other, will, I think, seem much more natural to the modern reader if the old spelling is retained.

I have, nevertheless, partially modernized the spelling of the texts along the lines established in my edition of Vicente's Castilian plays. I have retained the spellings used in the *Copilaçam,* except where it seemed evident that variations in spelling within the *Copilaçam* itself, or differences between the forms found there and those of the modern languages, are purely graphic variants which do not reflect corresponding differences in pronunciation. I have, however, retained the spelling *sam* for the first singular, present indicative of *ser* to distinguish it from the third plural, here transcribed as *são,* and have added a written accent to Spanish *al,* "something else," to distinguish it from the preposition *al.* Abbreviations have been silently expanded.

Additions to the text are given in brackets. Wherever the text has been changed, the reading found in the *Copilaçam* of 1562 is given in the tex-

---

[6] I say "in general" because Paul Teyssier has shown that popular and dialectal forms in Vicente's text are usually respected in the *Copilaçam;* see his discussion of this point, pp. 13-17.

[7] See James O. Crosby's preface to his edition of Quevedo's *Política de Dios,* pp. 18-23.

tual notes, preceded by a bracket. If the emendation calls for comment, it is discussed in the explanatory notes. The folio numbers in the right-hand margin of the text are those of the *Copilaçam* of 1562.

In annotating the plays, I have tried to clarify linguistic points which cannot be solved satisfactorily with the aid of a good modern dictionary and to provide a certain minimum of historical information. The historical notes have been limited to points which seemed essential to a proper understanding of the texts as literature; many persons and places mentioned in the plays have been identified only summarily, or even left without any annotation whatever. The linguistic notes include all Spanish words not found, or found only with a different meaning, in E. B. Williams's Spanish-English dictionary; for Portuguese words, those not found in James L. Taylor's Portuguese-English dictionary. The notes are not intended primarily as aids to the study of Hispanic dialectology or of historical grammar: I have not attempted to call attention to all the differences between Vicente's usage and that of modern Spanish or Portuguese. The works cited as authority for linguistic features have, for the most part, deliberately been limited to a few standard works, which should be familiar to every student of Vicente's theater. I hope my notes will provide a solid basis for assessing the stylistic values of Vicente's text. I have attempted, whenever possible, to distinguish between words which in Vicente's day were felt to have a dialectal or popular flavor and those which belonged to the usual literary language of the period. I have tried also to warn students whose primary interest is in Portuguese against the common error of assuming that, wherever Vicente's Spanish differs from modern Castilian usage and coincides with that of modern Portuguese, the explanation is to be found in his imperfect command of Spanish.

References to plays of Vicente not included in this volume and cited without an editor's name are to my own edition of Vicente's *Obras dramáticas castellanas* in the *Clásicos castellanos.* Books and articles cited in the notes are referred to only by the name of the author; if there is more than one work by the same writer, a short title is added; full titles of works cited may be found in the bibliography which begins on page 219.

A Fulbright research grant made it possible for me to spend the academic year 1966-67 in Madrid. I wish to express my gratitude to Professors Perry J. Powers, of the University of Oregon, Edward M. Wilson of Emmanuel College, Cambridge, and Arthur L.-F. Askins, of the University of California at Berkeley, all of whom read an earlier draft of much of the book and made a number of useful suggestions; to Sr. Eugenio Asensio, of Lisbon, for many kindnesses over a period of more than a dozen years; and to Mrs. Nancy Hayward, who typed the manuscript with exemplary efficiency and good humor.

Contents

5 Preface

Introduction

15 The Farces

35 The Festival Plays

64 Auto da Índia

87 Quem Tem Farelos?

111 Frágua de Amor

141 Cortes de Júpiter

167 O Triunfo do Inverno

217 Textual Notes

219 Bibliography

229 Index to the Notes

Introduction

The Farces

Gil Vicente's religious plays owe little, if anything, to the liturgical theater of the Middle Ages. His immediate sources are the shepherds' plays of the Salamancan dramatists Juan del Encina and Lucas Fernández. With Vicente's secular plays, however, we have no such clearly defined point of departure. I. S. Révah has suggested that when Vicente created the literary farce in Portugal, he could build upon the medieval tradition of *trebelhos, jogos* and *momos,* though he is careful to add that "si Gil Vicente n'a pas créé *ex nihilo* la farce portugaise, il lui a fait franchir la distance énorme qui va de l'improvisation plus ou moins spontanée à la création littéraire."[1] There are other possible antecedents in some little sketches by Anrique da Mota included in the *Cancioneiro geral* compiled by Vicente's friend Garcia de Resende, but we do not know whether Mota intended them to be acted before an audience; Eugenio Asensio has recently suggested that they may well be later than Vicente's earliest plays and indebted to them.[2]

The *Copilaçam* of 1562, which is our only source for almost all Vicente's plays, lists twelve works

[1] "Gil Vicente fondateur du théâtre portugais?," p. 172. I should add that the *momos* have more in common with Vicente's festival plays than with his farces.
[2] "Inés de Castro," pp. 347-349.

among the farces.[3] Of these twelve, two, the *Auto das fadas* and the *Auto das ciganas,* might, as Laurence Keates has suggested, more appropriately be called "court games."[4] Another, the *Auto da Fama,* I should place among the festival plays. I should do the same with the *Auto da Lusitânia.* Only the first scene, which presents a Jewish tailor and his family, really deserves to be called farcical; the rest is a play within a play, introduced as a work by Gil Vicente which might serve the Jewish community of Lisbon as a model for its celebration of the birth of John III's son, Manuel. It illustrates perfectly Révah's assertion that after 1521 Vicente's farces become more and more indistinguishable from his comedies, since both may involve allegorical elements.[5]

The fourfold division of Vicente's plays—*obras de devaçam, comédias, tragicomédias,* and *farsas*—in the *Copilaçam* was almost certainly not made by the playwright himself but by his son Luís Vicente, who prepared the text for publication nearly a quarter of a century after his father's death. The classification adopted in the *Copilaçam* does not reflect the very broad meaning of the term *farsa* usual in the early sixteenth century, when it was the ordinary word for any kind of play, secular or religious, and was by no means limited to comic works.[6] Eight of the twelve plays classed as *farsas* in the *Copilaçam* would surely qualify as farces in the modern sense of the word, "a light dramatic composition of satirical or humorous cast." To them we should need to add one other work, the *Romagem de Agravados,* which in the *Copilaçam* is placed among the tragicomedies.

Students of Vicente's theater have spent far too much time and energy on classifying his works.

---

[3] The *Auto dos Físicos,* though followed in the text by the words "Fim do quarto livro das farsas" (f. 249 v.), is omitted from the table of contents.

[4] *The Court Theatre of Gil Vicente,* p. 126.

[5] I. S. Révah, "La 'comédia' dans l'œuvre de Gil Vicente," p. 32.

[6] See N. D. Shergold, *A History of the Spanish Stage,* pp. 30-31. Vicente himself seems to use the word in this more general sense in *O Triunfo do Inverno* (line 69), but the precise meaning of the passage is not clear.

Classification is nevertheless a useful tool for literary analysis; indeed, E. D. Hirsch, Jr., has argued persuasively that every critical assertion about a literary work presupposes assigning it to a group of other, more or less similar works.[7] There may be some point in trying to divide Vicente's plays into a series of sub-groups, though our classification might never have occurred to the playwright himself and might have seemed absurd or even incomprehensible to him. I propose that we divide our nine farces into two groups.

One is made up of plays which resemble nothing so much as a series of comic vaudeville turns: *O Juiz da Beira, A Farsa dos Almocreves, O Clérigo da Beira, Romagem de Agravados, Auto dos Físicos.* In these plays we find a series of individual scenes linked by the presence of a single character who appears in all of them, like Pero Marques in *O Juiz da Beira* or Frei Paço in *Romagem de Agravados.* This central figure is sometimes assigned the rather passive role of a master of ceremonies. This is certainly true of Frei Paço and almost as true of Pero Marques; the same thing might be said of Winter in the *Triunfo do Inverno,* or of the devil in the *Auto das Barcas,* which Eugenio Asensio has aptly characterized as "el tipo de revista en que todo cabe."[8] Such plays may be seen as a kind of survey, a passing in review of the various types that made up the society of the period, a literary form much favored by the poets of the *cancioneiros.*[9] The social types are generally treated as comic figures; some of them appear in a number of different plays, often strikingly different in tone from one another. Thus, the proud though impoverished *fidalgo* of the *Farsa dos Almocreves* appears also in *Quem Tem Farelos?* and in the *Auto da Barca do Inferno*; the *alcouviteira* in the latter, and in *O Juiz da Beira, O Velho da Horta,* and the *Comédia de Rubena*; the *velho enamorado* in both the last two plays; and the old woman who seeks a

---

[7] *Validity in Interpretation,* chap. iii.
[8] "Las fuentes de las *Barcas,*" p. 216.
[9] See Pierre Le Gentil, *La poésie lyrique espagnole et portugaise à la fin du moyen âge,* I, 411-419.

young husband in *O Triunfo do Inverno* and in the *Auto da Festa.*

The five plays in our first group are thus not set off from the rest of Vicente's theater either by their dramatic structure or by the sort of characters they present. The other four plays—*Auto da Índia, O Velho da Horta, Quem Tem Farelos?,* and *Auto de Inês Pereira*—do share some common features that distinguish them both from the satirical reviews we have just been discussing and from Vicente's other plays. They offer a more nearly complete dramatic action than the plays in our first group. In the *Romagem de Agravados,* for example, one could change the order in which the characters appear without making other changes in the play.[10] One could not do so in any of the plays in the second group. Here the characters are drawn from the lower classes and the bourgeoisie, with an impoverished nobleman occasionally thrown in for good measure; the plot has to do with a relationship between a man and a woman which is a kind of parody of the fashionable code of courtly love. The lover's interest in his lady may be frankly sensual, as in *O Velho da Horta,* or frankly economic, as in the *Auto de Inês Pereira,* or both, as in *Quem Tem Farelos?*

The *Auto da Índia* is generally considered Vicente's first secular play and the first to be written partly in Portuguese. (Of its 514 lines, only 138, those assigned to the Castilian, Juan de Zamora, are in Spanish.) The *Copilaçam* assigns it to the year 1509, and this date has been accepted by Braamcamp Freire and by Révah.[11] The play may be seen as a kind of comic *Odyssey,* with a stupid

[10] This does not, of course, mean that the order is without dramatic significance, just as the separate numbers that make up a circus or music-hall program may be arranged more effectively in one order than in another. See William Empson, *Some Versions of Pastoral* (Norfolk, Conn., 1960), p. 25.

[11] Anselmo Braamcamp Freire, *Gil Vicente,* p. 81; I. S. Révah, "Gil Vicente fondateur du théâtre portugais?," pp. 175-176.

Odysseus and a clever though unfaithful Penelope. Its most immediately striking feature is its chaotic time scheme, which goes far beyond disregard for unity of time, never much respected in Vicente's theater. Not only do we not know how much time is supposed to elapse between the several scenes: we are given wholly incompatible statements about the matter. It is fair to say that most of the action of the play takes place in a single night, and equally fair to say that the beginning and end of that night are separated by the passage of two years.[12]

One might argue that the discrepancy is intentional and that it represents a dramatic foreshortening of a whole series of similar adventures with which the *ama* has amused herself during her husband's absence. This argument is not, however, very convincing; it is more likely that Vicente was unaware of the inconsistencies in his text, or confident that his audience would not notice them. One might also argue that his carelessness about establishing the time scheme of the play comes from his lack of experience in writing for the theater; if we accept the revised chronology of his works proposed by Révah, the *Auto da Índia* would be preceded only by the *Auto de la visitación* and the *Auto de San Martín,* surely the two simplest of his plays.[13] But this argument is not much more convincing than the first. In 1509, Vicente was probably in his forties; even his earliest plays can hardly be considered juvenilia.

The *Auto da Índia* reveals both a wonderful mastery of language and a sure feeling for theatrical effect. One notes, for example, the skillful charac-

[12] When the Castilian explains his visit by saying to the *ama* "Supe que vuesso marido/ era ido," she replies "Ant'ontem se foi" (lines 127-128). He accepts her invitation to return that same night; on his departure after his second visit, her servant remarks, in an aside, "Quantas artes quantas manhas,/ que sabe fazer minha ama!/ Um na rua, outro na cama!" (353-355); the aside is overheard by the *ama* who demands "Que falas? Que t'arreganhas?". The maid conceals her impertinence by replying "Ando dizendo entre mi/ que agora vai em dous anos/ que eu fui lavar os panos/ . . . / e logo partiu a armada" (lines 356-361).

[13] I. S. Révah, *Dicionário das literaturas,* p. 865.

terization of the Castilian, from the oratorical flair of his first line, "¡Paz sea 'n esta posada!," to his boastfulness and quickness to take offense when the *ama's* responses show that she is unwilling to take him as seriously as he takes himself. One notes, too, the way in which the *rima al mezzo* at the end of his first long speech in praise of the *ama* marks a transition from the conceits of courtly love to the more earthy concerns which have prompted his visit (lines 101-128). The dialogue is full of implicit stage directions, which are perhaps to be interpreted less as a sign of Vicente's desire to help the reader understand his work than as a measure of the vividness with which he imagined the scenes as performed by actors on a stage; he seems to have given little thought to publishing his plays, and it is unlikely that he contemplated their being performed under the direction of anyone else. An example might be the *ama's* sudden reproach to her servant, "Moça, tu que estás olhando?" (line 424), which shows us the latter's reaction to the unexpected reunion of her master and mistress, or, better still, Juan de Zamora's "Reís de lo que yo hablo?" (line 116,) which reveals at once the way in which the *ama* receives his attentions, his own exaggerated pride, and, in the following lines, his readiness to hang new rhetorical inventions on the peg which she offers him.

Vicente's skill in building up the character of Juan de Zamora may be partly due to the fact that he is presenting an established character type, that of the *miles gloriosus*. Juan, however, is less closely akin to the braggart soldier of Roman comedy than to Centurio in *La Celestina*. Like Centurio, and unlike the traditional *miles gloriosus*, Juan de Zamora is neither a soldier nor rich. We may suppose that he is shabbily dressed, for he assures Constança that

> aunque tal capa me veis,
> tengo más que pensaréis
> *(lines 194-195)*

The soldier of Roman comedy believes himself to be irresistible to women, while Centurio presents himself as a courtly lover, ready to obey any command from his lady. So does Juan de Zamora, though his anger at Constança breaks out several times and he finally leaves in a huff—understandably, since he has been kept waiting outside all night while she entertains his rival, the *escudeiro* Lemos. We have already noted Juan's delight in language; here, too, he is closer to Centurio than to the soldiers of Plautus and Terence, much less given to rhetorical exuberance than are the slaves and spongers who surround them.[14]

From Rojas's *tragicomedia,* too, Vicente may have learned to use the half-overheard aside which he exploits so brilliantly for comic effect in the *Auto da Índia* and in several later plays, notably the *Comédia de Rubena.*[15] The aside itself is, of course, a stock device in many kinds of literature; it is frequent in Roman comedy, though there seems no good reason to suppose that Vicente was familiar with the plays of Plautus and Terence nor, for that matter, with the humanistic comedy of the Renaissance, which also makes elaborate use of the aside. The special contribution of the *Celestina* is the frequency with which an aside is overheard by another character who fails to catch all the words and asks, or orders, that it be repeated to him; the repetition, while retaining some or most of the words originally spoken, is altered to make it more palatable to the person who has overheard it. Such asides are naturally most often assigned to servants or others who have reasons for speaking circumspectly in the presence of their betters. So used, the aside becomes at once a measure of the speaker's cleverness in finding a way to keep at least a part of the letter of his speech while transforming its spirit—an essential point, since he cannot be sure how much of it has been overheard—and of his listener's stupidity or willful-

---

[14] My discussion of the differences between Centurio and the *miles gloriosus* of Roman comedy is based on María Rosa Lida de Malkiel, *Estudios de literatura española y comparada,* pp. 176-177.

[15] In *Rubena,* however, the device is by no means limited to comedy, and, for just that reason, is more nearly comparable to its use in the *Celestina;* cf. lines 134-137, 158-160, 188-199 (though just where the last passage begins is not clear).

ness in accepting the message in its revised form.[16] This is exactly the way in which Vicente often uses it. Asides are rarely indicated in the *Copilaçam,* but the dialogue often makes clear which lines are to be spoken in this way.[17] In the following passage from the *Auto da Índia,* it is evident that the servant's lines must be spoken as asides, though the text does not mark them as such:

AMA Porque nao matas o fogo?
MOÇA Raivar, que este é outro jogo. [*Aparte*]
AMA Perra, cadela, tinhosa,
que rosmeas, aleivosa?
MOÇA Digo que o matarei logo.
(lines 406-410)

Exactly the same thing is found in an earlier exchange between Constança and her servant (lines 352-360).

I should not wish to lay too much stress on the bookishness of Vicente's sources. The boastful Castilian was not simply a literary type, but also, as we know from the reports of contemporary travelers, a human reality.[18] Andrea Navagero, who served as Venetian ambassador to Spain in 1525, says of the *caballeros* of Toledo that "pocos son los de gran renta, pero la suplen con la soberbia, o, como dicen, con la fantasía de la que abundan tanto que si sus facultades y medios igualaran con ella no bastaría todo el mundo contra ellos."[19] The unfaithful wife, too, is a familiar figure in folk-literature, but Vicente has placed the *ama* of the *Auto da Índia* in a very definite historical situation. The play has been considered an attack on the moral and social prob-

---

[16] See Marcel Bataillon, *"La Célestine" selon Fernando de Rojas,* pp. 83-92; María Rosa Lida de Malkiel, *La originalidad artística de "La Celestina,"* pp. 136-148.

[17] Two speeches in *Quem Tem Farelos?* are marked *passo* in the margin after the name of the character who speaks them (lines 197 and 268-269); there are, however, many more asides in the play.

[18] The same point has been made by Sra. Lida de Malkiel with respect to Rojas's Centurio: "El modelo de Centurio no se halla en la literatura latina sino en la realidad española de los tiempos del autor." *Estudios,* p. 184.

[19] Trans. Antonio María Fabié, quoted by F. Soldevila, *Historia de España,* III, 194.

lems precipitated by the voyages to India, a kind of preview of the speech of the Velho do Restelo in the *Lusiads* for whom the Portuguese adventures in the East were a "fonte de desamparos e adultérios" (IV,96).[20] To see the play in this way suggests that Vicente's treatment of his protagonist foreshadows that nineteenth-century realism so illuminatingly studied by Erich Auerbach, which represents man as "embedded in a total reality, political, social, and economic, which is concrete and constantly evolving."[21] Auerbach himself, however, would certainly not have seen Vicente's little play as a realistic work. Though it is easy to see how Constança's situation might have been presented problematically and even tragically, Vicente does not treat it in this way. The *Auto da Índia* is, after all, a farce and, as such, excluded from the class of works Auerbach would call realistic; it is rather an example of "the classical rule of distinct levels of style, which declared that everyday practical reality could find a place in literature only within the frame of a low or intermediate kind of style, that is to say, as either grotesquely comic or pleasant, light, colorful, and elegant entertainment."[22]

Just how much Vicente knew of the classical theory of the separation of styles is a matter about which we may well be somewhat skeptical. It is, nevertheless, hard to think of any earlier work with which Vicente might have been familiar which presents a heroine like his Constança as anything other than a comic figure. And Constança herself is, I am sure, to be regarded as a farcical creation.[23] She has

---

[20] A. J. Saraiva, *História da Cultura em Portugal,* II, 316, declares that in the *Auto da Índia* "as consequências da expansão ultramarina são vistas pelo seu lado negativo: a desordem familiar a que dá lugar a ausência dos maridos."

[21] *Mimesis,* p. 463.

[22] *Ibid.,* p. 554. See also E. C. Riley, *Cervantes's Theory of the Novel,* pp. 131-145.

[23] The same thing may be said, I think, of Inês Pereira, whom some modern critics have seen as the victim both of an absurd conception of romantic love and of a society which refuses to take seriously a woman's desire to shape her own destiny. See my article, "La estructura dramática del *Auto de Inês Pereira.*"

been called "uma mulher infiel e hipócrita."[24] Unfaithful she certainly is; Vicente's choice of a name for her is surely not without significance, nor is it without significance that we should learn her name, not at the beginning of the play, but later, in line 237, when we are in a position to appreciate its ironic appropriateness.[25] But is she really hypocritical? Certainly she resents her husband's leaving her, and leaving her just at this moment, in May "quando o sangue novo atiça" (line 92). She is resolved not to waste her youth in waiting for his return:

> O certo é dar a prazer.
> Pera que e envelhecer,
> esperando polo vento?
> Quant'eu, por mui nécia sento
> a que o contrairo fizer.
> *(lines 86-90)*

There is, however, no reason to suppose that his leaving will make it more difficult for her to satisfy her sexual appetites; indeed, her subsequent adventures seem to prove just the opposite. We know, too, from her own statement, that she has been unfaithful to him even before his departure for the East:

> Hi, se vai ele a pescar
> mea légua polo mar,
> isto bem o sabes tu,
> quanto mais a Calecu!
> Quem ha tanto de esperar?
> *(lines 77-81)*

Is it not possible that, despite her unfaithfulness to him in the past, she is genuinely upset by his departure, feels herself abandoned by him, and is therefore ready to turn her anger on him, as she does in the conversation with her servant which begins the play? May it not be precisely her anger over her

---

[24] Leif Sletsjöe, *O elemento cénico em Gil Vicente,* p. 95. See also Calado Nunes's note to lines 431 ff., quoted by Marques Braga, V, 112.

[25] Teyssier, however, believes that Vicente's choice of the name Constança was motivated solely by his need of a rhyme for *lembrança* in the following line (*La Langue de Gil Vicente,* p. 430).

husband's leaving her which, paradoxically, makes her fear that he will not really go after all? Again, how genuine is her joy at seeing him again when he returns at the end of the play? We may suppose that her attitude does not really change quite so suddenly as she makes it appear. The change is so abrupt that it leaves her servant open-mouthed with astonishment: "Moça, tu que estás olhando?" (line 424). Constança's sudden *volte-face* is perhaps prompted by her husband's innocent confidence in her. He greets her with a hearty "Abraçai-me, minha prima," only to be rebuffed with "Jesu! Quão negro e tostado!/ Não vos quero, não vos quero!" (lines 419-421). Here the use of the word *tostado* may represent a hasty attempt on Constança's part to cover her inadvertent use of *negro,* which may mean both "black" and "wretched, despicable," and to insure that her husband will take it in a literal, though hyperbolic, sense; a slight pause before the words "e tostado" would be enough to make this point unmistakably clear.[26] She is fighting for time, not quite sure how to receive him since she is not sure how much, if anything, he knows about her conduct during his absence. She becomes more certain of her ground with the revelation of his serene (and, of course, misplaced) confidence in her: "E eu a vós si quero, porque espero/ serdes mulher de recado" (lines 422-423). From this point on, her account of her behavior during his absence gains momentum as she goes along. Ironically, her first statement—"E eu, oh, quanto chorei,/ quando a armada foi de cá!" (lines 431-432)—is perfectly true, though we know, as her husband does not, that her tears were caused by fear that he would not go after all. Her self-assurance grows steadily greater, helped on by his smug "Assi havia de ser" in line 471. Her eloquence is so great that we almost wonder whether she has come to believe her own story and begin to ask ourselves whether her jeal-

[26] Cf. Covarrubias, *Tesoro de la lengua castellana,* s.v. *negro*: "Es color infausta y triste, y como tal usamos desta palabra, diziendo Negra ventura, negra vida, etc." For additional examples of *negro* used in a figurative sense in Vicente's works, see Teyssier, p. 439.

ousy and subsequent self-pity in lines 484-492 are wholly feigned. Only now does she venture to ask whether he has come back richer than he left her (line 499), but whether she does so by calculation or by accident we can hardly say; perhaps she herself could not at that moment have said with certainty.

In the *Copilaçam* of 1562 the *Auto da Índia* ends with the words "Vam se a ver a Nao & fenece esta primeyra farsa" (f. 191 r. [an error for 198 r.]). The same phrase is used at the end of *Quem Tem Farelos?*: "E com isto se recolhem & fenece esta primeyra farsa (f. 194 r.). The date of the first performance of *Quem Tem Farelos?* is given as 1505, four years before that of the *Auto da Índia*: "Foy representada na muy nobre & sempre leal cidade de Lixboa, ao muyto excelente & nobre Rey dom Manoel, primeyro deste nome, nos paços da ribeyra. Era do Senhor, de M.D.V. Annos" (f. 191 r. [unnumbered]). Braamcamp Freire points out, however that in 1505 the Ribeira Palace was not yet in use; it was still incomplete when King Manuel finally began to reside there in April or May of 1511. The *Copilaçam* must, therefore, be in error about either the date or the place of the first performance, and possibly about both; its *rúbricas* are often demonstrably wrong on both counts. Braamcamp Freire suggests that Ordoño's scornful remark about his master's cowardice in avoiding military service (lines 107-108: "Quando allende fue el rebate,/ nunca él entró en navío") refers to the calling up of troops for the reconquest of Algiers, which had been seized by the King of Fez in October 1508; the play must have been performed shortly afterward, either in the same year or early in 1509.[27] His suggestion has not, however, won general acceptance; Óscar de Pratt has proposed 1515 as the date of the play's first performance, arguing that MDV in the *Copilaçam* is simply a printer's error for MDXV.[28] His proposal has been adopted by Révah, who points out that Luís Vicente, in pre-

[27] Braamcamp Freire, p. 158.

[28] *Ibid.*, p. 162.

paring the *rúbricas* of the *Copilaçam,* subtracts ten years from the date of the *Auto da Alma,* giving it as 1508 rather than 1518.[29]

Braamcamp Freire further supposes that the play was first presented in public performances at Lisbon rather than at court, since the *Copilaçam* tells us that the title was not given by the author but by the public: "Este nome da farsa seguinte, quem tem farelos, pos-lho o vulgo." The title is certainly odd; it is the only one of Vicente's more than forty plays which takes its name from a line spoken in the play itself, in this case the very first line of the text. Moreover, there are other cases in which the title given a play in the *Copilaçam* seems not to be the one originally chosen by the playwright; thus, the play listed in the table of contents as "Auto chamado da Mofina mendez" is referred to differently in the friar's mock-sermon which introduces the play: "A qual obra he chamada/ os mysterios da Virgem" (f. 21 r.). Again, the play identified in the *Copilaçam* as *A Farsa do Clérigo da Beira* is listed in the *Rol dos Livros Defesos* of 1551 as *O Auto de Pedreanes*; it is, however, by no means certain that the play really was given its title by *o povo.*[30] We do not know to what extent Vicente's plays were performed other than at court. We do know that some of them were published during his lifetime and that others were published in the years following his death but prior to the appearance of the *Copilaçam;* the titles of some of these *edições avulsas* may have been chosen by the printers and may reflect a tradition already established in public performances of the plays.

Carolina Michaëlis de Vasconcelos has suggested that the farces may have been written *para o povo,* that is, for performances before an audience very different from that which saw them performed at court, and further that Vicente's decision to seek a wider public was perhaps undertaken at the suggestion of the Queen Mother, Dona Leonor.[31] There is not much reason to accept either assumption.

[29] "Gil Vicente fondateur du théâtre portugais?," p. 175.
[30] Pratt, pp. 246-247.
[31] *Notas Vicentinas,* p. 477.

One might suppose that some of the recurrent figures in the farces—for example, the poor *escudeiro* who dreams of marrying a rich wife or of establishing himself at court—would have been far funnier to a courtly than to a popular audience.

Quem Tem Farelos? is, if anything, even slighter than the *Auto da Índia.* Its plot can be summed up by saying that a poor *escudeiro* serenades a girl only to be driven off by a torrent of abuse from her mother; the latter, in turn, is then treated to an equally scathing attack by her daughter. Nothing more. We may suppose that the *escudeiro* will serenade the girl and that she will be just as ready to listen to him, or that, at the very least, both he and she will repeat the scene with other partners. None of the characters comes so close to being a fully realized individual as the young wife Constança in the *Auto da Índia.* And yet I think one can argue that *Quem Tem Farelos?* is in some ways an even finer achievement than the earlier play.

Gil Vicente's talent has often been said to be lyric rather than dramatic. Some critics have attempted to account for his deficiencies as a playwright by insisting that the Portuguese temperament is ill-suited to dramatic expression, which calls less for introspection than for clear-headed observation and the ability to imagine oneself in someone else's place and to see things as he sees them; others have argued that Vicente, though he inherited a rich and varied tradition in lyric poetry, was obliged in writing for the theater to discover everything for himself. The second position, that of Dámaso Alonso in his sensitive study of "La poesía dramática en la *Tragicomedia de Don Duardos,*" is, I think, much closer to the truth, though I should add that Gil Vicente is a better playwright than he is generally credited with being.[32] Objections to the occasional "incoherence" or "lack of proportion" of his plots can often be met in the same way that we have learned, thanks to the work of some British Hispanists, most notably E. M. Wilson and A. A. Parker, to meet the charge that the sub-plots of many Span-

[32] Gil Vicente, *Tragicomedia de Don Duardos,* ed. D. Alonso, pp. 17, 26-27.

ish plays of the *siglo de oro* are a disturbing excrescence which prevents the playwright from achieving either unity of action or unity of tone. For the moment, however, I should like to pursue another tack by arguing that Vicente's genius, if not precisely dramatic, is at least thoroughly theatrical. The distinction is not easy to sum up in a phrase; I shall try to explain what I mean by it through an examination of *Quem Tem Farelos?*

By theatrical I do not mean that the play contains any strikingly dramatic, or even unexpected, turn of events. Nor do I mean that it makes use of spectacular stage effects, as the festival plays do. The whole action is played in a single setting, and the only property needed is Aires Rosado's *viola.* I mean rather that the action has been planned with a view to presentation by actors before an audience; one might well apply to *Quem Tem Farelos?* the tired old phrase "it's the kind of play one has to see to appreciate." Consider, for example, the half-overheard asides, which we have already discussed with reference to the *Auto da Índia,* here effectively combined with one of Aires Rosado's songs (lines 218 ff.); or the way in which another of his songs is interrupted first by the dogs and cats of the neighborhood and then by the mother of the girl whom he is serenading. Consider, too, Aires's conversation with the girl, Isabel. She remains out of sight in her room; we do not hear her answers directly, but must infer them from the way Aires responds to them. This is, of course, wholly unrealistic; since he obviously hears what she has to say, there is no very good reason why we should not hear it, too.[33]

---

[33] See António José Saraiva and Maria Teresa Rita, "Diálogo," pp. 716-717. Sra. Rita observes that there are "certas cenas de *Quem Tem Farelos,* em que as relações entre as personagens são . . . puro jogo, sem respeito pela verosimilhança. No namoro de janela do Escudeiro com a sua dama, em vez de assistirmos a um diálogo a duas vozes, como seria natural, a presença da donzela é criada apenas através do Escudeiro, único que se ouve falar,—dos seus risinhos, dos seus ardores, dos seus silêncios. É um processo muito importante para o teatro contemporâneo que rompeu deliberadamente com a tradição naturalista. A mesma falta de respeito pela verosimilhança se manifesta no encadeamento

Vicente's method, nevertheless, has two advantages; first, it speeds up the tempo of the scene, since the pauses in Aires's speech need not correspond to the time needed for the girl's replies, and second, it postpones the appearance of Isabel herself and allows us to wonder a little longer just what sort of girl it is to whom Aires is paying court. Isabel's appearance, when it does come, brings a stream of words directed at her mother, which forms a kind of echo to the latter's abuse of Aires earlier in the play; the resemblances between the two speeches would be easy to bring out in performance, for example, by having Isabel imitate her mother's gestures and intonation.

Vicente's theatrical inventiveness is matched by his rhetorical virtuosity, surely very great, though perhaps one need not agree with Giuseppe Tavani that it reveals the author's *cultura tecnica.*[34] It is most apparent in the speech of Isabel's mother, ingeniously analyzed by Paul Teyssier, who compares it with a similar passage from the *Auto do Nascimento* of Baltazar Díaz and concludes that:

> La supériorité de Gil Vicente est éclatante. Sous l'incohérence des mots une sorte d'idée directrice se fait jour, ponctuée par une série de termes qui, tous, évoquent une fuite à travers une campagne hostile . . . Or ce qui avait réveillé la Vieille, c'est la chanson chantée par l'Ecuyer sous les fenêtres d'Isabel . . . L'on voit que les imprécations de la Vieille ne sont autre chose que la transposition de l'idée exprimée dans ce texte. L'Écuyer invitait Isabel à une poétique fuite dans la nuit . . . Mais ce fil directeur, s'il relie les associations d'idées

de situações. Um exemplo também tirado de *Quem Tem Farelos*: o criado do Escudeiro convida um colega a assistir as 'sandices' poéticas do amo; automáticamente, e sem mais preparos, este aparece em cena a ler o seu cancioneiro. Em vez de os colocar na situação de surpreender a intimidade de Aires pelo buraco da fechadura de um estratagema qualquer, Gil Vicente dá à realidade teatral o seu direito de viver por si, de dar de ombros à verosimilhança" (p. 717).

[34] Gil Vicente, *Comédia de Rubena,* ed. Giuseppe Tavani, pp. 29-31.

> dans un certain ordre, s'entortille perpétuellement dans une foule d'images et de mots les plus imprévus du monde, dont le seul élément commun est qu'ils expriment toutes sortes de calamités. Si l'on étudie le morceau de Baltazar Díaz, on n'y trouve rien de tel : c'est une énumération de maux divers, en particulier de maladies, et la seule "constante" qui s'y manifeste est une recherche systématique de l'ordure et de l'obscénité,—trait qui est au contraire rigoureusement absent de la tirade de Gil Vicente.[35]

I am not sure Vicente's audience would have recognized the thematic unity of the *velha's* attack on the poor *escudeiro,* but they could hardly have failed to respond to the brilliance of its rhythmic and rhetorical effects. M. Teyssier again sums up the essential points :

> Si nous considérons maintenant la forme des deux "malédictions," la supériorité du texte vicentin n'est pas moins évidente. Sous les quatrains d'*octosílabos* c'est un rythme endiablé qui s'impose à la lecture : aux reprises allitératives de *mao, má* le poète a ajouté d'innombrables rimes intérieures, par lesquelles les termes s'appellent, s'enchaînent, se combinent en une sarabande infernale. On finit même, dans deux vers, par oublier le rythme binaire pour adopter un rythme ternaire qui fait disparaître entièrement l'*octosílabo* ("má morte, má corte, má sorte").[36]

One might further point out that the song with which Aires tries to drown out the *velha's* diatribe is appropriate to the situation, so much so, indeed, that the refrain "Garrido amor !" takes on a markedly ironic tone :

> Eu amei ũa senhora
> de todo meu coração.
> Quis Deus e minha ventura

---

[35] Teyssier, pp. 505-506.
[36] *Ibid.*, p. 506.

que não ma querem dar, não.
Garrido amor!
(lines 416-421)

Whether Aires himself is aware of the irony is doubtful. Much of the comedy in the play can perhaps be best accounted for in terms of Bergson's notion that rigidity is the fundamental comic trait. Thus, Aires is annoyed by the dogs' barking but goes on singing, asking his servant to quiet them by throwing them a bit of bread, though he must know that Apariço has none; so, too, he can think of no reply to the *velha's* flood of abuse and begins to sing again, thus providing a kind of comic counterpoint to her threats. Some of Vicente's uses of the half-overheard aside in *Quem Tem Farelos?* may be seen as an indication that Aires is too much preoccupied with playing a role to pay proper attention to what is being said around him: he surely knows how little chance he has of impressing his servant Apariço, but for the sake of consistency he must remain true to the image he has tried to create for himself.[37] Moreover, he can still think of the impression he hopes to make on Apariço's fellow servant Ordoño.

Aires's need to try to impress even another man's servant doubtless tells us something both about his own personality and about conditions in Vicente's Portugal. The first point is perhaps reinforced by the name Vicente has chosen for his protagonist; it suggests both the phrase *darse aires* or, in Portuguese, *dar-se ares,* "to put on airs," and the verb *rosar-se,* "to blush; to feel ashamed." Aires's reluctance to admit the gap between the reality of his existence and his desires is matched by Apariço's hope that his master will be able to secure a place for him at court ("Diz que m'há-de dar a el-Rei," line 82), though he knows perfectly well that Aires's claims of enjoying *privança* are only empty boasts ("Deitam-no fora da sala," line 323); we may be tempted to see Apariço's mixture of belief and unbelief in his master's claims as a kind of anticipation

[37] See Lionel Gossman, *Men and Masks, A Study of Molière.*

of Sancho's attitude toward the *ínsula* promised him by Don Quijote.

Here there is doubtless a hint of genuine social criticism. An excessive preoccupation with service at court and with a real or fancied social position, to the detriment both of one's own interests and those of Portugal, is a recurrent theme in Vicente's theater, as well as in other literature of the period.[38] It is clearly related to the equally frequent theme of the necessity of a hierarchically ordered society, a point to which we shall return in our discussion of the festival plays. Isabel's rebellion against her mother's authority is doubtless another facet of the same thing. She attacks her mother for her hypocrisy in wanting her daughter to make herself attractive to men without herself feeling any sort of sexual desire:

> Vos quereis que mate a gente,
> de fermosa e avisada:
> quereis que não fale nada,
> nem ninguém em mim atente?
> Quereis que creça e que viva
> e não deseje marido?
> . . .
> Quereis que seja discreta
> e que não saiba d'amores?
> *(lines 469-472, 475-476)*

Her arguments sound strikingly modern, so much so that we may need to remind ourselves that they go precisely counter to the notions of proper behavior which were then generally accepted. This need not mean that Vicente felt no sympathy for Isabel's position; *Quem Tem Farelos?* gives us no reason to suppose that he would have ranged himself unqualifiedly on the side either of Isabel or of her mother. The *Auto de Inês Pereira,* performed

[38] Cf. *A Farsa dos Almocreves,* where the theme is developed at length. Claims to hold a social position which is not one's birthright are mocked by Garcia de Resende in his *Miscellania,* pp. 369-370: "Os Reys por acrescentar/ as pessoas em valia,/ por lhe serviços pagar, vimos a huõs o dom dar,/ e a outros fidalguia:/ ja se os Reys non haã mester,/ pois toma dom quẽ ho quer,/ e armas nobres tambem/ toma quem armas nam tem,/ e da ho dom ha molher."

a few years later, in 1523, does, however, make it quite clear that he was aware of the dangers inherent in Isabel's attitude.[39]

Isabel, indeed, may be seen as a precursor of Inês Pereira, just as Aires Rosado may be said to foreshadow the *escudeiro* who becomes Inês's first husband. The play is closer to being a comedy of character than of intrigue, more like certain plays of Molière than like a typical Spanish *comedia*; it is significant that many of Vicente's plays, like those of Molière and unlike those of the Spanish dramatists, take their title from the name of the protagonist, or from a phrase which serves to identify him (for example, *O Juiz da Beira* or *O Velho da Horta*). But if we can see Isabel as a forerunner of Inês, we can also see her as a variation on the theme announced by Constança in the *Auto da Índia*: both represent the woman who is wholly uninterested in questions of morality and only a little more concerned with what other people may say about her. Aires's servant Apariço is given some of the attributes of Constança's servant in the *Auto da Índia,* notably the insolence which neither makes more than a half-hearted effort to conceal; we shall meet him again in the person of the *escudeiro's* servant in the *Auto de Inês Pereira,* as we shall meet Isabel's mother in the figure of Inês's mother. Constança's husband, too, may foreshadow the trusting and not very bright Pero Marques, who marries Inês Pereira after the death of the *escudeiro;* the analogy is, however, less close here than in the other cases we have dealt with, for though Constança's husband may be played as a simpleton, and indeed was so played in the one performance of the *Auto da Índia* I have seen in Portugal, the lines Vicente gives him do not demand this interpretation, while those he assigns Pero Marques certainly do. The two earlier farces are not only delightful in their own right; they also help us to see the separate elements which were to be so masterfully combined in the *Auto de Inês Pereira,* surely the finest of Vicente's farces and perhaps of all his plays.

[39] For a fuller discussion, see my article "La estructura dramática del *Auto de Inês Pereira.*"

The Festival Plays

FOR THE PORTUGUESE, Gil Vicente is one of the glories of their national literature, second in importance only to Camões. He is honored above all as a dramatist, both for the excellence of many of his plays and for his historical role as founder of the Portuguese theater. To Spanish readers, on the other hand, and doubtless to most foreign students of Spanish literature, Vicente is far better known as a lyric poet than as a playwright. His lyrics have become familiar through their inclusion in a long series of anthologies; in our own day they have won new readers through the reawakening of interest in *poesía de tipo tradicional*; and they have been echoed in the works of distinguished contemporary poets, notably Rafael Alberti.

An important consequence of this tendency to think of Gil Vicente as a poet who wrote plays rather than as a playwright whose works contain a great deal of wonderful poetry is an overemphasis on the popular elements in his theater. One of Vicente's great strengths is the wealth of delightful songs scattered throughout his plays. Many of them belong to the kind of poetry that Spanish scholars, following the example of Dámaso Alonso in his famous anthology,[40] usually call *poesía de tipo*

[40] *Poesía de la edad media y poesía de tipo tradicional.* The book was first published in Spain in 1935.

tradicional. To say that a song is of the traditional type is to imply that we do not know whether it has been transmitted orally from one singer to another over a period of many years—if we know that in fact it *has* done so, we shall, of course, call it simply a traditional song—or whether it is the work of a single poet, whose name we may, or may not, chance to know. This caution is especially necessary in dealing with the songs of Gil Vicente. All of them come from his plays, and by far the greater number have a real function in the play from which they come; one must agree with C. M. Bowra that in most cases "Vicente's lyrics belong to the dramatic action and do something for it."[41] It is, however, often impossible to say with assurance whether a given song is Vicente's own work, a new creation though one that adheres closely to the conventions of popular poetry, or whether it has been taken directly from popular tradition with perhaps some slight modification to make it fit its new role as part of a play.

Vicente's obvious affection for traditional poetry is not something peculiar to him. On the contrary, it is a taste he shared with other poets and musicians of the period, men who, like Vicente himself, were often dependent for a livelihood on court patronage. And, again like Vicente, neither poets nor musicians were content simply to admire the beauties of the traditional songs; rather, they tried to make the songs their own by using them as a point of departure for original compositions. The poets often used fragments of popular songs as pegs upon which to hang compositions which are courtly both in language and content. The musicians did much the same thing; they gratefully accepted the simple melodies of the folksongs as a basis for elaborate polyphonic compositions. But since they were not much concerned with the words of the songs they adapted, they were often content, unlike the poets, to leave the texts as they found them. Vicente's practice is closer to that of the musicians than to that of the poets. Doubtless he often added a *glosa* of his own to a traditional refrain or modified a

---

[41] *Inspiration and Poetry,* p. 91.

traditional lyric to make it heighten a moment of dramatic intensity or help in characterizing the person who sings it in the play; but in doing so he almost always remained faithful to the established conventions of popular poetry.[42]

The literary tastes of the court were not, of course, identical with those of the common people, though some scholars tend to exaggerate the differences between them. One who does not do so is Margit Frenk Alatorre, whose painstaking studies of the relations between popular and courtly lyrics are of the greatest importance for our understanding of Gil Vicente. She has pointed out that sixteenth-century readers do not seem to have drawn the sharp distinctions we are accustomed to make between *lo popular* and *lo cortesano*: most of the songbooks and poetic anthologies of the period contain both kinds of poetry, and both courtly and popular elements are often found within the limits of a single poem, as if neither the poets nor their readers were aware of the differences between the two kinds of poetry.[43]

The presence of popular elements in Vicente's plays does not, then, constitute a denial of their essentially courtly character. Almost all the plays were written for performance at the Portuguese court; in most cases, this performance must have been the only one foreseen by the playwright. I can find no reason to assume, with Carolina Michaëlis de Vasconcellos, that the farces were written for a popular audience, nor to accept her suggestion that it was perhaps at the suggestion of the Queen Mother, Dona Leonor, that Vicente first sought an audience wider than the court itself.[44] I find it equally impossible to agree with António José Saraiva that the publication of some of Vicente's plays in the form of *folhas volantes* represents a deliberate attempt by the poet to free himself from depending solely on court patronage.[45]

---

[42] See Margit Frenk Alatorre, "Glosas de tipo popular," pp. 304-305.

[43] Margit Frenk Alatorre, "Dignificación de la lírica popular," pp. 39-40.

[44] *Notas Vicentinas,* p. 477.

[45] *História da Cultura,* II, 243.

Though almost all the plays were written to be performed at court, one group of them is bound to particular events at court in a rather special way which illustrates very nicely Huizinga's contention that "the Middle Ages knew only applied art. They wanted works of art only to make them subservient to some practical use."[46] That "practical use," in Vicente's case, was often to celebrate some important moment in the life of the court. The occasion might be one of the great feasts of the liturgical year, Easter or Epiphany or, most often, Christmas. Sometimes, however, the play was performed to celebrate a special event which was not tied to the fixed round of the seasons: the birth of a prince or princess, a royal marriage, or simply the king's entrance into a city after a prolonged absence. It is this second group of works that I shall call festival plays. They are *Cortes de Júpiter* (1521); *Frágua de Amor* (1524); *Templo de Apolo* (1526); *Nau de Amores* (1527); *Comédia sobre a Divisa da Cidade de Coimbra* (1527); *Tragicomédia Pastoril da Serra da Estrela* (1527); *Triunfo do Inverno* (1529); and *Auto da Lusitânia* (1532).[47]

The festival plays have not been very attractive to scholars. None of them, so far as I know, has ever been subjected to detailed critical analysis, and more than one writer has expressed his regret that Vicente was obliged by his patrons to turn away from the farces and religious plays he handled with such consummate skill only to waste his gifts on these court pageants. It is, of course, obvious that Vicente, in writing these plays, was working to order, providing the court with the kind of entertainment it demanded to celebrate its great occasions. Today we tend to think that working to order is a violation of the artist's freedom, but there is plenty of evidence that medieval and renaissance writers felt nothing of the kind.[48] Leo Spitzer has

---

[46] J. Huizinga, *The Waning of the Middle Ages,* p. 244.

[47] The dates are those given by I. S. Révah, *Dicionário das literaturas,* p. 866.

[48] See the illuminating discussion of the relationship between the artist and his patron in Edgar Wind, *Art and Anarchy,* chap. VI.

given us a salutary warning against the too easy assumption that the things we do not like, or do not understand, in a writer were dictated by the taste of the times, that is, by the demands of his audience —implying, of course, that the writer himself must have felt just as we do, and would certainly have omitted the troublesome features, or handled them differently, if only he had been free to do so.[49] Perhaps Gil Vicente did feel that the energies he spent on writing and staging the festival plays might have been better spent in perfecting the kind of plays he had already attempted with such happy results. But there is no evidence whatever that he felt this way, and one could argue just as plausibly that his was the kind of artistic temperament that delights in experimenting with an endless succession of new forms.[50]

In the festival plays, we see most clearly the special blend of courtly and popular elements which constitutes one of the most striking features of Vicente's theater. Folk materials are everywhere, sometimes on the surface, as in the many fine *canciones de tipo tradicional,* or the figure of the enchanted Moorish princess Tais in the *Cortes de Júpiter*; sometimes just beneath it, as in the ritual combat between Winter and Spring, which may have served as a point of departure for the *Triunfo do Inverno.*

In the festival plays, too, we see Vicente most clearly as a Portuguese writer. J. P. W. Crawford long ago pointed out the importance of Manuel I, and of his successor John III, for the development of Vicente's theater.[51] Festival plays needed a patron, not simply, as Crawford suggests, because they were expensive to stage, but because they were addressed to a special kind of audience, the ladies and gentlemen of the court, and because a large part of their *raison d'être* was precisely praise of the sovereign.[52] Praising him implies praising his achieve-

---

[49] "Dos observaciones sintáctico-estilísticas," p. 11, n. 16.
[50] See Eugenio Asensio, "Las fuentes de las *Barcas,"* p. 209.
[51] *Spanish Drama before Lope de Vega,* pp. 62-63.
[52] See Dolora Cunningham, "The Jonsonian Masque as a Literary Form," pp. 171-173.

ments and those of his predecessors; many songs and speeches in the festival plays celebrate the great deeds of the Portuguese in a way that to many readers will seem to foreshadow Camões. But there is more than simply praise. The incompetence and greed that made the Portuguese voyages to India a cause of so much needless heartbreak and suffering are clearly presented in the *Triunfo do Inverno,* just as the corruption of the courts is symbolized by the twisted figure of Justice in the *Frágua de Amor*. Though it is doubtless fair to apply to the festival plays Enid Welsford's remark that the masque was "chiefly appreciated as an advertisement of wealth and an opportunity for flattery and political propaganda," one must add immediately that the demands of flattery and propaganda did not completely rule out any possibility of criticism.[53] Vicente offers us a picture of Portuguese society both as it was and as it should be, with the implication that, thanks to the king, the gap between the two is about to be closed once and for all.

One reason for scholarly neglect of Vicente's festival plays is doubtless that they do not correspond very closely to anything in contemporary Spanish literature. N. D. Shergold declares that "it is perhaps misleading to talk of a court theater at all in the sixteenth century, for Charles V and Philip II were not interested in the drama, and did not give it their patronage. It is only with Philip III that the 'comedia' begins to develop as a court entertainment, and that a particular kind of court play, dependent largely on spectacular effect, comes into existence."[54] Vicente's plays appear much less isolated if we look at them in the context of European literature, and not just the literature of Spain and Portugal. We see then that the difficulties we meet in interpreting the festival plays—and the difficulties are great, for these plays make us feel most keenly the long span of years that separates us from Vicente and from his intended audience—are much like those we find in the court theater and the court poetry of other European countries. Here we can

[53] *The Court Masque,* p. 247.
[54] Shergold, p. 236.

turn for help to Huizinga's *Waning of the Middle Ages,* and to a number of studies of English literature and especially of the masque.[55]

It has often been remarked that the masque is set apart from other types of theatrical performances by a unique kind of relationship between the actors and the audience: "[The Masque] attempted from the beginning to breach the barrier between spectators and actors, so that in effect the viewer became part of the spectacle. The end toward which the masque moved was to destroy any sense of theater and to include the whole court in the mimesis . . . The most common method of effecting this transformation was to have the production culminate, dramatically and literally, in the revels, the dance between the masquers and members of the audience. But this was by no means the only method, and we find a number of entertainments that approach the same ends by different means, appearing to be masques in structure though not employing the customary dances and revels. These are not masques *manqués,* but other kinds of the same form, which developed along with the masque Miss Welsford describes and were thought of as analogous entertainments."[56]

Although many of Vicente's plays end with a dance, there is none in which actors and audience dance together. There are, however, a number in which the line that divides the actors from the spectators is overstepped in the course of the play. Vicente's first play, the *Auto de la visitación,* is a good example. It was performed on the evening of June 7, 1502, to celebrate the birth of Prince John, the future King John III, which had taken place the day before. The play is obviously indebted to the shepherds' plays of Juan del Encina, but its structure seems to derive also from the tradition of the early court masque. The king and queen are at once members of the audience and essential, though

[55] In addition to Miss Welsford's book, already cited, see John Stevens, *Music and Poetry in the Early Tudor Court*; C. L. Barber, *Shakespeare's Festive Comedy*; Stephen Orgel, *The Jonsonian Masque; A Book of Masques.*
[56] Orgel, pp. 6-7; see also Shergold, pp. 555-556.

silent, participants in the action; much of the comedy in the play must have come from the mixture of familiarity and awe with which the *vaquero* addresses them. The play ends with a presentation of gifts to the newborn prince, another traditional feature of the court masque, and one Vicente employs often in the festival plays.

The *Auto de la visitación,* however, is not really typical of Vicente's festival plays; in them, as in the masque generally, music and dancing, and, most of all, lavish spectacle seem always to be threatening the primacy of the text. This is clear from the only contemporary description of a performance of one of Vicente's plays that has come down to us, that given by Garcia de Resende in his elaborate account of the festivities surrounding the departure of Princess Beatrice from Lisbon in the summer of 1521 to become Duchess of Savoy. The play can only be the *Cortes de Júpiter,* but Resende gives neither the title of the play nor the name of the author. The omission is surely not because he disliked the play; he tells us that it was "hũa muyto boa, e muyto bem feita comedia de muytas figuras muyto bem atauiadas e muy naturaes, feyta, e representada ao casamento, e partida da senhora Infante, cousa muyto bem ordenada e bem a proposito, e com ella acabada se acabou o serao."[57] Clearly, what mattered to Resende was not so much the play itself as its appropriateness to the occasion, and above all the care which had gone into its production. The latter is, of course, a tribute to Gil Vicente as director and producer of his own play, but it is much more a tribute to the wealth and liberality of his patron King Manuel. Significantly, Resende gives much less space to his account of the play than to the fitting out of the ships which were to take the princess to her new home; the preparation of the ships obviously involved a far greater outlay of money.

The history of the masque in other countries shows that there, too, the splendor of the production and the expense it implied were what most caught the attention of the spectators.[58] The splendor was

[57] Garcia de Resende, *Miscellania,* p. 326.
[58] Welsford, p. 247; Stevens, p. 248.

destined to last only a few hours, like Michelangelo's statue made of snow in which Enid Welsford sees reflected "no small part of the artistic activity of several centuries;" one measure of the monarch's liberality was his willingness to spend great sums of money on a single evening's entertainment.[59] The ephemeral nature of the masque is constantly stressed in contemporary comments on it, nowhere perhaps more clearly than in Ben Jonson's preface to his first published masque, *The Masque of Blacknesse,* which begins "The honor, and splendor of these *spectacles* was such in the performance, as could those houres have lasted, this of mine, now, had been a most unprofitable worke."[60] Jonson is far more articulate than most of his contemporaries, but it is worth emphasizing that what is peculiar to him is not his conviction that the masque is by its very nature a desperately impermanent work of art.[61] It is, rather, his belief that there may be a way of salvaging at least part of it from the ravages of time by bringing its text to the level of great poetry.

It is Jonson, too, who points out another quality of the masque, one which forms perhaps the greatest single barrier to our understanding of Gil Vicente's festival plays. In his preface to *Chloridia* he tells us that "the King, and Queenes Majesty, having given their command for the Invention of a new argument, . . . it was agreed, it should be the celebration of some Rites, done to the Goddesse *Chloris* . . . Upon this hinge, the whole Invention mov'd." On this passage Miss Welsford comments that it "expresses very neatly a characteristic of the masque that differentiates it from drama. The drama is a story with crisis and dénouement; the masque is an invention moving upon a hinge, or, to put it another way, it is the logical working out of an idea which has to be taken for granted. The hinge of a masque was as a rule some riddling compliment of the sovereign, or an actual event, which was repre-

---

[59] Welsford, p. 247.

[60] [Works], VII, 169, lines 1-3.

[61] See Inga-Stina Ewbank, "'These Pretty Devices'," pp. 419-420.

sented as taking place in Olympus or Arcadia or as being so magnificent an affair that divinities were brought down to celebrate it."[62]

Vicente's *Cortes de Júpiter* exactly fits the latter part of Miss Welsford's definition of the kind of hinge upon which a masque may move: an actual event, represented as so magnificent that divinities are brought down to celebrate it. In the play, Providence enlists the aid of Jupiter to assure a safe journey for Princess Beatrice as she leaves Portugal for Savoy to meet her new husband. Jupiter, in turn, calls on the Sun, the Moon, Venus, and Mars to help him in his task. The rest of the play is a sort of preview, transferred to the plane of fantasy, of the princess's sailing, which was to take place a few days after the performance. Finally, the Moon and Venus are sent to wake the Moorish girl, Tais, from her enchanted sleep; she will bring three magic gifts for the princess, a ring, a thimble, and a sword. The gifts are, as we have already noted, a traditional ending for the masque; here, as often, they represent qualities supposed to be possessed by the person to whom the gifts are offered.

If we compare Vicente's play with Garcia de Resende's very detailed account of the princess's departure, or with the briefer one given by Damião de Góis, we shall see at once that Vicente gives us something quite different, something that is by no means merely a retelling in verse of what the chroniclers say in prose, but a richly imaginative work of poetic fiction which offers both less and more than they. Less, of course, in the sense that we should not read Vicente's play to find out how many ships accompanied the princess—Resende tells us there were eighteen—or to learn what sort of armament they carried, something Resende also tells us in great detail. Resende stresses the magnificence, and therefore the expense, of the preparations for the journey, and the very real dangers it involved.[63]

---

[62] Welsford, p. 256.

[63] The armament the ships carried was not just for decoration. The distinction we make between piracy and organized warfare was not so clearly or consistently drawn in the sixteenth century; pirates were then, and for many years

Vicente's treatment is quite different. He stresses rather the gaiety of the occasion and the role played by nature, personified by the ancient gods and goddesses, in assuring the princess a safe journey. The gods, in turn, are simply obeying the command of the one true God, who reveals once more his concern for the Portuguese, a reward for their faithful service to him in the past. The point is made in a long speech by Mars, who emphasizes also that God has chosen the Portuguese to play a role in the modern world analogous to that of the Romans in the ancient world (lines 530-579). Both points were, of course, made repeatedly by sixteenth-century Portuguese poets and historians; both were to receive their finest treatment from Camões in *Os Lusíadas* a half century after Vicente's play.

Vicente's treatment of his theme involves nothing that can be called dramatic conflict. Indeed, the very fiction he takes for his point of departure makes any threat to the princess's safety or happiness quite out of the question. The whole point of the play is to show how God has ordered all things to pay homage to the princess and to shield her from harm. In the *Cortes de Júpiter,* as so often in the court literature and court ritual of the period, there is no hard and fast dividing line between secular and religious elements, since everything connected with the royal family is touched by the sovereign's role as a divinely appointed ruler, God's vicar on earth.[64]

An even more striking example of the fusion of secular and religious ceremonial is found in another of the festival plays, the *Nau de Amores,* performed early in 1527 to celebrate the return of the court to Lisbon after an absence of four years because of plague in the city. The opening scene presents Lisbon herself, personified as a princess who greets

---

afterward, an ever-present threat in Mediterranean waters. (See Braudel, II, 101.) There were other dangers. In the small ships of the time, bad weather might have disastrous consequences; Góis tell us that one of the ships which accompanied the princess lost its rigging in a storm and had to put in at Cartagena, though no lives were lost. (*Crónica de D. Manuel,* pt. IV, chap. lxx.).

64 Stevens, pp. 236-237.

the King and Queen with a speech in which she associates their entry into the city with the creation of the world and with the Incarnation and Resurrection of Christ:

> Ó alto e poderoso em grande grandeza
> meu Rei precioso per graça divina!
> De mi apartado por eu não ser dina,
> por minha mofina se foi vossa alteza.
> Venhais em tal ponto, em tal dia, em tal
> hora
> como aquela em que Deos incriado
> criou todo mundo tão bem acabado
> como será e foi até agora.
>
> Venhais em tal hora como ele encarnou;
> venhais em tal hora como ele naceo;
> venhais em tal hora como esclareceo
> aquela menhã em que resuscitou.
> Ó flor da floresta dos Emperadores,
> preciosa Rainha, venhais em tal hora
> como aquela em que Nossa Senhora
> achou o seu filho antre os doutores.
>
> Venhais em tal hora como a em que
> naceram
> todas as castas e virgens do céo;
> venhais em tal hora como Deos recebeo
> na glória aqueles que a mereceram.
> Venhais em tal hora como Gabriel
> veio à Virgem, Nossa Senhora;
> senhores infantes, venhais em tal hora
> como Deos veio remir Israel.[65]

The *Cortes de Júpiter* differs from Vicente's other festival plays only in that it lacks the elaborate pageant wagons found in most of them. None of the plays has a real plot; all, in Jonson's phrase, move upon a hinge. In the *Frágua de Amor,* for example, the point of departure is nothing more solid than the word-play on "castle" and "Castile." The King of Portugal is determined to conquer "un castillo que hay en Castilla" (line 68). The castle is Charles V's

[65] F. 145 v.; ed. Marques Braga, IV, 57-58.

younger sister, Catherine of Austria, whose betrothal to John III was celebrated at Tordesillas in August 1524. There is, however, no need to take the castle by force, thanks to the intervention of Cupid—a graceful way of saying that the union of John and Catherine was a marriage for love and not one undertaken solely for reasons of state. Cupid's appeal to the princess is not the climax of the play; the surrender of the castle takes place before the play begins. The audience is never in doubt as to the success of Cupid's mission; understandably, since the play was performed to celebrate the betrothal that, in the fiction of the play, Cupid has taken it upon himself to arrange. The play is concerned rather with the festivities Cupid organizes to celebrate his success as a matchmaker. Since the coming of the new queen marks the beginning of a new epoch in the history of Portugal, he proposes building a forge of love, in which the Portuguese may be made new and, by implication, more worthy of their new sovereign. From this point on, the play becomes a series of comic vaudeville turns as one person after another steps forward to be reshaped in the forge of love. As always, our delight in the play comes, not from wondering how the story will turn out—there is no story—but from the grace and humor of the individual scenes. The scenes, though dramatically discrete, are thematically related. The theme is the new and more harmonious society which the new queen will help to create in Portugal. Enid Welsford's remark that "harmony, particularly social harmony, is the underlying theme of most of the masquing and pageantry of our period" is true also of Gil Vicente's festival plays, though with the important proviso that in them harmony is more often seen as an ideal to be sought than as an achieved reality.[66]

The festival plays, like the other kinds of plays that make up Vicente's theater, differ greatly in length, in complexity, and in aesthetic value. The

[66] Welsford, p. 397.

longest and perhaps the finest of all is the *Triunfo do Inverno,* performed to celebrate the birth, on April 28, 1529, of Princess Isabel, the second daughter of John III and Catherine of Austria. The play is a kind of synthesis of Vicente's theater, combining elements from almost the whole range of his dramatic works and conferring upon them a high degree of thematic unity.

The play has been called an adaptation of the Medieval Latin *Conflictus hiemis et veris.*[67] There is, however, no proof that Vicente knew the *Conflictus*; his treatment is radically different from any of the other poems on this theme.[68] The other poems deal with the contrasting pleasures of the two seasons, Winter praising the delights of good food and wine before a blazing fire, Summer those of amorous dalliance in a field of flowers. Vicente's Winter, in contrast, does not proclaim the pleasures of his season, but rather its hardships; he exults in his power to make men suffer. The point of the play lies in the contrasting personalities of Winter and Spring and in the different ways men react to the challenges offered them by the two seasons.

The play begins, like so many of Vicente's plays, with a prologue, here assigned to the *autor,* the playwright-producer; the role may possibly have been played by Vicente himself. The *autor* contrasts the sadness which now dominates the life of every-

---

[67] Crawford asserts that in it Vicente "[uses] as a background the well-known medieval debate of winter and spring" (p. 66). (In the first edition [Philadelphia, 1922], he had said that the play "presents with a rustic setting the familiar *Conflictus veris et hiemis*" [p. 73].)

[68] Poetic debates between Winter and Summer are found in French and English; the latter is contemporary with Vicente. There may well have been others in Spanish or Portuguese. None of the vernacular versions known to me has much in common with the Latin *Conflictus.* The Latin poem, sometimes attributed to Alcuin, is discussed by F. J. E. Raby, *A History of Secular Latin Poetry in the Middle Ages,* I, 208-209. Two different French versions are included in Anatole de Montaiglon, *Recueil de poésies françaises des XVe et XVIe siècles,* VI, 190-195, and X, 40-53. The English "Debate and Stryfe betwene Sommer and Wynter" is in W. Carew Hazlitt, ed., *Remains of the Early Popular Poetry of England,* II, 33-39.

one in Portugal with the gaity of twenty years before. Then, he declares, there was a tambourine in every house and a bagpipe in every hay loft. Now, however, there are neither pipes nor pipers, and melancholy reigns everywhere: "agora Geremias/ é nosso tamborileiro" (lines 9-10).

The *autor's* speech has sometimes been cited by students of Vicente's theater as an indication of the temper of Portuguese thought in the 1520s.[69] There were plenty of reasons for unhappiness in the history of the times. Protestantism was rapidly gaining strength in Northern Europe, while the countries of Catholic Europe became politically more and more divided; the year before the presentation of the play had seen the sack of Rome by the troops of Charles V. Closer home, the 1520s had brought famine and plague to Portugal.[70] It has been suggested, too, that the prologue may reflect the difference in temperament between Vicente's two patrons, John III and his father Manuel the Fortunate, and, finally, that it may reveal the natural pessimism of a man in the declining years of his life; we do not know Vicente's age when he wrote the play, but he can hardly have been less than fifty-five and may have been considerably older.

This line of reasoning is nevertheless unsatisfactory on several grounds. It falls into the error, frequent in studies of Vicente's theater, of identifying the views of a character in one of the plays with those of the playwright; the error is no less grave in this case because the character in question is called the *autor* and may perhaps have been played by Vicente himself. Even if we grant that Vicente, for reasons of age or health or because of his concern over the events of the day, may have had good cause to be unhappy, we shall still have to explain why he chose to talk about these things at just this point in this particular play—and if we can justify the *autor's* speech in terms of its appropriateness to the rest of the play, then we shall have no need to

---

[69] See Keates, pp. 130-132; Bell, *Estudos Vicentinos,* pp. 36, 85, 135.

[70] See Frei Luís de Sousa, *Anais de D. João III,* I, 64-67.

account for it by appealing to the events of Vicente's personal life, about which we know so very little.

One might argue that the speech is a variation on the traditional theme of affected modesty.[71] Given the prevailing sadness, the *autor* declares, it is useless to hope that the birth of the little princess will be celebrated as it deserves to be. If only she had been born twenty years before! Nevertheless, he will do what he can to make up for the deficiencies of his compatriots by composing a play in her honor. Since the prevailing mood is one of bleak despair, he has thought it appropriate to take as his subject the triumph of winter, though he is careful to point out that spring's turn will come later in the play. The *autor's* choice of theme is deliberate; it is not forced upon him by the mood of the times, but is rather a challenge to that mood, a reminder that things may not be so bad as they seem. He gives no cause for the prevailing melancholy, insisting that no one has taken the trouble even to ask what became of the joy that once existed in Portugal. The tone of the prologue, moreover, is comic; though the *autor* tells us that neither music nor dancing is now to be found in Portugal, the play is full of both. He interrupts his own complaint to sing a gay little folk song, much like our nursery rhyme "The House that Jack Built," as an example of the sort of thing one used to hear sung in Portugal; the contrast between the mood of the song and that of the speech in which it is inserted must have been far more apparent to those who saw the play than it is to us who merely read the text silently. There is doubtless comedy, too, in the fact that the song the *autor* cites as an example of current taste seems to be a Judeo-Spanish lament, "Terra frida, déismelo; no me neguéis mi consuelo;" the Jews's fondness for mournful songs was frequently ridiculed in the sixteenth century.[72]

The *autor* now introduces Winter, who will act as a sort of master of ceremonies for the first part of the play, that which presents his "triumphs,"

---

[71] See Ernst Robert Curtius, *European Literature and the Latin Middle Ages,* pp. 83-85.

[72] See Manuel Alvar, *Endechas judeo-españolas,* pp. 32-33.

the demonstration of his powers. Winter's opening speech offers a fine example of Vicente's gifts as a poet of nature. His countryside is very different from the ideal landscape of the pastoral tradition; it is, at least in winter, a most unpleasant place. Winter's speech exemplifies the superb quality of Vicente's nonlyric verse. There is a real danger that the beauty of his songs may make us overlook the excellence of his dramatic poetry; we sometimes need to remind ourselves how much of our pleasure in reading his plays is a specifically rhetorical pleasure, which would be lost in any prose rendering of the text, however skillful. Winter's speech is not just a catalogue of the discomforts of cold weather. Keen observation there is in plenty, but there is also a wild fantasy, an exuberant play of imagination, which seems at times to be led from one topic to another by nothing more than the chance associations called forth by the rimes. Winter tells us proudly that he is

> dios de los fríos vapores,
> y señor de los ñublados,
> . . . pastor de las tempestades,
> . . . maestre sala de la luna,
> *(lines 90-91, 95, 98)*

but he also tells us, on quite a different plane, that he is

> assador mayor de patos,
> alcahuete de los gatos,
> y partero de las gatas.
> *(lines 82-85)*

Winter's monologue helps the play along by revealing the dominant traits of his personality: his pride in his manifold powers, his love of rhetorical display, and, most of all, his delight in the sufferings he causes. He proudly calls himself "agravio de las viejas dueñas" (line 89) and "tormiento de los pastores" (line 93), and exults in his power to

> [quitar] las sombras graciosas
> debaxo de los castaños;
> *(lines 106-107)*

he takes delight in saying

> hago llorar las huertas
> la muerte de los jardines.
> *(lines 120-121)*

The *autor* had introduced him to the audience with the line "o Inverno vem salvagem" (line 73), and he himself declares that his appearance is that of "un salvage bruto" (line 103); he doubtless appeared dressed in furs, a conventional way of suggesting the hairiness of the wild man. As a wild man, he has a double tie with tradition, on the one hand with the ritual battles between Summer and Winter which seem once to have existed all over Europe, and on the other with the opposition, frequent in courtly literature, between the wild man and the courtier, who will appear later in Vicente's play in the figure of Spring.[73] He is, appropriately enough, something of a bully, and he has a bully's inability to imagine himself in the position of his victims. At the same time, he does not lack a certain rough good humor; he seems to regard the hardships of the winter season as so many practical jokes. All these qualities are brought out still more clearly in his conversation with the shepherd Brisco Pelayo which constitutes his first "triumph." He praises Brisco for cursing him so eloquently—understandably, since the violence of Brisco's attack is the best possible testimony to Winter's power—and challenges him to a *juego de pullas,* the mocking exchange of insults and curses which was an established convention of the shepherds' play.

The following scene introduces a second shepherd, Juan Guijarro. Like Brisco, Juan enters singing a folk song, and, again like Brisco, he separates the verses of his song by spoken passages in which he complains bitterly of the cold. There is, nevertheless, an essential difference between the two

---

[73] For the ritual battles between summer and winter, see Richard Bernheimer, *Wild Men in the Middle Ages,* pp. 55-56, and chap. iii for the wild man in the folk-theater of various European countries; for the opposition between wild man and courtier, see A. A. Parker, "An Age of Gold: Expansion and Scholarship in Spain," p. 241, and A. D. Deyermond, "El hombre salvaje."

shepherds: though both turn to music as a partial relief from their wretchedness, Brisco is simply making the best of a bad situation which has come about through no fault of his own, while Juan has good reason to regret his own folly. The summer before he had fallen in love with a girl and had spent all he had on gifts for her. He now curses love for making him forget that cold weather would come and find him unprepared, without cloak or shoes or money to buy them. He begs Brisco to lend him his cloak for a moment, but Brisco refuses, saying smugly that a man is a fool to give away something he needs for himself, and adding that if Juan had taken his advice he would not now have to dance to keep from freezing. The whole scene is a displacement, to use Northrop Frye's term, of the old fable of the grasshopper and the ant, given a conventionally pastoral setting and neatly tied to the theme of the play.[74] At this moment Winter announces the approach of the old woman, Brásia Caiada. She has fallen in love with a much younger man and has proposed to him, only to have him insist, as a condition for accepting her proposal, that she cross the mountains in winter while they are covered with snow and, moreover, that she do so barefoot. As Juan had forgotten that summer will not last the whole year through, so the old woman

[74] See Northrop Frye, *Anatomy of Criticism*, pp. 136-140, and his essay "Myth, Fiction, and Displacement," in *Fables of Identity*, pp. 21-38. For a Spanish version of the fable of the grasshopper and the ant, cf. *Libro del sabio & clarisimo fabulador ysopo historiado & annotado* (Seville: Juan Cronberger, 1533), folios 33v.-34, where it is given with the marginal heading "El perezoso siẽpre esta menesteroso": "De la hormiga y de la cigarra. En el tiẽpo del inuierno la formiga sacaua al sol el trigo que en el verano avia cogido. La cigarra llegãdo a ella cõ hãbre rogauale que le diesse vn poco de aquel trigo porque no muriesse. A la qual dixo la formiga. Amiga que heziste en el estio? Respondio la cigarra. No tuue para coger espacio porque andaua por los setos [sic] cantãdo. La formiga riẽndose della: & metiẽdo su trigo en su casilla dixo le. Si cantaste en el verano: dança agora en el inuierno. Esta fabula enseña al perezoso que trabaje quãdo puede y es tiẽpo: porque despues faltandole de comer no pida a otros: los quales antes se reyran de el que darle algo."

has refused to admit that she has entered the winter of her life. Like Juan, she shows the folly of refusing to adapt one's actions to one's circumstances; the point is not that love is a bad thing in itself, but simply that it is not for all seasons.

In *The Triumph of Winter,* the harmony which is the underlying theme of all the festival plays is shown, more explicitly than in any of the others, to embrace not only the social order but the order of nature as well. Harmony demands that every man accept the place assigned him in the hierarchical order of the universe; both nature and society are simply partial manifestations of that divinely established order. Up to this point the play has stressed the importance of a proper regard for the powers of nature, in this case the rigors of winter. The next scene combines this motif with the more usual one of the need to accept one's place in the established social order, which means, of course, accepting not only privileges but also responsibilities. The shepherds become spectators as Winter invites them to see his second "triumph," a storm on the Gulf of Guinea which threatens to destroy a Portuguese ship bound for India. The scene may have been introduced primarily to give an opportunity for spectacular stage effects; ships seem always to have been favorite properties for the masque. It is also wonderfully funny. The crew, with a single exception, is hopelessly incompetent; the pilot, who does not know how to do his own job, is irritated less by his shipmates's inability to do theirs than by their refusal to talk like sailors and call things on shipboard by their true names. But the scene does not just provide an interlude of riotous comedy: it creates a bridge between the motif of accepting one's place in the order of nature and that of accepting one's place in the order of human society. Juan Guijarro and the old woman had come to grief because their love had made them heedless of the rigors of winter; the ship runs into danger not so much because of the fury of the storm as because the captain's greed and pride have led him to choose an incompetent crew. He owes his place to favors bought and sold at court by men who, like himself, put their own gain above their duty to their country and their fellows. The offense was by no means imaginary nor even unusual; a great many Portuguese ships in the Indian trade were lost through what can only be called criminal negligence on the part of those responsible for them.[75] Nevertheless, there is, in *The Triumph of Winter,* no criticism of Portuguese institutions. Though the blame for the ship's desperate situation is clearly placed on the captain, and thus ultimately on the men at court who obtained his post for him, Vicente obviously sees no inconsistency in inserting an attack on corruption at court in a play which, like court plays in other countries, is largely given over to praise of the sovereigns. The reason is surely that he sees the hope of reforming society not in institutional reforms but in persuading individual men and women to act differently. He does not think of creating new social institutions, nor even of transforming old ones, but rather of returning to the spirit of the established forms, in the firm conviction that, if only everyone will accept the obligations of his place in society, things will surely run smoothly once more. It is, of course, a conviction he shared with almost all his contemporaries, and not only in Portugal.[76]

We are not told what happens to the ship, though the audience which saw the play may not have been left in doubt; the staging may have made its fate perfectly clear. There is perhaps a hint that it is saved in the sirens's song which comes immediately after the storm at sea. Its theme is that calm weather always follows a storm,

> que todas bonanças buenas
> son después de la tormenta.
> *(lines 878-879)*

One must not lose hope that things will turn out all right, however desperate one's situation:

> Por más que la vida pene,
> no se pierda el esperança,
> porque la desconfiança,

[75] See James Duffy, *Shipwreck and Empire,* chaps. IV-VI.
[76] See Le Gentil, I, 411-412.

sola la muerte la tiene.
(lines 880-883)

The song, like so many of Vicente's songs, sums up one of the central themes of the play ; we shall return to it a little later.

Winter now proposes that he take the sirens to see the king and queen. They alone, he declares, have shown themselves unafraid of his storms by sending out their ships to conquer the seas. The lines seem ironic when we think of the poor merchantman buffeted by the storm in the preceding scene, but the irony was doubtless not noticed by the audience.[77] Winter himself cannot stay long in the presence of the sovereigns, for their radiance destroys him. He tells them that

delante tal claridad
mi fuerça se consumió

and a moment later,

va enflaquesciendo
mi fuerça delante vos ;
(lines 927-928 ; 934-935)

the underlying image, of course, is that of ice melted by the sun. The sovereigns are presented as exempt from the rule of the seasons ; at the same time, they are, somewhat illogically, associated with one particular season, Spring, both because of the implicit metaphor of ice and sun and because Winter's departure is the signal for the appearance of his rival, whom he calls

mi enemigo mayor
y capitán de Cupido.
(lines 1017-1018)

The association of the monarchs with Spring is found elsewhere in Vicente's theater and is a common feature of court plays in other countries. In a number of Elizabethan pageants the queen is given

---

[77] See C. V. Wedgwood, "The Last Masque," for an account of a masque in which flattery of the king openly contradicted what the spectators knew about the state of the kingdom.

the rôle of a supreme summer lady to whom the figures in the play come to do homage. She is sometimes greeted with verses which suggest that her coming brings with it the annual renewal of nature in spring. When she departs,

> Leaves fall, grass dies, beasts of the wood
> hang head,
> Birds cease to sing, and every creature
> wails
> To see the seasons alter with this change:
> for how can Summer stay, when Sun
> departs?[78]

Just as often, the sovereigns are declared to stand outside the order of nature, magically free from the regular changing of the seasons. The conceit is nowhere developed more beautifully than in Summer's charge to Winter near the end of Nashe's *Summer's Last Will and Testament*:

> And, Winter, with thy writhen frosty
> face,
> Smooth up thy visage, when thou look'st
> on her;
> Thou never look'st on such bright
> majesty.
> A charmed circle draw about her court,
> Wherein warm days may dance, and no
> cold come.[79]

In *The Triumph of Winter,* Vicente seems for a moment to be following both traditions at once, but, as we shall see, this is not really the case.

The second part of the play presents the triumphs of Spring. It is much shorter than the first part; some scholars have considered it a later addition.[80] Vicente's Spring is very different from his Winter. Winter is a braggart and a bully, exulting in his powers and ready to run roughshod over anyone who gets in his way; Spring is a polished courtier, eager to give pleasure to others and confident of

---

[78] Barber, pp. 32-33.
[79] Barber, pp. 84-85.
[80] See Pratt, pp. 239-244; Crawford, p. 66.

his ability to do so. Like every perfect courtier, he knows the rules of the game of courtly love, as we see in his conversations with the Serra de Sintra, the beautiful range of mountains near Lisbon which Vicente here personifies as a lovely woman. John Stevens's remark that "much of what we today call the 'literature' of medieval England is a *symptom* of a certain kind of social activity" holds just as true for Vicente's Portugal. So does his further remark that "of no literature is this more true than of the literature of courtly love . . . Courtly love provided the aristocracy not only with a philosophy and a psychology of love but also with a code of social behavior. It was a school of manners, of 'politeness,' of 'chere of court.' In this code . . . the sexual attraction between man and woman was the central motif . . . Even if you were not a lover, you must—at least in mixed company—*act the lover*."[81] It is this desire to please, to play the game of courtly life according to the rules that is, I think, the dominant force in the personality of Vicente's Spring. His conversations with the Serra de Sintra have much more the quality of an exquisite game than of a deeply felt passion. It is not that Spring is insincere; rather, he has learned to play the game so well that for him the question of sincerity does not arise at all.

One feels that Spring could never willingly displease anyone. Yet he is perhaps more dangerous than Winter, for his charm may make men forget that his reign is fleeting, and this, indeed, has happened to Juan Guijarro and to the old woman, Brásia Caiada. Winter had declared that the discomforts he brings must be accepted with confidence that they will not last forever:

> que todas bonanças buenas
> son después de la tormenta.

As we must not despair over the hardships of Winter, so we must not cling too eagerly to the delights of Spring, for they, too, will last only a short time. The play ends by rejecting the special association of the monarchs with Spring which had seemed for

---

[81] Stevens, p. 151.

a moment to be affirmed when Winter took his leave of the king and queen.

The ending of the play is thoroughly conventional, the presentation of a gift to the sovereigns. The gift is a magic garden, kept intact by the Serra de Sintra for a thousand years. It will be presented by a prince, awakened from his enchanted sleep for just this purpose. Spring, however, interrupts his speech of presentation asserting that all gardens, even those which bear "las flores más reales," (line 1367) are subject to him. His claim is rejected instantly and brusquely. The prince insists that though what Spring says may be true of other gardens, it is not true of this one, for this is "o santo jardim de Deus" (line 1375); its flowers are the unchanging Christian virtues, which will last as long as the world itself. Winter had been forced to recognize that the splendor of the sovereigns would outlast his own brief reign; now it is Spring's turn to learn the same lesson. The king and queen are at last shown to be exempt from the cycle of the seasons, and thus implicitly to be exempt from the natural laws which govern everyone else; but they are also shown, more explicitly than in most other court plays, to be exempt from them precisely because they are identified with the Christian moral order, which transcends the order of nature.

A. A. Parker has taught us the importance for a proper understanding of the Spanish drama of the Golden Age of distinguishing between the action of a play and its theme. The Spanish dramatists, he declares, offer us "not a series of complete characters, but a complete action. By a complete action, I do not only mean one that hangs together, that ties up at the end all loose strands, I mean an action that is a significant whole, one that discloses a theme that has a significant bearing on experience, a theme that can be taken out of the particular action and universalized in the form of an important judgment on some aspect of human life."[82] Professor Parker

[82] *The Approach to the Spanish Drama of the Golden Age,* p. 5.

goes on to argue for the "primacy of theme over action, with the consequent irrelevance of realistic verisimilitude."[83] Now in Vicente, too, we can, I think, argue for the primacy of theme over action, though we shall have to add at once that, at least in the festival plays, there is nothing like a complete action in Professor Parker's sense of the term. Once more we are led back to the distinction between a play, a story with a beginning, a middle, and an end, and a masque, an invention moving upon a hinge. The *Triunfo do Inverno* has no plot at all. Its characters come and go without ever really establishing any sort of relationship with one another. And it has plenty of loose ends. We are not told whether Juan Guijarro survives the winter, nor whether the old woman succeeds in crossing the mountains, nor, perhaps, even whether the ship goes down in the storm. Yet for all that the play does have a kind of unity; its scenes are not to be equated with the separate numbers that make up a music-hall show.

Can we say that the theme of the *Triunfo do Inverno* "can be . . . universalized in the form of an important judgment on some aspect of human life"? The theme of Vicente's play is harmony, which in this context means each man's duty to accept the place assigned him in the hierarchical order of the universe. From our modern point of view this demand may well seem unreasonable; it leaves no room for the idea of progress, no room for the individual to change his situation and become what he himself would choose to be. Enid Welsford has remarked that "the Tudor and Stuart masque was bound up with creeds and institutions that the staunchest modern Tory would hardly wish to revive"; the *Triunfo do Inverno* must strike many readers in exactly the same way.[84] The reason is doubtless that, unlike most medieval and many renaissance thinkers, we no longer find it easy to conceive the whole universe as a single organism; in particular, we are reluctant to believe that any set of social institutions is a direct expression of the

---

[83] *Ibid.*, p. 27.
[84] *Op. cit.*, p. 399.

will of God, created out of His love for men to guide them to salvation. Yet the premise that one must accept one's lot as something given by God, though not, of course, all the political and economic consequences that have been drawn from it, is very old, and has proved attractive to some very gifted minds; one thinks immediately of Boethius, whose book *The Consolation of Philosophy* played an important part in forming the men of Vicente's generation, as of many others.[85]

I should argue that what matters most in the play, aside from the beauty of the verse and the effectiveness of some of the individual scenes, is the theme, and not the story. *O Triunfo do Inverno* is fundamentally a moral play. Gil Vicente would no doubt have agreed with Ben Jonson that "all Repræsentations, especially those of this nature in court, publique Spectacles, eyther have bene, or ought to be the mirrors of mans life, whose ends, for the excellence of their exhibiters (as being the donatives of great Princes, to their people) ought alwayes to carry a mixture of profit, with them, no lesse then delight."[86]

---

[85] He might have read it in the translation by Fray Alberto de Aguayo, *Libro de Boecio Severino intitulado de la consolacion de la philosophia* (Seville: Juan Cromberger, 1518), listed by Norton, p. 168.

[86] *Loves Triumph*, lines 1-7 (*Works*, VII, 735).

Auto da Índia

Auto da Índia

A farsa seguinte chamam Auto da Índia. { *f. 195 r.* }
Foi fundado sobre que ũa molher, estando já embarcado pera a Índia seu marido, lhe vieram dizer que estava desaviado, & que já não ia, & ela de pesar está chorando, & fala-lhe ũa sua criada. Foi feita em Almada, representada à muito católica rainha dona Lianor. Era de M.D. IX anos.

Entram nela estas figuras: Ama, Moça, Castelhano, Lemos, Marido.

MOÇA Jesu, Jesu, que é ora isso?
É porque se parte a armada?
AMA Olhade a mal-estreada!
Eu hei-de chorar por isso?

Before line 1 *ũa,* 'uma.' The form *ũa,* with nasal *u,* was usual in the sixteenth century; it is still found in popular speech in Northern Portugal. (See Vázquez Cuesta, p. 55; Williams, 78, 4, D.)
Before line 1 *pera.* Both *pera* and *para* are usual in sixteenth-century texts. Vicente uses both forms.
Before line 1 *seu marido.* In the sixteenth century, the definite article was much less often used with possessive pronouns than it is today. See Meier, pp. 373-374.
Before line 1 *está chorando.* Both *está chorando* and *está a chorar* were usual in the sixteenth century. Both are used in modern Portuguese, though the former is today often considered a Brazilianism.
2 *se parte a armada.* The *Garça,* on which, as we learn in line 388, the *ama's* husband sailed to India, left Lisbon on Palm Sunday (April 6), 1506, as part of the fleet commanded by Tristão da Cunha. See Révah, *BHTP,* I (1950), 176.
3 *olhade,* 'olhai.' The imperative *olhade* had already ceased to be employed in cultivated speech in Vicente's day. According to Teyssier, pp. 182 ff., it is used in the plays as a stylistic device to mark the social class of the speaker, "l'indicatif des commères." Tavani, however, observes that it is not found with the same frequency in all Vicente's women of the people and argues convincingly that "una 'caratterizzazione delle commari' non [esiste] nel senso indicato dal Teyssier, cioè come intenzionale creazione di una categoria distinta linguisticamente: [esistono] piuttosto singole individuazioni espressive di quei personaggi femminili sui quali il poeta desiderava richiamare, con maggiore o minore insistenza, l'attenzione divertita del suo pubblico per mezzo di un elemento linguistico che, per la sua arcaicità e rozzezza, doveva predisporre l'uditorio al riso" (p. 25).

MOÇA Por minha alma, que cuidei 5
e que sempre imaginei
que choráveis por noss' amo.
AMA Por qual demo ou por qual gamo
ali má-hora chorarei?

Como me leixa saudosa! 10
Toda eu fico amargurada.
MOÇA Pois porque estais anojada?
Dizei-mo por vida vossa.
AMA Leixa-m' ora eramá!
Que dizem que não vai já! 15
MOÇA Quem diz esse desconcerto?
AMA Dixeram-mo por mui certo
que é certo que fica cá.

O Concelos me faz isto!
MOÇA Se eles já estão em Restelo, 20
como pode vir a pêlo?

---

8 *gamo,* here 'cuckold.' Cf. *Inês Pereira,* ed. Révah, lines 1130-1132: "Bem sabedes vós, marido,/ quanto vos amo;/ sempre fostes percebido/ pera gamo." The synonym *cervo* occurs in line 1140. The image was a commonplace; cf. *Cancionero musical,* No. 387, lines 60-67: "Venistes vos, marido,/ de Sevilla./ Cuernos os han nacido/ de maravilla./ No ay ciervo en esta villa/ de cuernos tales,/ que no caben en casa/ ni en los corrales."
9 *má-hora.* This interjection is found in a number of variant forms in Vicente's plays. *Índia* itself offers *eramá* (15) and *muitieramá* (259). The phrase *ira má* (76) is explained by Révah (*Recherches,* II, 221) as a popular etymology based on *eramá.*
10 *leixa,* 'deixa.' The form *leixar* (from Latin LAXARE) was usual in the first third of the sixteenth century. Révah, *Recherches,* II, 98-99, suggests that the preponderance of *deixar* in the *Copilaçam* is due to the intervention of Luís Vicente or of the printer and reflects the usage of the 1560s.
17 *dixeram,* 'disseram.' Vicente uses both forms with *-x-* and forms with *-ss-*; there seems to have been no stylistic distinction between the two. See Teyssier, pp. 81-82.
19 *O Concelos.* Jorge de Vasconcelos was entrusted with arming and provisioning the ships of the *carreira da Índia* by King Manuel in 1501; he died in 1525. See Braamcamp Freire, pp. 143-144.
20 *Restelo.* The *praia de Restelo,* near Belém, just west of Lisbon, was the last familiar landmark for sailors bound for India.

Melhor veja eu Jesu Cristo!
Isso é quem porcos há menos.
AMA Certo é que bem pequenos
são meus desejos que fique. 25
MOÇA A armada está muito a pique.
AMA Arreceo al de menos.

Andei na má-hora e nela
a amassar e biscoutar
pera o o demo levar 30
à sua negra canela.
E agora dizem que não!
Agasta-se-m' o coração,
que quero sair de mim.
MOÇA Eu irei saber se é assim. 35
AMA Hajas a minha benção!

Vai a moça e fica a ama dizendo:

AMA A Santo António rogo eu
que nunca mo cá depare.
Não sinto quem não se enfare
de um diabo Zebedeu. 40
Dormirei, dormirei,
boas novas acharei.
São João no ermo estava

---

23 Correas's *Vocabulario* gives both "Kien puerkos á menos, grúñenle tras kada seto," and "Kien puerkos á menos, ke gruñen se le antoxa, i los oie lexos" (p. 408).
26 *está muito a pique,* "is about to sail.' See *Barca do Inferno,* ed. Révah, n. 22.
27 *arreceo,* 'arreceio.' Cf. *mea,* 'meia' (78); *veo,* 'veio' (236). The change from *e* to *ei* seems to have taken place in the early sixteenth century; it is possible that Vicente's spelling no longer corresponded to the actual pronunciation. See Williams 35, 7, A; *Inês Pereira,* ed. Révah, n. 368.
27 *arreceo al de menos,* 'I'm afraid that isn't the worst of it.' Cf. Modern Portuguese *isso é o de menos,* 'that isn't the worst of it.' *Al* in medieval and classical Portuguese, as in early Spanish, means "something else."
40 *de um diabo Zebedeu.* The reference is not clear; Carolina Michaëlis points out that in the New Testament Zebedee is the father of James and John, but this seems hardly relevant here.
41 Cf. Correas's *Vocabulario,* p. 332; "Dormiré, dormiré, buenas nuevas hallaré."

e a passarinha cantava.
Deus me cumpra o que sonhei! 45

[*Ouve-se a voz da moça, cantando.*]

AMA Cantando vem ela e leda.
[*Entra a moça.*]
MOÇA Dai-m' alvíssaras, senhora!
Já vai lá de foz em fora.
AMA Dou-te ũa touca de seda.
MOÇA Ou quando ele vier 50
dai-me do que vos trouxer.
AMA Ali muitieramá!
Agora há-de tornar cá?
Que chegada e que prazer!

MOÇA Virtuosa está minha ama! [*Aparte.*] 55
Do triste dele hei dó.
AMA E que falas tu lá só?
MOÇA Falo cá com esta cama.
AMA E essa cama, bem, que há?
Mostra-me essa roca cá, 60
siquer fiarei um fio.
Leixou-me aquele fastio
sem ceitil.
MOÇA Ali eramá! [*Aparte.*] *f. 195 v.*

Todos ficassem assi!
Leixou-lhe pera três anos: 65
trigo, azeite, mel e panos.
AMA Mau pesar veja eu de ti!
Tu cuidas que não te entendo?

---

61 *siquer*, 'at least.' Cf. *Auto da Alma*, lines 353-356: "Sequer dai dous passos ora/ até onde mora/ a que tem o mantimento/ celestial."
64 *assi*, 'assim.' The form *assi* is frequent in Vicente's plays, as is *si* for Modern Portuguese *sim* (e.g., in *Índia*, 444). Williams, 112, explains the nasal vowel of *sim* as having arisen under the influence of *não*, but it might equally well have been influenced by the numerous monosyllables in which the [ĩ] is etymologically justified (e.g., *fim, vim*).
67 *Mau pesar veja eu de ti!* Cf. *Inverno*, line 1147, and *Farelos*, line 162. Campos de Andrada's note on the latter passage explains that "o povo acreditava, e acredita ainda, na eficácia do *mau pesar* (desgôsto) que alguém deseja a outrem."

MOÇA Que entendeis? Ando dizendo
que quem assi fica sem nada 70
coma vós, que é obrigada . . .
Já me vós is entendendo.

AMA Ha ha ha ha ha ha!
Estará bem graciosa!
Quem se vê moça e fermosa 75
esperar, pola ira má!
Hi, se vai ele a pescar
mea légua polo mar, . .
isto bem o sabes tu,
quanto mais a Calecu! 80
Quem há tanto de esperar?

Milhor, Senhor, sê tu comigo
à hora de minha morte!
Que eu faça tão peca sorte . . .
guarde-me Deus de tal perigo! 85
O certo é dar a prazer!
Pera que é envelhecer,
esperando polo vento?
Quant'eu, por mui nécia sento
a que o contrairo fizer. 90

Partem em Maio daqui,

---

71 *coma,* 'como.' Vicente generally uses the modern form. Cf. Révah, *Recherches,* I, 97.
75 *fermosa,* 'formosa.' The usual medieval and classical form; the pretonic *e* arose from dissimilation caused by the following *o.*
76 *pola,* 'pela.' Vicente uses both forms, apparently with no stylistic distinction. See Teyssier, p. 135.
82 *milhor,* 'melhor.' The spelling with *i* was common in the sixteenth century and reflects the actual pronunciation of the word, then as now. For the change of pretonic *e* to *i* before a palatal consonant, see Williams, 41, 3, A.
89 *quant'eu,* 'na minha opinião.' Elsewhere, Vicente uses the spelling *cant'eu* (line 368), which may reflect the usual pronunciation of the phrase; see *Barco do Inferno,* ed. Révah, n. 71. *nécia,* 'néscia.'
90 *contrairo,* 'contrário.' Such methathesized forms, still common in popular speech (see Vázquez Cuesta, p. 55), were not substandard in Vicente's day.
91 *Partem em Maio daqui.* In fact, the fleet sailed on Palm Sunday, April 6, 1506. The error may be involuntary, and

quando o sangue novo atiça:
parece-te que é justiça?
Milhor vivas tu, amém,
e eu contigo também! 95
Quem sobe por essa escada?
[*Entra o Castelhano.*]

CASTELLANO ¡Paz sea 'n esta posada!
AMA Vós sois? Cuidei que era alguém.
CASTELLANO A según esso, soy yo nada.

AMA Bem, que vinda foi ora esta? 100
CASTELLANO Vengo aquí en busca mía,
que me perdí en aquel día
que os vi hermosa y honesta,
y nunca más me topé.
Invisible me torné, 105
y de mí crudo enemigo;
el cielo imperio es testigo
que de mí parte no sé.

Y ando un cuerpo sin alma,
un papel que lleva el viento, 110
un pozo de pensamiento,
una fortuna sin calma.

---

might not have been noticed by the audience. Note, however, that it *may* help to characterize the *ama*, whose anger at being left alone causes her to exaggerate. May was traditionally associated with love; cf. Torner, pp. 193-194, and *Cancionero musical*, No. 76.

92 *sangue novo.* Cf. the speech of Verano (=Primavera) in the *Auto de los cuatro tiempos:* "Agora reina Cupido/ desque vido/ la nueva sangre venida;/ ahora da nueva vida/ al namorado perdido" (lines 203-207). Bartholomaeus Anglicus, whose *Libro de proprietatibus rerum* (Toulouse, 1494) is drawn upon by Vicente for many details in the *Cuatro tiempos*, explains that "en el verano la sangre se comiença de multiplicar al cuerpo & los umores que en el yvierno estavan encogidos por la frialdad se comiençan de estender & mover por la calor del tiempo del verano" (Book IX, chap. 5).

99 *a según,* 'según.' Both *a según* and *a segundo* are found in medieval Spanish; the latter is used by Juan del Encina and, in Portuguese, by Camões (*Lusíadas*, VI, 2 and VI, 33). Vicente's repeated use of *a según* in Spanish may thus be a *lusismo*. See *Don Duardos*, ed. Alonso, n. 624.

112 *fortuna,* 'tempestad.' In this sense the word is an Italianism; see Gillet, III, 94, n. 40. Cf. *infra*, line 430.

¡ Pese al día en que nascí !
Vos y Dios sois contra mí
y nunca topo el diablo . . . 115
¿ reís de lo que yo hablo ?

AMA Bem sei eu de que me ri.

CASTELLANO Reísvos del mal que padezco,
reísvos de mi desconcierto,
reísvos que tenéis por cierto 120
que miraros no merezco.

AMA Andar em bo-hora.

CASTELLANO ¡ Oh, mi vida y mi señora,
luz de todo Portogal,
tenéis gracia especial 125
para linda matadora !

Supe que vuesso marido
era ido.

AMA Ant'ontem se foi.

CASTELLANO ¡ Al diablo que lo doy,
el desestrado perdido ! 130
¿ Qué más India que vos ?
¿ Qué más piedras preciosas ?
¿ Qué más alindadas cosas
que estardes juntos los dos ?

---

115 *nunca topo el diablo.* Vicente omits the preposition *a* before a personal object almost as often as he uses it. The omission is perhaps a *lusismo* (see Teyssier, pp. 386-387), though it need not be : sixteenth-century Spanish texts offer many examples.

122 *Andar em bo-hora.* Not, as in MPtg. *andar embora,* 'go away !' but rather 'continue, go on with what you were saying.'

127 *vuesso,* 'vuestro.' According to Keniston, the form *vuesso* was used in the 16th century only in the phrase *vuestra merced;* cf. Juan de Valdés, *Diálogo de la lengua,* pp. 91-92. Vicente's usage does not conform to Keniston's rule ; cf. *Casandra,* lines 662-663 : "Cessen las lágrimas vuessas :/ no llorará vuestra madre."

130 *desestrado,* 'desastrado.' Cf. *Barca de la Gloria,* lines 464-465 : "Barquero tan desestrado/ no ha obispos de passar." Covarrubias defines *desastrado* as "el hombre que en su nacimiento no tuvo estrella bien puesta que le favoreciesse, y assí sería de poco valor y consideración."

134 *estardes juntos,* 'estar juntos vosotros.' The use of the inflected infinitive is common in Vicente's Castilian texts and in those of his Portuguese contemporaries. See Teyssier, pp. 375-380.

No fue él Juan de Çamora, 135
que arrastrado muera yo
si por quanto Dios crio
os dexara media hora.
Y aunque la mar se humillara,
y la tormenta cessara, 140
y el viento me obedeciera,
y el quarto cielo se abriera,
un momiento no os dexara.

Mas como evangelio es esto:
que la India hizo Dios 145
sólo porque yo con vos
pudiesse passar aquesto;
y sólo por dicha mía, *f. 196 r.*
por gozar esta alegría,
la hizo Dios descobrir, 150
y no ha más que dezir,
¡por la sagrada María!

AMA Moça, vai àquele cão
que m'anda naquelas tigelas.
MOÇA Mas os gatos andam nelas. 155
CASTELLANO ¡Cuerpo del cielo con vos!
¡Hablo en las tripas de Dios,
y vos habláisme en los gatos!
AMA Se vós falais desbaratos,
em que falaremos nós? 160

CASTELLANO No me hagáis derreñegar

---

143 *momiento.* Like all the sixteenth-century Portuguese who wrote in Castilian, Vicente is frequently led astray by the many words in which Portuguese *e* and *o* correspond to Spanish *ie* and *ue,* respectively. See Teyssier, pp. 361-367.
147 *aquesto,* 'esto.' Both forms were current in sixteenth-century Castilian.
157 *hablo en,* 'hablo de.' Perhaps a *lusismo* (Portuguese *falar em*), but there are many examples in sixteenth- and seventeenth-century Spanish texts. See *Don Duardos,* ed. Alonso, n. 337; Corominas, s. v. *hablar;* Teyssier, p. 328.
159 *desbaratos,* 'defeats.' Cf. *Farelos,* lines 97-98: "Habla en roncas, picas, dalles,/ en guerras y desbaratos." Perhaps a *lusismo,* but *desbarato,* 'derrota,' is also found in sixteenth-century Spanish; see Corominas, s. v. *baratar.*
161 *derreñegar,* 'derrenegar.' Despite the *ñ* for Castilian *n,* the form is not *sayagués,* but an analogical extension of a

o hazer un desatino.
¿Vos pensáis que soy devino?
Soy hombre y siento el pesar.
Trayo de dentro un león 165
metido en el coraçon;
tiéneme el ánima dañada
de ensangrentar esta espada
en hombres, que es perdición.

Ya Dios es importunado 170
de las ánimas que le embío,
y no es en poder mío
dexar uno acuchillado.
Dexé bivo allá en el puerto
un hombrazo alto y tuerto, 175
y después fuilo a encontrar;
pensó que lo iva a matar,
y de miedo cayó muerto.

AMA Vós queríeis ficar cá?
Agora é cedo ainda; 180
tornareis vós outra vinda,
e tudo se bem fará.

CASTELLANO ¿A qué hora me mandáis?

AMA Às nove horas e nô-mais,

---

palatalization favored by the *ie* of such forms as *reñiego* and *reñiega*. See Teyssier, p. 69.

163 *devino,* 'divino.' The Castilian texts included in the *Copilaçam* offer many examples of *e* for pretonic *i* and of *o* for pretonic *u*; so do works in Spanish by other Portuguese authors. The phenomenon is, nevertheless, not a *lusismo*; it is frequent in sixteenth-century Spanish writers and is still often found in the following centuries. See Lapesa, *Historia de la lengua,* p. 187; Teyssier, pp. 323-325.

164 *trayo,* 'traigo.' The usual form in Old Spanish, it was still occasionally used by sixteenth-century writers. See Menéndez Pidal, *Manual,* paragraph 113, 2; Gillet, III, 95, n. 44.

171 *embío,* 'envío.' Cf. *bivo,* 'vivo' in line 175. Vicente (or the printers of the *Copilaçam*) often uses *b* where modern Spanish spelling, following the etymology of the words, demands *v*. Many sixteenth and seventeenth-century Spanish texts do the same, especially when an initial *v* is followed by another *v* in the next syllable (e.g., in *vivo, volver,* which often appear as *biuo, boluer*).

184 *nô-mais.* Medieval and classical form of *não mais.* Cf.

e tirai ũa pedrinha, 185
pedra muito pequenin[h]a,
à janela dos quintais.

Entonces vos abrirei
de muito boa vontade.
Pois sois homem de verdade, 190
nunca vos falecerei.

CASTELLANO ¿Sabéis qué ganáis en esso?
El mundo todo por vuesso;
que aunque tal capa me veis,
tengo más que pensaréis, 195
y no lo toméis en gruesso.

Bésoos las manos, señora.
Voyme con vuessa licencia
más ufano que Florencia.

AMA Ide e vinde muit' em bo-hora. 200

MOÇA Jesu, como é rebolão!
Dai, dai ò demo o ladrão!

AMA Muito bem me parece ele.

MOÇA Não vos fieis vós naquele,
porque aquilo é refião. 205

AMA Ja lhe eu tenho prometido.

MOÇA Muito em bo-hora seja assi.

AMA Um Lemos andava aqui,
meu namorado perdido?

Camões, *Os Lusíadas*, III, 67: "Sendo êstes que fizeram tanto abalo/ Nô-mais que só sessenta de cavalo." Further examples in Sousa da Silveira, p. 127.
188 *entonces*, 'então.' *Entonces* is frequent in sixteenth-century texts alongside the more usual *então*. There seems to have been no stylistic distinction between the two forms. See Teyssier, pp. 140-141; *Inês Pereira*, ed. Révah, n. 380.
195 Correas's *Vocabulario*, p. 34, gives several versions of this proverbial expression; the one most like Vicente's is "aunke me veis kon este kapote, otro tengo allá en el monte."
202 *ò*, 'ao.' The pronunciation *ò* seems to have been usual in sixteenth-century Portuguese; cf. Fernão de Oliveira, *Gramática da lingoagem portuguesa* (Lisbon, 1536), quoted by José G. Herculano de Carvalho, p. 22. It is still often heard in Portugal.
205 *refião*, 'rufião.' The pretonic *e* is perhaps caused by confusion with the many words in *re-*.

MOÇA Quem? O rascão do sombreiro? 210
AMA Mas antes era escudeiro!
MOÇA Seria, mas bem çafado;
não sospirava o coitado
senão por algum dinheiro.

AMA Não é ele homem dessa arte. 215
MOÇA Pois inda ele não esquece?
Há muito que não parece.
AMA Quant'eu, não sei dele parte.
MOÇA Como ele souber, à fé,
que nosso amo aqui não é, 220
Lemos vos vesitará.
LEMOS Ó de casa!
AMA Quem é lá?
LEMOS Subirei?
AMA Suba quem é.

[*Entra Lemos.*]

LEMOS Vosso cativo, senhora.
AMA Jesu! Tamanha mesura! 225
Sou rainha porventura?
LEMOS Mas sois minha emperadora.
AMA Que foi do vosso passear,
com luar e sem luar,
toda a noite nesta rua? 230
LEMOS Achei-vos sempre tão crua,
que vos não pude aturar. *f. 196 v.*

Mas agora como estais?

---

210 *rascão,* 'mandrião, vadio." See *Inês Pereira,* ed. Révah, n. 691.
211 *escudeiro,* 'título honorífico, que designa o grau mais inferior de nobreza' (Morais). Cf. Covarrubias, s. v. *escudero:* "el hidalgo que lleva el escudo al cavallero, en tanto que no pelea con él. . . . En la paz, los escuderos sirven a los señores de acompañar delante sus personas, asistir en la antecámara o sala; otros se están en sus casas y llevan acostamiento de los señores, acudiendo a sus obligaciones a tiempos ciertos."
212 *çafado,* 'safado.'
216 *inda,* 'ainda.' Both forms are found in sixteenth-century texts.
216-217 Cf. the proverb "Quem não aparece, esquece" (Chaves, p. 350.)

AMA Foi-se à Índia meu marido,
e depois homem nacido 235
não veo onde vós cuidais.
E, por vida de Costança,
que se não fosse a lembrança
MOÇA Dizei já essa mentira. [*Aparte.*]
AMA que eu vos não consentira 240
entrar em tanta privança.

LEMOS Pois que agora estais singela,
que lei me dais vós, senhora?
AMA Digo que venhais em bo-hora.
[*Ouve-se tirar uma pedra à janela.*]
LEMOS Quem tira àquela janela? 245
AMA Meninos que andam brincando,
e tiram de quando em quando.
LEMOS Que dizeis, senhora minha?
AMA Metei-vos nessa cozinha,
que me estão ali chamando. 250

CASTELLANO Ábrame vuessa merced
que estoy aquí a la vergüença,
¿Esto úsase en Sigüença?
Pues prometéis, mantened.
AMA Calai-vos, muitieramá, 255
até que meu irmão se vá!
Dissimulai por hi entanto.
Ora vistes o quebranto?
Andar muitieramá!

LEMOS Quem é aquele que falava? 260
AMA O Castelhano vinagreiro.
LEMOS Que quer?
AMA Vem polo dinheiro
do vinagre que me dava.
Vós queríeis cá cear,
e eu não tenho que vos dar. 265
LEMOS Vá esta moça à ribeira
e traga-a cá toda enteira,

---

261 *vinagreiro*. Cf. Modern Portuguese *vinagre,* 'pessoa de génio ou modos desabridos' (*Pequeno Dicionário,* s.v.) Morais, s. v. *vinagre,* gives "*Estar com os vinagres,* estar mal disposto, arreliado." In the *Barca do Inferno,* ed. Révah, line 270 the parvo addresses the Devil as "Pero Vinagre."

que toda s'há-de gastar.

MOÇA Azevias trazerei?
LEMOS Dá ò demo as azevias; 270
não compres, já me enfastias.
MOÇA O que quiserdes comprarei.
LEMOS Traze ũa quarta de cereijas
e um ceitil de briguigões.
MOÇA Cabrito?
LEMOS Tem mil barejas. 275

MOÇA E ostras? Trazerei delas?
LEMOS Se valerem caras, não:
antes, traze mais um pão
e o vinho das Estrelas.
MOÇA Quanto trazerei de vinho? 280
LEMOS Três pichéis deste caminho.
MOÇA Dais-me um cinquinho nô-mais?
LEMOS Toma aí mais dous reais.

Vai e vem muito emproviso.
[*Canta.*]
Quem vos anojou, meu bem, 285
bem anojado me tem.
AMA Vós cantais em vosso siso?
LEMOS Deixai-me cantar, senhora.
AMA A vizinhança que dirá?
Se meu marido aqui não está 290
e vos ouvirem cantar,
que rezão lhe posso eu dar
que não seja muito má?

---

269 *azevias,* 'dabs, flounders.'
274 *briguigões,* 'berbigões.' Cf. Morais, *s. v.*
275 *barejas,* 'varejas.' Cf. Morais, *s. v.*
282 *cinquinho.* Cf. Viterbo, *Elucidário,* s.v.: "Eram cinco réis de prata. Esta moedinha fez lavrar el-rei D. João II, e seu sucessor el-rei D. Manuel."
292 *rezão,* 'razão.' *Rezão* is the usual form in medieval and classical Portuguese; the *e* may come from confusion with the prefix *re-* (cf. n. 205), though Williams, 40, 2, A, gives a different explanation, arguing that "the *e* of such forms as *menhã* and *rezão,* which arose in the late fifteenth or early sixteenth century, developed by dissimilation."
292 *lhe,* 'lhes.' *Lhe* for *lhes* is common in classical Portuguese (Sá de Miranda, Camões), as is *le* for *les* in sixteenth-century Castilian. See Gillet, III, 105-106, n. 39.

CASTELLANO ¡ Reniego de Marenilla!
¿ Esto es burla o es burleta? 295
¿ Queréis que me haga trompeta
que me oiga toda la villa?
[*Fala a ama a Lemos:*]
AMA Entrai vós ali, senhor,
que ouço o corregedor.
Temo tanto esta devassa! 300
Entrai vós ness'outra casa,
que sinto grande rumor.

Chega à janela.

Falai vós passo, micer!
CASTELLANO ¡ Pesar ora de San Pa[b]lo!
¿ Esto es burla o es diablo? 305
AMA E eu posso-vos mais fazer?
CASTELLANO ¿ Y aun en esso está ahora
la vida de Juan de Çamora?
Son noches de Navidá;
quiere amanecer ya, 310
que no tardará media hora.

AMA Meu irmão cuidei que se ia.
CASTELLANO Ah señora, ¿ y reísvos vos?

---

303 *Falai vós passo, micer!* 'falai baixo, senhor.' The same phrase, *hablar passo,* is found in Old Spanish and still occurs in texts of the *siglo de oro;* see Corominas, s. v. *pasa.* Covarrubias, s. v. *passo,* glosses *hablar passo* with *hablar quedo. Micer* is a borrowing from Italian *messer,* or, rather, from a dialectal form *misser,* perhaps by way of Catalan *misser.* In Castilian, *micer* was often used in the fifteenth and sixteenth centuries to refer to Italians and Catalans; it may be significant that Constança uses it in addressing the Castilian Juan de Zamora. See Corominas, s. v. *señor.*
304 *San Pablo.* The *Copilaçam* has *Sam Palo,* but the rhyme with *diablo* shows that this is an error, caused perhaps by the custom of invoking imaginary saints, often with comically inappropriate or suggestive names. See Gillet, III, index, s. v. "saints (fantastic)."
309 *Navidá,* 'Navidad.' The omission of final *-d* is frequent in sixteenth-century Spanish texts.
313 *reísvos vos,* 'os reís.' Cf. Lapesa, "La lengua de la poesía epica," p. 8: "Los romances viejos, no obstante habernos llegado en pliegos sueltos posteriores casi todos a 1525, o en colecciones que datan de 1547 en adelante,

	¡ Ábrame, cuerpo de Dios!	*f. 197 r.*
AMA	Tornareis cá outro dia.	315
CASTELLANO	¡ Assossiega, coraçón;	
	adormiéntate, león!	
	No eches la casa en tierra,	
	ni hagas tan cruda guerra	
	que mueras como Sansón.	320
	¡ Esta burla es de verdad,	
	por los ossos de Medea!	
	¡ Si no, que arrastrado sea	
	mañana por la ciudad,	
	por la sangre soverana	325
	de la batalla Troyana!	
	Y juro a la casa santa . . .	
AMA	Pera que é essa jura tanta?	
CASTELLANO	¿ Y aun vos estáis ufana?	
	Quiero destruir el mundo,	330
	quemar la casa, es la verdad;	
	después, quemar la ciudad:	
	señora, en esto me fundo.	
	Después, si Dios me dixere,	
	quando allá con él me viere,	335
	que por sola una muger. . . .	

---

responden al estado lingüístico del siglo XV: . . . muy repetidos, *non* y *vos* átono ('¿De qué *vos* reís, señora? ¿de qué *vos* reís, mi vida[?]')." Vicente may have been unaware of the archaism.

320 *Sansón.* The *Copilaçam* has *San Son,* doubtless a copyist's or printer's error, suggested by the tradition mentioned in n. 304.

322 *ossos,* 'huesos.' The use of the Portuguese word here may be simply a printer's error; Vicente elsewhere uses the correct Castilian form (*Barca de la Gloria,* line 25; *Auto de los cuatro tiempos,* lines 53, 134).

333 *me fundo.* Cf. *Amadís,* lines 785-788, where Amadís, in answer to the hermit's question "¿ Y queréis ser ermitaño?", answers "Padre, en esse bien me fundo,/ porque el mundo en que me daño/ nunca fue para mí mundo,/ sino una mar de engaño." Vicente uses the phrase several times in Portuguese, e. g. in *Auto da Alma,* ed. Sousa da Silveira, line 168, and in *Barca do Inferno,* line 225. Révah's note on the latter passage cites Morais's definition of *fazer fundamento:* "fazer caso, ter tenção, e resolução assentada para algum fim." Spanish examples are cited by Gillet, III, 57, n. 21.

Bien sabré qué responder,
quando a esso viniere.

AMA Isso são rebolarias.
CASTELLANO Séame Dios testigo 340
que vos veréis lo que digo
antes que passen tres días.
[*Vai-se o Castelhano.*]
AMA Má viagem faças tu
caminho de Calecu,
praza à Virgem consagrada! 345
LEMOS Que é isso?
AMA Não é nada.
LEMOS Assí viva Berzabu!

AMA I-vos em bo-hora, senhor
que isto quer amanhecer.
Tudo está a vosso prazer, 350
com muito dobrado amor.
[*Vai-se Lemos.*]
[MOÇA] Oh que mesuras tamanhas! [*Aparte.*]
Quantas artes, quantas manhas,
que sabe fazer minha ama!
Um na rua, outro na cama! 355
AMA Que falas? Que t'arreganhas?

MOÇA Ando dizendo entre mi
que agora vai em dous anos
que eu fui lavar os panos
além do chão d'Alcami; 360
e logo partiu a armada,
domingo de madrugada.
Não pode muito tardar
nova se há-de tornar
noss'amo pera a pousada. 365

---

348 *I-vos,* 'ide-vos.' *I* is the usual medieval and classical form.
352 In the *Copilaçam,* the *moça's* speech begins with the following line.
357 *mi,* 'mim.' Both forms are found in the *Copilaçam* and in the works of other sixteenth-century writers, among them Camões. Fernão de Oliveira observes: "*mi.* alghũs o acabão co esta letra .til. assi .mĩ." (cited by Révah, *Inês Pereira,* n. 87).

AMA Asinha?
MOÇA Dous anos há
que partiu Tristão da Cunha.
AMA Cant'eu ano e meo punha.
MOÇA Mas dous e mais haverá.
AMA Vai tu comprar de comer. 370
Tens muito pera fazer;
não tardes.
MOÇA Não, senhora;
eu virei logo ness'hora
(se me eu lá não detiver). [*Aparte.*]

[*Vai-se a moça.*]

AMA Mas que graça que seria, 375
se este negro meu marido
tornasse a Lixboa vivo
pera minha companhia!
Mas isto não pode ser,
que ele havia de morrer 380
sòmente de ver o mar.
Quero fiar e cantar,
segura de o nunca ver.

[*Entra a moça.*]

MOÇA Ai senhora! Venho morta!
Noss'amo é hoje aqui! 385
AMA Má nova venha por ti,
pe[r]ra escomungada torta!
MOÇA A *Garça,* em que ele ia,
vem com mui grande alegria;
per Restelo entra agora. 390
Por vida minha, senhora,
que não falo zombaria.

E vi pessoa que o viu

---

366 *Dous anos há.* Here and in line 369 the *Copilaçam* has *três,* not *dous.* The fleet which left Lisbon in April, 1506, returned in July, 1508. See Révah, *BHTP,* I (1950), 176.
387 *escomungada,* 'excomungada.' The spelling *s* for pre-consonantal *x* is frequent in the *Copilaçam;* so is the reverse (e.g., *Lixboa* for *Lisboa*). In this position, written *s* and *x* were probably already pronounced [ʃ] ([ʒ] before a voiced consonant), just as in Modern Portuguese; see Hart, "Notes," pp. 414-415.

	gordo que é pera espantar.	
AMA	Pois, casa, se te eu caiar,	395
	mate-me quem me pariu!	
	[*À moça.*]	
	Quebra-me aquelas tigelas	
	e três ou quatro panelas!	*f. 197 v.*
	Que não ache em que comer!	
	Que chegada e que prazer!	400
	Fecha-me aquelas janelas;	
	deita essa carne [a] esses gatos;	
	desfaze toda essa cama.	
MOÇA	De mercês está minha ama;	
	desfeitos estão os tratos.	405
AMA	Porque não matas o fogo?	
MOÇA	Raivar, que este é outro jogo.	[*Aparte.*]
AMA	Perra, cadela, tinhosa,	
	que rosmeas, aleivosa?	
MOÇA	Digo que o matarei logo.	410
AMA	Não sei pera que é viver!	
	[*Chama-se à porta.*]	
MARIDO	Olá!	
AMA	Ali, má-hora, este é.	
	Quem é?	
MARIDO	Homem de pé.	
AMA	Gracioso se quer fazer.	
	Sobi, sobi pera cima!	415
MOÇA	É noss'amo como rima!	
AMA	Teu amo! Jesu! Jesu!	
	Alvíssaras pedirás tu!	
	[*Entra o marido.*]	
MARIDO	Abraçai-me, minha prima.	
AMA	Jesu! Quão negro e tostado!	420
	Não vos quero, não vos quero!	
MARIDO	E eu a vós si, porque espero	
	serdes molher de recado.	

---

409 *rosmeas,* 'resmungas' (Morais, s. v. *rosmear*).
423 *de recado,* 'prudente.' Morais, s.v. *recado,* explains: "*Homem de recado* . . . (fig.) Pessoa prudente, capaz de desempenhar o que está à sua conta, de acertar no que pede discrição." Chaves offers a proverb: "Mulher de bom recado enche a casa até ao telhado" (p. 237).

AMA Moça, tu que estás olhando?
Vai muito asinha saltando, 425
faze fogo, vai por vinho,
e a metade dum cabretinho,
enquanto estamos falando.

[*Vai-se a moça.*]

Ora, como vos foi lá?
MARIDO Muita fortuna passei. 430
AMA E eu, oh, quanto chorei,
quando a armada foi de cá!
E quando vi desferir,
que começastes de partir,
Jesu, eu fiquei finada! 435
Três dias não comi nada;
a alma se me queria sair.

MARIDO E nós, cem léguas daqui,
saltou tanto sudueste,
sudueste e oest-sudueste, 440
que nunca tal tromenta vi.
AMA Foi isso à quarta-feira,
aquela logo primeira?
MARIDO Si, e começou na alvorada.
AMA E eu fui-me de madrugada 445
a Nossa Senhora d'Oliveira.

E com a memória da cruz
fiz-lhe dizer ũa missa,
e prometi-vos em camisa
a Santa Maria da Luz; 450
e logo à quinta-feira

---

441 *tromenta,* 'tormenta.' Vicente uses both forms; see Teyssier, pp. 352-353. For the corresponding Spanish forms used by Vicente (*tormento, tromento, tormiento, tromiento*), see Teyssier, pp. 354-355.
445 The *Copilaçam* assigns this speech to the husband.
449 *em camisa.* Morais offers only "*Em camisa,* sem outro vestuário senão ela," which is hardly applicable here. Marques Braga, in his note on this line, explains that Constança has promised the church a sum of money equal to her husband's weight in wax, but cites no authority for this interpretation.

fui ao Spirito Santo
com outra missa também.
Chorei tanto que ninguém
nunca cuidou ver tal pranto. 455

Correstes aquela tromenta?
Andar.

MARIDO Durou-nos três dias.

AMA As minhas três romarias,
com outras mais de quarenta.

MARIDO Fomos na volta do mar 460
quasi quasi a quartelar;
a nossa *Garça* voava,
que o mar se espedaçava.

Fomos ao rio de Meca;
pelejámos e roubámos, 465
e muito risco passámos,
a vela árvore seca.

AMA E eu cá esmorecer,
fazendo mil devações,
mil choros, mil orações. 470

MARIDO Assi havia de ser.

AMA Juro-vos que de saudade
tanto de pão não comia
a triste de mi cada dia.
Doente, era ũa piedade; 475
já carne nunca a comi.
Esta camisa que trago
em vossa dita a vesti,
porque vinha bom mandado.

Onde não há marido 480
cuidai que tudo é tristura.

---

452 *Spirito Santo. Espíritu* is spelled in several different ways in the *Copilaçam: spirito, esprito, spiritu, espiritu, sprito.* That the stress was on the next-to-last syllable is proved by the rhymes *gritos: espritos* and *spirito: infinito;* see Teyssier, p. 347.
467 *a vela árvore seca.* Cf. *correr em árvore seca,* 'to scud, be driven swiftly before a gale.'
469 *devações,* 'devoções.' The usual medieval and classical form.

Não há prazer nem folgura:
sabei que é viver perdido.
Alembrava-vos eu lá? [*f 198 r.*]

MARIDO E como!

AMA Agora, aramá! 485
Lá há Índias mui fermosas;
lá faríeis vós das vossas.
E a triste de mi cá,

encerrada nesta casa,
sem consentir que vezinha 490
entrasse por ũa brasa,
por honestidade minha.

MARIDO Lá vos digo que há fadigas,
tantas mortes, tantas brigas,
e perigos descompassados, 495
que assi vimos destroçados,
pelados coma formigas.

AMA Porém vindes vós muito rico?

MARIDO Se não fora o capitão,
eu trouxera a meu quinhão 500
um milhão, vos certifico.
Calai-vos, que vós vereis
quão louçã haveis de sair.

AMA Agora me quero eu rir
disso que me vós dizeis. 505

Pois que vós vivo viestes,
que quero eu de mais riqueza?
Louvada seja a grandeza
de vós, Senhor, que mo trouxestes!
A nau vem bem carregada? 510

MARIDO Vem tão doce, embandeirada!

AMA Vamo-la, rogo-vo-lo, ver.

MARIDO Far-vos-ei nisso prazer?

AMA Si, que estou muito enfadada.

Vão-se a ver a nau e fenece esta primeira farsa.

---

498 The verse is a syllable too long. One might emend it either by omitting *vós* or by replacing *muito* with *mui.*

Quem Tem Farelos?

Quem Tem Farelos?

Este nome da farsa seguinte, Quem Tem Farelos?, *pôs-lho o vulgo. É o seu argumento que um escudeiro mancebo, per nome Aires Rosado, tangia viola e a esta causa, ainda que sua moradia era muito fraca, continuadamente era namorado. Trata-se aqui de uns amores seus per cinco figuras, s[cilicet] Ordonho, Apariço, Aires Rosado, Isabel, e ũa velha, sua mãe. Foi representada na mui nobre e sempre leal cidade de Lixboa ao muito excelente e nobre rei Dom Manuel, primeiro deste nome, nos Paços da Ribeira. Era do Senhor de M.D.V. anos.* { [*f. 191 r.*] }

Vêm Apariço e Ordonho, moços de esporas, a buscar farelos, e diz logo Apariço: { [*f. 191 v.*] }

APARIÇO Quem tem farelos?
ORDOÑO ¿Quién tiene fareles?
APARIÇO Ordonho, Ordonho, espera-m'hi.
Ó fideputa roim!
Çapatos tens amarelos!
Já não falas a ninguém! 5
ORDOÑO ¿Cómo te va, compañero?
APARIÇO Se eu moro c'um escudeiro,
como me pode a mi ir bem?

ORDOÑO ¿Quién es tu amo? Di, hermano.

Before line 1 *moradia,* 'pensão concedida pelo Rei aos moradores de sua Casa.' Cf. *infra,* n. 329. The date for the first performance given here (1505) is in all probability incorrect; see Introduction, p. 26.
Before line 1 *Apariço.* A popular form of *Aparício.*
Before line 1 *moços de esporas.* Cf. Morais, s.v. *espora*: "*Moço de esporas,* o que acompanhava o amo a pé, pegava na estribeira e lhe calçava e descalçava as esporas."
Before line 1 *buscar farelos.* "A-fim-de fazerem a palhada (mistura de palha, farelos e água) para as montadas de seus amos" (Campos de Andrada). Cf. *infra,* line 140.
2 *hi,* 'ali.' See *Júpiter,* n. 214. Ordoño's first speech rhymes with no other line in the stanza, and is ametrical, as is Apariço's. I have counted the two as forming a single line, following Campos de Andrada, who suggests that they may have been spoken simultaneously.
7 *escudeiro.* See *Índia,* n. 211.
8 *mi,* 'mim.' See *Índia,* n. 357.

APARIÇO É o demo, que me tome. 10
Morremos ambos de fome
e de lazeira todo ano.
ORDOÑO ¿Con quién bive?
APARIÇO Que sei eu?
Vive assi per hi, pelado
coma podengo escaldado. 15
ORDOÑO ¿De qué sirve?
APARIÇO De sandeu.

Pentear e jejuar,
todo dia sem comer,
cantar e sempre tanger,
sospirar e bocijar. 20
Sempre anda falando só;
faz ũas trovas tão frias,
tão sem graça, tão vazias,
que é cousa pera haver dó.

E presume de embicado, 25
que com isto raivo eu.

---

12 *todo ano.* The omission of the definite article after *todo* is frequent in sixteenth-century texts; cf. *infra,* line 18.
14 *assi,* 'assim." See *Índia,* n. 64. *per,* 'por.' In the older language, *per* was used, like Latin *per,* to indicate the space in which an action takes place. The distinction between *per* and *por* was lost in the course of the sixteenth century, the former surviving only in certain set phrases. The distribution of the two forms in the *Copilaçam* may not represent Vicente's own usage but rather a partial modernization of it. See Révah, *Recherches,* I, 162.
15 *coma,* 'como.' See *Índia,* n. 71.
20 *sospirar e bocijar,* 'suspirar e bocejar.' Sixteenth-century Portuguese texts offer many examples of *o* and *e* for pretonic *u* and *i* together with examples of *u* and *i* for pretonic *o* and *e.* For a similar phenomenon in sixteenth-century Castilian, see *Índia,* n. 163.
22 *ũas,* 'umas.' See *Índia,* note preceding line 1.
24 *pera,* 'para.' See *Índia,* note preceding line 1.
25 *embicado.* Cf. Morais, s.v.: "Inclinado, embeiçado, embevecido: 'Andavam todos, pois, embicados nela e Baltasar com as entranhas em vivo fogo,' Camilo, *O Santo da Montanha,* cap. 10, 89." Cf. also the verb *embicar-se,* defined as 'arriçar-se, dirigir galanteios' by Morais, who illustrates its use with the following sentence from Jorge Ferreira de Vasconcello's *Ulíssipo*:"O meu Barbosa embicava-se pera a moça."

Três anos há que sam seu,
e nunca lhe vi cruzado;
mas, segundo nós gastamos,
um tostão nos dura um mês. 30

ORDOÑO ¡Cuerpo de San! ¿Qué coméis?

APARIÇO Nem de pão não nos fartamos.

ORDOÑO ¿Y el caballo?

APARIÇO Está na pele,
que lhe fura já a ossada;
não comemos quási nada 35
eu e o cavalo, nem ele.
E se o visses brasonar,
e fingir mais de esforçado,
e todo o dia aturado
se lhe vai em se gabar. 40

Estoutro dia, ali num beco,
deram-lhe tantas pancadas,
tantas, tantas, que aosadas . . . !

ORDOÑO ¿Y con qué?

APARIÇO C'um arrocho seco.

ORDOÑO ¡Hi hi hi hi hi hi hi! 45

---

27 *sam.* 'sou.' *Sam* is the phonologically regular development of Latin SUM; *sou* developed by analogy with *estou* and *vou,* in order to avoid homonymy with the third plural. Fernão de Oliveira, in his grammar of 1536, mentions four forms (*som, são, sou* and *so*), of which he prefers the last. See Williams, 198, 3. In this edition I keep the old spelling *sam* for the first singular, to distinguish it from the third plural *são*; both are regularly spelled *sam* in the *Copilaçam* of 1562.

30-31 For the rhyme *mês*: *coméis,* see Teyssier, pp. 173-174.

31 *¡Cuerpo de San!* Similar oaths with *cuerpo* (*de Dios, de nos, de tal,* and many other variations) are very frequent in sixteenth-century dramatic texts in both Spanish and Portuguese. See Gillet, III, 344, n. 130.

32 *Nem . . . não.* The use of *não* before the verb after such negative expressions as *nem, ninguém,* and *nenhum* was common in medieval and classical Portuguese. Cf. *infra* lines 67-68, 233, 468.

35 *quási,* 'quase.'

43 *aosadas.* Morais glosses this old form as 'ousadamente, certamente, com seguridade.' For the corresponding Castilian form, see *Frágua,* n. 539.

APARIÇO Folguei tanto!
ORDOÑO ¿Y él, callar?
APARIÇO E ele calar e levar,
assi assi, má-hora, assi!

Vem alta noite de andar,
de dia sempre encerrado; 50
porque anda mal roupado,
não ousa de se mostrar.
Vem tão ledo —sus, cear!
como se tivesse quê;
e eu não tenho que lhe dar, 55
nem ele tem que lhe eu dê.

Toma um pedaço de pão
e um rábão engelhado,
e chanta nele bocado
coma cão. 60
Não sei como se mantém,
que não está debelitado.
ORDOÑO Bástale ser namorado,
en demás se le va bien.

APARIÇO Comendo ò demo a molher! 65
Nem casada, nem solteira,
nenhũa negra tripeira
não-no quer.
ORDOÑO ¿Será escudero peco
o desdichado? 70
APARIÇO Mas, a poder de pelado,
dá em seco!

---

48 *má-hora.* See *India,* n. 9.
63 *namorado,* 'enamorado.' Vicente uses both *namorar* and *enamorar,* apparently without being aware that the former is a dialectal form (*sayagués*), since he uses it in works, like this one, which have nothing to do with the pastoral tradition; the form is thus probably to be classed as a *lusismo* (Portuguese *namorar*). See Teyssier, pp. 66, 368.
65 *ò,* 'ao.' See *India,* n. 202.
68 *não-no quer.* The form *no* is now used only after verbal forms which end in a nasal vowel, but was formerly found also after certain other words ending in a nasal, such as *não, bem, quem,* and *sem.* See Williams, 143. 4. B.
69 *peco. Lusismo*; Port. *peco,* 'néscio, bronco.'

Todas querem que lhe dêem,
e não curam de cantar.
Sabe que quem tem que dar 75
lhe vai bem.
Querem mais um bo presente
que tanger
nem trovar nem escrever *f. 192 r.*
discretamente. 80

ORDOÑO Y pues ¿por qué estás con él?
APARIÇO Diz qu m'há-de dar a el-Rei,
e tanto farei farei . . . .
ORDOÑO ¡Déxalo, reñiega de él!
¡¿Y tal amo has de tener?! 85
APARIÇO Bofá, não sei qual me tome.
Sou já tão farto de fome
coma outros de comer.

ORDOÑO Poca gente de esta es flanca.
Pues el mío es repeor; 90
suéñase muy gran señor,
y no tiene media blanca.
Júrote a Dios que es un cesto,
un badajo contrahecho,

---

74 *não curam de cantar.* For *curar* in this sense, see Morais, s.v.: "importar-se com; interessar-se por."
77 *bo,* 'bom.' Frequent in medieval and classical Portuguese, *bo* occurs several times in the *Copilaçam.* See *Inês Pereira,* ed. Révah, n. 173.
83 Cf. Correas, *Vocabulario*: "Nadie no diga 'haré, haré,' ke más vale un 'toma' ke dos 'te daré' " (p. 228); "Faré, faré; más kiero un toma ke dos te daré" (p. 339).
84 *reñiega,* 'reniega.' See *Índia,* n. 161.
86 *Bofá,* 'a boa fé.' For this popular form, see Teyssier, p. 141.
89 *flanca,* 'franca." A *lusismo,* caused by the very frequent correspondence of initial consonant plus *r* in Portuguese to consonant plus *l* in Castilian, as in *branco*: *blanco, praça*: *plaza, praia*: *playa,* etc. See Teyssier, pp. 358-361.
92 *media blanca.* For the value of this coin, and of the *maravedi* mentioned in line 229, see Gillet, III, 198, n. 588.
93 *cesto.* Cf. Covarrubias, s.v. *cesta*: "Por afrenta se dize a uno que es un cesto, por quanto está vacío del licor de sabiduría y discreción, como hombre incapaz, que lo que oye le entra por un oydo y se le sale por el otro; como acontecería si uno quisiesse echar agua en cesto, que se toma por cosa perdida y sin provecho."

galán mucho mal dispuesto, 95
sin descanso y sin provecho.

Habla en roncas, picas, dalles,
en guerras y desbaratos;
y se pelean allí dos gatos,
ahuirá montes y valles. 100
Nunca viste tal buharro:
cuenta de los Anibales,
Cepiones, Roçasvalles,
y no matará un jarro.

Apuéstote que un judío 105
con una beca lo mate.
Quando allende fue el rebate,
nunca él entró en navío,
y quando está en la posada,
quiere destruir la tierra. 110
Siempre sospira por guerra,
y todo su hecho es nada.

Y presume allá en palacio
de andar con damas el triste.
Quando se viste, 115
toma dos horas de espacio;

---

95 *mucho mal dispuesto,* 'muy mal dispuesto.' Both constructions are found in sixteenth-century Castilian, though the former is much less frequent, as it is also in Vicente's Castilian texts. Vicente, however, uses it much more often than his Spanish contemporaries, doubtless because both constructions were still very much alive in Portuguese. See Teyssier, pp. 329-330.

97 *habla en,* 'habla de.' See *Índia,* n. 157; *roncas,* 'armas parecidas a las partesanas,' that is, halberds. *dalles.* Cf. Covarrubias, s.v.: "Arma enastada, y el hierro es una cuchilla taxante, de ambos cortes, ancha al principio y termínase en una punta muy aguda, con la qual hiere."

99 *se,* 'si.' *Lusismo,* frequent in Vicente's Castilian texts and in those of other Portuguese writers. See Teyssier, p. 335.

102 *Anibales.* For the accentuation, see *Frágua,* n. 627.

103 *Cepiones,* 'Escipiones.' *Roçasvalles,* 'Roncesvalles.'

112 *todo su hecho es nada. Nada* is frequently used without a preceding *no* in sixteenth-century Castilian; see Keniston, 40.453.

116 *de espacio.* Cf. Covarrubias, s.v. *espacio*: "Vale lugar .... También sinifica el intervalo del tiempo, y dezimos por

y quanto el cuitado lleva,
todo lo lleva alquilado,
y como se fuesse comprado,
ansí se enleva. 120

Y tambien apaña palos
como qualquier pecador;
y sobre ser el peor,
burla de buenos y malos.

APARIÇO Par Deus, roins amos temos! 125
Tem o teu mula ou cavalo?

ORDOÑO Mula, seca como un palo;
alquílala, y d'ahí comemos.

Mas mi amo tiene un bien:
que, aunque le quieran hurtar, 130
no ha hi de que sisar,
ni el triste no lo tien.

APARIÇO É músico?

ORDOÑO Muy de gana.
Quando haze alguna mueca,
canta como pata chueca; 135
otras vezes, como rana.

APARIÇO Meu amo tange viola.
Ũa voz tão requebrada . . .

ORDOÑO Quiérome ir a la posada.

APARIÇO E os farelos?

ORDOÑO Paja sola. 140

APARIÇO Mas vem comigo e verás
meu amo como é pelado,
tão doce, tão namorado,
tão doudo, que pasmarás.

---

espacio de tiempo de tantas horas, etc. . . . Caminar de espacio. Hablar de espacio, etc. No ay espacio, no ay tiempo."
120 *se enleva,* 'está contento.' *Lusismo* (Portuguese *enlevar,* 'to enrapture, enchant').
125 *Par Deus,* 'por Deus.' For the corresponding construction in sixteenth-century Castilian, see Gillet, III, 345, n. 143.
131 *ha hi,* 'hay.' *Lusismo.* For the corresponding construction in Portuguese, see *Júpiter,* n. 314.
132 *tien,* 'tiene.' See *Inverno,* n. 186.
135 *chueca. Lusismo*; cf. Ptg. *galinha choca,* 'setting hen,' and the verb *chocar,* 'to hatch.'

ORDOÑO ¿Cómo ha nombre tu señor? 145
APARIÇO Chama-se Aires Rosado;
eu chamo-lhe asno pelado,
quando me faz mais lavor.
ORDOÑO ¿Aires Rosado se llama?
APARIÇO Neste seu livro o lerás; 150
escuta tu e verás
as trovas que fez à dama.

Anda Aires Rosado só, passeando pola casa lendo no seu cancioneiro desta maneira:

AIRES *Cantiga d'Aires Rosado*
a sua dama,
e não diz como se chama, 155
de discreto namorado.

Senhora, pois me lembrais,
não sejais desconhecida, *f. 192 v.*
e dai ò demo esta vida
que me dais. 160

Ou me irei ali enforcar,
e vereis mau pesar de quem,
por vos querer grande bem,
se foi matar.
Então lá no outro mundo 165
veremos que conta dais
da triste da minha vida
que matais.

Outra sua.

Pois amor me quer matar
com dor, tristura e cuidado, 170
eu me conto por finado,
e quero-me soterrar.

Fui tomar ũa pendença
com ũa cruel senhora,
e agora 175

Before line 153 *pola*, 'pela." See *Índia*, n. 76.
162 *mau pesar*. See *Índia*, n. 67.
173 *pendença*, 'pendência.'

acho que foi pestelença.
Chore quem quiser chorar!
Saibam já que sam finado
sem finar,
e quero ser soterrado. 180

Outra sua, estando mal com sua dama.

Senhora mana Isabel,
minha paixão e fadiga,
mando lá esse papel
que vo-la diga.

Volta.

Se quiser dizer verdade, 185
dir-vos-á tantas paixões,
que em sete corações,
não couberam ametade.
Estou coa candeia na mão,
senhora minha, Isabel; 190
mando lá esse papel,
que vos diga esta paixão.

Fala Aires Rosado co' seu moço:

AIRES Como tardaste, Apariço!
APARIÇO E tanto tardei or'eu?
AIRES Apariço, bem sei eu 195
que te faz mal tanto viço.
[APARIÇO] E desd'ontem não comemos! [*Aparte.*]
AIRES Vilão farto, pé dormente.
APARIÇO Ó Ordonho, como mente! [*Aparte.*]
ORDOÑO Otro mi amo tenemos. [*Aparte.*] 200

Canta o escudeiro:

AIRES Ré mi fá sol lá so[l] lá.
APARIÇO Vês ali o que te eu digo. [*Aparte.*]
AIRES Que diabo falas tu?
Canta:
Fá lá mi ré ut.

---

188 *couberam*, 'caberiam.' The use of the pluperfect indicative instead of the conditional in the result clause of a conditional sentence is still permissible in literary style.
196 *viço*, 'pleasure, idleness.' See Gillet, III, 623, n. 66, and Corominas, s.v. *avezar*.
198 Cf. Correas, *Vocabulario*, p. 523: "Villano harto, pie entumido."

Fala:
Não rosmees tu comigo! 205
Canta:
"Un día era, un día . . ."
APARIÇO Ó Jesu! Que agastamento! [*Aparte.*]
AIRES Dá-me cá esse estromento.
APARIÇO Ó que cousa tão vazia! [*Aparte.*]
AIRES Agora que estou desposto, 210
irei tanger a minha dama.
APARIÇO Já ela estará na cama . . .
AIRES Pois entonces é o gosto!

Tange e canta na rua à porta de sua dama Isabel, e em começando a cantar "Si dormís, donzella," ladram os cães:

CÃES Hão! Hão! Hão! Hão!
AIRES Apariço, mat'esses cães, 215
ou vai, dá-lhe senhos pães!
APARIÇO E ele não tem meo pão. [*Aparte.*]

Canta o escudeiro:

AIRES Si dormís, donzella,
despertad y abrid

APARIÇO Ò diabo que te eu dou, [*Aparte.*] 220
que tão má cabeça tens!
Não tem mais de dous vinténs,
que lhe hoje o cura emprestou.

Pros[s]egue o escudeiro a cantiga:

AIRES Que venida es la hora,
si queréis partir. 225

APARIÇO Má partida venha por ti! [*Aparte.*]
E o cavalo suar! *f. 193 r.*

---

205 *rosmeas.* See *Índia,* n. 409.
208 *estromento,* 'instrumento.'
213 *entonces,* 'então.' See *Índia,* n. 188.
216 *senhos,* 'one apiece.' 'cada um o seu.' This form, usual in Old Portuguese, was apparently not yet felt as an archaism in Vicente's time; cf. Old Spanish *seños* (Modern Spanish *sendos*). For *lhe,* 'lhes,' see *Índia,* n. 292.
217 *meo,* 'meio.' See *Índia,* n. 27.

ORDOÑO ¿Y no tienes qué le dar?
APARIÇO Não tem um maravedi.

Pros[s]egue o escudeiro a cantiga:

AIRES Si estáis descalça, 230
APARIÇO Eu má-hora estou descalço. [*Aparte.*]
Canta [o escudeiro]:
AIRES Não curéis de vos calçar,
APARIÇO Nem tu não tens que me dar. [*Aparte.*]
Arrenego do teu paço!

Pros[s]egue a cantiga:

AIRES Que muchas aguas 235
tenéis de passar . . .
APARIÇO Não g'eu cant'a em teu poder! [*Aparte.*]
AIRES Ora andar!
APARIÇO Antes de muito.
Pois não espero outro fruito, [*Aparte.*]
caminhar! 240

Pros[s]egue a cantiga:

AIRES Aguas d'Alquebir,
que venida es la hora,
si queréis partir.

Aqui lhe fala a moça da janela, tão passo que ninguém a ouve, e polas palavras que ele responde se pode conjecturar o que lhe ela diz:

AIRES Senhora, não vos ouço bem. —
Oh! Que vos faço eu aqui? — 245
Que é, senhora? — Eles a mi?
Não hei medo de ninguém!
Olhai, senhora Isabel,
inda que tragam charrua,
eu só lhes terei a rua 250
com ũa espada de papel!

---

237 *g'eu,* 'já eu.' *cant'a,* 'quanto a.' See *Índia,* n. 89.
Before line 244 *passo,* 'baixo.' See *Índia,* n. 303. *polas,* 'pelas'. See *Índia,* n. 76.
249 *charrua.* Cf. Morais, s.v.: "Navio grande de guerra empregado no transporte de tropas, munições e víveres."

Que são? Que são? — Rebolarias?
E mais rides-vos de mi? —
Eu porque m'hei-d'ir daqui?
Faço-vos descortesias? — 255
Mana Isabel! Ouvis? —
Eu, que difamo de vós?
Oh pesar nunca de Deus!
Vós tendes-me em dous ceitis? —

Não sabeis que me digais? — 260
Sabeis quê? — Bem vos entendo.
Inda me não arrependo,
com quanto mal me queirais. —
Há hi mais que me perder?
Pera que são tais prefias? — 265
Bem dizeis; porém meus dias
nisto hão-de fenecer.

[Apariço] passo:

APARIÇO Dou-te ò demo essa cabeça;
não tem siso por um nabo.
AIRES Senhora, isso do cabo 270
me dizei ante que esqueça.
Mais resguardado está aqui
o meu grande amor fervente —
Que tendes? — Um pé dormente?
Oh que grão bem pera mi! 275

Hi hi hi! — De que me rio?
Rio-me de mil cousinhas,
não já vossas, senão minhas.
APARIÇO Olhai aquele desvario! *[Aparte.]*
CÃES Hão! Hão! Hão! Hão! 280

---

258 *Oh pesar nunca de Deus!* According to Campos de Andrada, the use of the oath "pesar de Deus" (or "de Nossa Senhora, dos Santos, da Fé Cristã") is forbidden in the *Ordenações Manuelinas* (Livro V, título 34). For similar oaths "neutralized" by *no, nunca, no digo,* etc., see Gillet, III, 477, n. 30.
264 *há hi,* 'há.' See *Júpiter,* n. 314.
265 *prefias,* 'porfias.' Vicente uses four different forms of this word (*perfia, prefia, porfia, profia*), apparently without stylistic distinction but with a marked preference for the first. See Teyssier, pp. 355-56.

AIRES Não ouço com a cainçada!
Rapaz, dá-lhe ũa pedrada,
ou fart'os, eramá, de pão!

APARIÇO Coas pedras os ajude Deus!
CÃES Hão! Hão! Hão! Hão! 285
AIRES Pesar não de Deus cos cães!
Rapazes, não lhes dais vós?
Senhora, não ouço nada.
Dou-me ò demo que me leve!
APARIÇO Toda esta pedra é tão leve — 290
tomai lá esta seixada!

CÃES Hãi! Hãi! Hãi! Hãi!
APARIÇO Perdoai-me vós, senhor.
AIRES Ora fizeste peor!
Ah pesar de minha mãe! 295
Não vos vades, Isabel —
está vossa mercê hi?
Nunca tal mofina vi
de cães! — Que sam cruel? . . .

Não há cousa que mais m'agaste 300
que cães! — E gatos também! *f. 193 v.*
GATO Miau! Miau!
AIRES Oh que bem!
Quant'agora m'aviaste!
Falai, senhora, a esses gatos,
e não sejais tão sofrida, 305
que antes queria a vida
toda comesta de ratos! —

Ja tornais ao defamar?
Quem é o que fala nisso? —
Senhora, sabei que é um riso 310
quanto podeis sospeitar. —

---

283 *eramá.* See *Índia,* n. 9.
303 *m'aviaste.* Cf. *Barca do Inferno,* ed. Révah, n. 70: "*aviado estou:* me voilá bien! Cf. les vers 414 et 691 *'ora estás bem aviado'* que l'on retrouve souvent dans le théâtre portugais du XVIe siècle et le commentaire de Morais: 'loc. fam. usada por antiphrase, ou ironia, para exprimir o mau estado, ou aperto em que alguem se acha."
307 *comesta,* 'comida' (past participle of *comer*).

Que tenham olhos e molhos!
Vós andais pera me ferir;
eu ando pera vos servir,
mana, meus olhos. — 315

Vós andais pera me matar!
Mana Isabel, olhai:
que o saiba vosso pai
e vossa mãe. Hão-de folgar,
porque um escudeiro privado, 320

APARIÇO Mas pelado. [*Aparte.*]

AIRES como eu sou,
e de parte meu avô
sou fidalgo afidalgado.

Já privança com El-Rei,
a quem outrem vê nem fala. 325

APARIÇO Deitam-no fora da sala. [*Aparte.*]

AIRES Senhora, com vosso pai falarei;
lá depois d'acrecentado,
não quero que me dêem nada.

APARIÇO Oh como será aviada, [*Aparte.*] 330
e seu pai encaminhado!

AIRES Que tenhais, que não tenhais,
tenho mais tapeçaria,
cavalos na estrebaria,
que não há na corte tais! 335

---

312 *Que tenham olhos e molhos!* 'Let them look all they want to!' (Literally, 'let them have eyes and plenty of them!'). Campos de Andrada cites the phrase *a molhos,* 'em abundância,' used by Camões in his *Filodemo*: "Outro dia lhe ouvirão lançar suspiros a molhos."

323 *fidalgo afidalgado,* that is, one whose rank came to him by right of birth and not because it had been conferred upon him by the King. Cf. Covarrubias, s.v. *fidalgo* and Morais, s.v. *fidalgo* and *fidalgo de linhagem.*

329 *acrecentado.* Cf. Morais, s.v. *acrescentado*: "Ant. A que se aumentou a moradia [a pensão que se dava aos fidalgos]: 'Todos seus filhos como são de idade pera irem ao Paço, logo têm parte das moradias de seus pais e como passam de vinte anos são *acrescentados* à moradia, que seus pais tem.' Gavi de Mendonça, *Cêrco de Mazagão,* IX, 30, vs., ed. de 1607."

Vossa camilha dobrada!
Não tendes em que vos acupar,
senão sòmente enfiar
aljofre já de enfadada!

APARIÇO Ó Jesu! Que mau ladrão! [*Aparte.*] 340
Quer enganar a coitada.
AIRES Ide ver se está acordada.
Que estas velhas pragas são! [*Aparte.*]
GALO Cacaracá! — Cacaracá!...
AIRES Mea-noite deve ser. 345
APARIÇO Já fora rezão comer,
pois os galos cantam já.

Escudeiro cantando:

AIRES Cantan los gallos,
yo no me duermo,
ni tengo sueño. 350

Fala:

Como? Vossa mãe vem cá?
Cá à rua? Pera quê?
Não me dá, por minha fé!
Venha, que aqui m'achará!

[*Entra a velha e diz:*]

VELHA Rogo à Virgem Maria, 355
que quem me faz erguer da cama,
que má cama e má dama,
e má lama negra e fria,
má mazela e má courela,
mau regato e mau ribeiro, 360
mau silvado e mau outreiro,
má carreira e má portela,

Mau cortiço e mau somiço,

---

336 *camilha.* Morais defines it as "cama aparatosa" and cites Camões, *Lusíadas,* VII, 57: "aquele potente Imperador/ Nũa camilha jaz, que não se iguala/ De outra algũa no preço e no lavor."
337 *acupar,* 'ocupar.'
346 *rezão,* 'razão.' See *Índia,* n. 292.

maus lobos e maus lagartos,
nunca de pão sejam fartos! 365
Mau criado, mau serviço,
má montanha, má companha,
má jornada, má pousada,
má achada, má entrada,
má aranha, má façanha, 370

Má escrença, má doença,
má doairo, má fadairo,
mau vigairo, mau trintairo,
má demanda, má sentença,
mau amigo e mau abrigo, 375
mau vinho e mau vezinho,
mau meirinho e mau caminho,
mau trigo e mau castigo,

Ira de monte e de fonte,
ira de serpe e de drago, 380
perigo de dia aziago
em rio de monte a monte,
má morte, má córte, má sorte,
má dado, má fado, má prado, *f. 194 r.*
mau criado, mau mandado 385
mau conforto te conforte!

Rogo às dores de Deus
que má caída lhe caia,
e má saída lhe saia!
Trama lhe venha dos céus! 390
Jesu! Que escuro que faz!
Ó mártere São Sadorninho!
Que má rua e que má caminho!
Cego seja quem m'isto faz!

Hui! Amara, percudida, 395
Jesu, a que m'eu encandeo!

---

371 *escrença.* A popular form of *excrescência,* 'tumor.'
372 *má doairo.* Campos de Andrada explains that "a apócope *má* em vez de *mau, maus, más* ainda hoje é corrente na linguagem plebeia: 'Má raios te partam.'" *doairo.* Morais gives *doairo* both as a synonym of *donaire* and as meaning 'rosto, semblante.' Either would be appropriate here.

Esta praga donde veo?
Deus lhe apare negra vida!

Canta o escud[eiro]:

AIRES Por mayo era, por mayo.
VELHA Hui! hui hui! E que mau lavor! 400
Quem é este rousinol,
picanço ou papagaio?

Que má-hora começaram
os que má saída lhe saia!
I, eramá, cantar à praia! 405
Más fadas que vos fadaram
a maldição de Madorra,
de Bitão e d'Abirão,
e de minha maldição!
Oh, Santa Maria m'acorra! 410

Escudeiro cantando:

AIRES Apartar-me-ão de vós,
garrido amor!
VELHA Má partida, má apartada,
mau caminho, má estrada,
má lavor te faça Deus! 415

Escudeiro cantando:

AIRES Eu amei ũa senhora
de todo meu coração.

---

399 *Por mayo era, por mayo.* The first line of the *romance* of *El prisionero.* See *Cancionero musical,* No. 85.
405 *i,* 'ide.' See *Índia,* n. 348.
407 *Madorra.* A popular deformation of Gomorra, according to Campos de Andrada, who offers no evidence to support this assertion. Though the word is written with a capital *M* in the *Copilaçam,* it may not be a proper name; cf. *Índia,* n. 320, where the capitalization found in '1562' is probably to be attributed to the printer's failure to understand the text. Note that the meaning of the common noun *madorra* would be perfectly appropriate here: 'drowsiness, sluggishness, apathy.'
408 *de Bitão e d'Abirão. Bitão* is presumably a corruption of Dathan, who, with Abiram, was swallowed up by the earth for refusing to obey Moses (Numbers 16.1-35).

Quis Deus e minha ventura
que não ma querem dar, não.
Garrido amor! 420

VELHA Má cainça que te coma,
mau quebranto te quebrante
e mau lobo que te espante!
Toma duas figas, toma!
Nunca a tu hás-de levar. 425
Pára, bargante rascão,
que não te fartas de pão,
e queres musiquiar.

Pros[s]egue o escudeiro a cantiga:

AIRES Não me vos querem dare,
irme-ei a tierras agenas 430
a chorar meu pesare.
Garrido amor!

VELHA Vai-t'ò demo com sa mãe,
e dormirá a vezinhança.
Ò demo dou eu de ti a criança, 435
e esse te cá aportou.
APARIÇO Dizei-lhe que vá comer, [*Aparte.*]
que não comeu hoje bocado.
VELHA Vai comer, homem coitado,
e dá ò demo o tanger. 440

E, demais, se não tens pão,
que má-hora começaste,
aprenderas a alfaiate
ou siquer a tecelão.

---

424 *toma duas figas.* Cf. Covarrubias, s.v. *higa*: "Es una manera de menosprecio que hazemos cerrando el puño y mostrando el dedo pulgar por entre el dedo índice y el medio." See also Gillet, III, 285, n. 455.
430 *agenas,* 'alheias.' For a similar example of a Castilian word inserted in the text of a Portuguese song, cf. *Inverno,* line 1402; for a historical explanation of this practice, used repeatedly by Vicente, see Teyssier, pp. 424-425.
433 *sa mãe,* 'sua mãe.' This archaic form of the possessive adjective survived in Vicente's day only in popular and rustic speech. See Teyssier, pp. 123-125.
444 *siquer.* See *Índia,* n. 61.

Pros[s]egue a cantiga:

[AIRES] Já vedes minha partida; 445
os meus olhos já se vão.
Se se parte minha vida,
cá me fica o coração.

Vai-se o escudeiro, e fica a velha dizendo à filha:

[VELHA] Isabel, tu fazes isto;
tudo isto sai de ti. 450
Isabel, guar-te de mi,
que tu tens a culpa disto.
ISABEL Pois si! Eu o fui chamar?
VELHA Ai! Maria! Maria Rabeja!
ISABEL Trama a quem o deseja, 455
nem espera desejar!

VELHA Que dirá a vezinhança?
Dize, má molher sem siso!
ISABEL Que tenho eu de ver co'isso.
VELHA Como tens tão má criança? 460
ISABEL Algum demo valho eu, *f. 194 v.*
e algum demo mereço,
e algum demo pareço,
pois que cantam polo meu?

Vós quereis que me despeje, 465
vós quereis que tenha modos,
que pareça bem a todos

---

445 ff. For Spanish and Portuguese analogues to Aires's song, see Torner, pp. 138-142.
451 *guar-te,* 'guarda-te.' Apocopated forms of the imperative were common in Old Portuguese and are occasionally found in Vicente. See *Barca do Inferno,* ed. Révah, n. 239. For the corresponding phenomenon in Castilian, see *Inverno,* n. 795.
455 *Trama a quem o deseja! Trama,* originally 'plague,' is used by Vicente in the general sense of 'calamity, misfortune.' Cf. *Comédia de Rubena,* ed. Tavani line 227: "que maa trama que lhes naça!"; *Inês Pereira,* ed. Révah, line 159: "Trama te dê na garganta!" and the editors' notes on these two passages.
464 *polo meu,* 'por minha causa.' Cf. *Barca do Inferno,* ed. Révah, lines 463-464: "E a senhora Frorença/ po-lo meu entrará lá!"

e ninguém não me deseje?
Vós quereis que mate a gente,
de fermosa e avisada: 470
quereis que não fale nada,
nem ninguém em mi atente?

Quereis que creça e que viva
e não deseje marido?
Quereis que reine Copido, 475
e eu seja sempre esquiva?
Quereis que seja discreta,
e que não saiba d'amores?
Quereis que sinta primores,
mui guardada e mui secreta? 480

VELHA Tomade-a lá! Hui, Isabel!
Quem te deu tamanho bico,
rostinho de cerolico?
És tu moça ou bacharel?
Não deprendeste tu assi 485
o verbo d'*Anima Christe*
que tantas vezes ouviste!

ISABEL Isso não é pera mi.

VELHA E pois quê?

ISABEL Eu vo-lo direi:
Ir a meúde ao espelho, 490
e poer do branco e vermelho,
e outras cousas que eu sei:
pentear, curar de mi
e poer a ceja em dereito,

---

470 *fermosa.* See *Índia,* n. 75.
491 *poer,* 'pôr.' This medieval form was already considered old-fashioned in Vicente's day; Fernão de Oliveira, in his Portuguese grammar of 1536, declares that "este verbo *ponho pões* faz o seu infinitivo ẽ *.or.* dizẽdo *.por.* o qual todauia ja fez *poer* e ainda o assi ouuim[os] a alghũs velhos" (cited by Révah, *Inês Pereira,* n. 1117). Both forms are found in the *Copilaçam. do branco.* The use of the partitive indefinite, formed with *de* and the definite article, is frequent in sixteenth-century texts, both in Castilian and in Portuguese. See Gillet, III, 529, n. 178.
494 *ceja,* 'sobrancelha,' or, perhaps, 'pestana.' Portuguese *celha* has both meanings, unlike Spanish *ceja,* which is used only in the sense of 'eyebrow.' Campos de Andrada takes

e morder por meu proveito 495
estes beicinhos assi.

Ensinar-me a passear
pera quando for casada:
não digam que fui criada
em cima d'algum tear. 500
Saber sentir um recado,
e responder emproviso,
e saber fingir um riso
falso e bem dissimulado.

VELHA E o lavrar, Isabel? 505
ISABEL Faz a moça mui mal feita,
corcovada, contrafeita,
de feição de meo anel;
e faz muito mau carão,
e mau costume d'olhar. 510
VELHA Hui! Pois jeita-te ao fiar
estopa, ou linho, ou algodão,

Ou tecer, se vem à mão!
ISABEL Isso é pior que lavrar!
VELHA Enjeitas tu o fiar? 515
ISABEL Que não hei-de fiar, não.
Eu sou filha de moleira?
Em roca me falais vós?
Ora, assi me salve Deus,
que tendes forte cenreira! 520

---

ceja here to mean 'eyebrow,' and explains that "as damas já usavam rapar, ou, talvez mesmo, pintar as sobrancelhas," citing Ferreira de Vasconcellos's *Comédia Eufrosina,* Act III, scene 6: "Que maneira tendes para trazer uma sobrancelha tão bem feita?" Teyssier takes it to mean 'eyelash': "Isabel, comme les belles dames de son temps, voudrait bien pouvoir se farder les cils. Et elle le dit en employant le mot espagnol *ceja* parce que l'espagnol est la langue distinguée, celle de la cour et des grands personnages. Cet hispanisme, comme on voit, est du même genre que certains gallicismes du portugais moderne (ex.: *rouge*). Il caractérise une époque et une société" (p. 405).
505 *lavrar,* 'bordar.' Isabel's dislike for embroidering is shared by Inês Pereira; cf. *Inês Pereira,* ed. Révah, lines 3-4: "Renego deste lavrar/ e do primeiro que o usou!"
520 *cenreira,* 'teima, birra' (Morais).

VELHA Aprende logo a tecer.
[ISABEL] Então bolir co fiado?!
Achais outro mais honrado
ofício pera eu saber?
Tecedeira viu alguém 525
que não fosse boliçosa,
cantadeira, presuntuosa?
E não têm nunca vintém!

E quando lhe quebra o fio,
renega coma beleguim. 530
Mãe, deixai-me vós a mim,
vereis como me atavio.
Isto vai sendo de dia;
eu quero, mãe, almoçar.
VELHA Eu te farei amassar! 535
ISABEL Essa é outra fantesia!

E com isto se recolhem e fenece esta primeira farsa.

---

530 *renega,* 'curses, swears.' For a similar use of *renegar* in 16th-century Spanish, see Gillet, III, 576, n. 300.
533 *Isto vai sendo de dia.* For the use of *isto* in this construction, see *Don Duardos,* ed. Alonso, n. 886.
536 *fantesia,* 'presunção.' See J. E. Gillet, "Spanish *fantasía* for *presunción*" and *Barca do Inferno,* ed. Révah, n. 86.

Frágua de Amor

Frágua de Amor

Tragicomédia representada na festa do { *f. 151 r.* } *desposório do muito poderoso e católico Rei de gloriosa memória Dom João, o terceiro deste nome, com a sereníssima Rainha Dona Caterina nossa senhora, em sua ausência, na cidade de Evora, na era de Cristo nosso Senhor de M.D.XXV. A qual tragicomédia é chamada* Frágua d'Amor. *E o castelo de que aqui se fala é per metáfora, porque se toma castelo por Caterina.*

Primeiramente entra um peregrino dizendo:

PEREGRINO Un castillo me han loado
alto y muy esclarecido,
por los Césares fundado,
torreado y nobrecido,
en buen sino edificado, 5
de siete cercas murado:
Fe, Caridad, las primeras,
Esperança y sus parceras
virtudes de que es cercado,

Before line 1 The actual date of the first performance must have been 1524, not 1525. See Braamcamp Freire, pp. 184-185.
1ff For the metaphor of the lady as a castle threatened with attack by the lover, cf. *Cancionero musical,* No. 341, "Torre de la niña, y date,/ si no, dart'e yo conbate; ibid., No. 414; *Cancionero llamado Flor de Enamorados,* folios 83v.-84 r. Further examples in Gillet, IV, 54-55.
4 *nobrecido,* 'ennoblecido.' For the *r,* see Teyssier, pp. 358-361. The apheresis of *en-* may be a *lusismo* (cf. the frequent use of *namorado,* 'enamorado'), but note that *noblecer* existed alongside *ennoblecer* in pre-classical Spanish; Nebrija gives both forms.
5 *sino,* 'signo' [del Zodíaco]. Cf. Juan de Valdés, p. 78: "quando escrivo para castellanos, y entre castellanos, siempre quito la *g* y digo *sinificar* y no *significar, manífico* y no *magnífico, dino* y no *digno,* y digo que la quito, porque no la pronuncio."
8 *parceras,* 'compañeras.' The meaning "companion," found in medieval and classical Spanish, survives today only in western dialects of the Peninsula. See Corominas, s.v. *aparcero.*
9 *es cercado,* 'está cercado.' Cf. Keniston, 35.23: "By the sixteenth century *estar* has become definitely established

lo guardan de mil maneras. 10

Diz que tiene, y bien hermosas,
quatro torres muy derechas,
fuertes, lindas, tan graciosas,
que sobran todas las cosas *f. 151 v.*
que en el mundo fueron hechas; 15
estas quatro muy perhechas
torres, con cubos y almenas,
y todas quatro tan buenas,
que no pueden ser deshechas.

La una es genelosía, 20
y la otra gravedad,
otra liberalidad,
la otra sabedoría.
La más alta es la bondad,
las puertas de honestidad, 25
las llaves de devoción,
los petrechos de razón,
las armas de santidad.

Dizen que es tan bien fundada
su torre del homenage, 30

---

in Spanish as the normal mode of expressing the state which results from an action. But the older use of *ser* continues with diminishing frequency throughout the century."

11 *diz que,* 'se dice, dicen.' Cf. Juan de Valdés (p. 126): "Dezimos *diz que* por *dizen,* y no parece mal." Covarrubias, at the beginning of the seventeenth century, s.v. *dizque,* calls it a "palabra aldeana, que no se deve usar en Corte. Vale tanto como dizen que." It survives in many parts of the Hispanic world; see Rosenblat, pp. 311-313.

16 *per[h]echas,* 'perfectas.' See Teyssier, p. 354.

17 *cubos.* Cf. Covarrubias, s.v.: "Cubo es el torreón de la muralla o fortaleza, por ser redondo o ochavado o quadrado."

18 *todas quatro.* The omission of the definite article in this construction, rare in sixteenth-century Castilian, is frequent in contemporary Portuguese texts. See *Farelos,* n. 12; Keniston, 21.2.

20 *genelosía,* 'genealogía.' Vicente uses the same form in *Don Duardos,* line 2023; it is used by Santillana in *Bias contra Fortuna.* See Gillet, III, 651, n. 58.

23 *sabedoría,* 'sabiduría.' See *India,* n. 163.

27 *petrechos. Lusismo* (Portuguese *petrechos,* 'tools, implements, utensils.')

tan noblemente lavrada,
con piedra de tal linage
que primero fue sagrada;
y que de dentro es forrada
de muy santos pensamientos, 35
y que tiene los cimientos
para siempre ser loada
por muchos merecimientos.

La cava, en suma grandeza,
y profunda en descrición; 40
y dizen que a Salamón
ni Dios ni la natureza
no le dio más prefeción.
Castillo sin división,
gracioso, fuerte, terrible, 45
hermoso quanto es possible,
dichoso quanto es razón.

Quando vi andar bolando
su fama por las montañas,
per palacios y cabañas 50
estas cosas pregonando
con alegrías tamañas,
engendróse en mis entrañas
desseo sin detener
de ir a Castilla por ver 55
esta flor de las Españas.

Encontra-se com um romeiro e diz [*o peregrino*]:

¿Vas o vienes, padre honrado?

---

40 *descrición*, 'discreción.' *Lusismo* (Portuguese *discrição*). For the meaning of *discreción* in medieval and Renaissance texts, see A. A. Parker's appendix to his edition of Calderón's *No hay más fortuna que Dios*, pp. 77-92.
42 *Natureza*, 'naturaleza.' *Lusismo*; Vicente never uses the correct Castilian form. See Teyssier, p. 309.
43 *prefeción*, 'perfección.' Vicente uses both *perfeción* and *prefeción*. For the metathesis of the *r* see Teyssier, pp. 351-356. *Perfeción* is common in sixteenth-century Castilian; for the simplification of the consonant cluster, see Lapesa, *Historia de la lengua*, pp. 241-242.
50 *per*, 'por.' *Lusismo*. For the use of *per* and *por* in sixteenth-century Portuguese, see *Farelos*, n. 14. For Vicente's use of *per* in Castilian texts, see Teyssier, pp. 397-398.

ROMERO Vo y vengo y ahora estó.
PEREGRINO ¿Adó vas?
ROMERO Hermano, vo
ver un príncipe afamado, 60
el que en Portugal reinó,
porque dizen por allá
que es un rey tanto facundo,
que conquista todo el mundo,
y que todo se le da, 65
y es Alexandre segundo.

Dizen que quiere tomar
un castillo que hay en Castilla,
tan fuerte y en tal lugar
que si él lo conquistar, 70
gran rey es a maravilla.
PEREGRINO Mas creo que es ya tomado,
a según la nueva suena,

---

58 *estó,* 'estoy.' Forms without final *-y* were already considered old-fashioned in the first half of the sixteenth century. Cf. Juan de Valdés, p. 121: "*Yo so,* por *yo soy,* dizen algunos, pero, aunque se pueda dezir en metro, no se dize bien en prosa." With few exceptions, among them *vo,* 'voy,' in this line, Vicente uses the forms without *-y* only in rime. See Teyssier, p. 326.
59 *adó,* 'adónde.'
59-60 *vo ver un príncipe,* 'voy a ver a un príncipe.' Vicente often omits the preposition *a* before an infinitive introduced by a verb of motion. He may have been influenced by Portuguese usage, but note that the preposition was often omitted in medieval Spanish and in Lucas Fernández. See *Don Duardos,* ed. Alonso, n. 421-422. For the omission of *a* before a personal object, see *India,* n. 115.
61 *reinó,* 'ha reinado.' The use of the preterite with the force of a perfect tense, common in Old Spanish, is rare in the sixteenth century; see Keniston, 32.52. Vicente's use of it here is probably a *lusismo*; the preterite is still used in this way in Modern Portuguese.
63 *facundo.* See *Júpiter,* n. 591.
66 *Alexandre.* See *Júpiter,* n. 283.
70 *conquistar,* 'conquistare.' Forms of the future subjunctive without final *-e,* as in Portuguese, are frequent in Vicente and in the Castilian works of other Portuguese writers. See Teyssier, pp. 373-374. For the construction (*si* + future subjunctive, followed by present indicative), see Keniston, 31.23.
73 *a según,* 'según.' See *India,* n. 99.

y gran tiempo ha que tan buena
no llegó a este reinado 75
de ninguna tierra agena.

ROMERO ¿Tan aína y tan sin pena?
¿Quién haría esse lavor?
PEREGRINO El mayor dios del amor,
que todos bienes ordena; 80
pero éste es el mayor.
ROMERO Pues tal castillo venció,
cierto es lo que dizen de él,
que todo hombre que lo vio
dize: "Cred que yo vi aquel 85
en que no cabe sinó."

PEREGRINO Para te hablar verdad,
por fuerça no fue vencido,
mas el capitán Copido
le pedió la voluntad, 90
y diola sin más roido: *f. 152 r.*
vino del cielo, escondido
de su madre Venus diesa,

---

77 *aína,* 'pronto.' Covarrubias, s.v. *madrugar,* cites the proverb "Por mucho madrugar no amaneze más aína."
78 *esse lavor.* Vicente always uses *lavor* as a masculine noun (Portuguese *o lavor*). Though a number of common words are of different genders in Castilian and in Portuguese, Vicente rarely makes an error of this kind. See Teyssier, p. 384.
85 *cred,* 'creed.' Vicente consistently uses forms with only one *e,* like those of the corresponding Portuguese verb *crer.* See Teyssier, pp. 380-381.
85-86 *aquel en que no cabe sinó,* 'the one who leaves nothing to be desired.' *Sinó* is a *lusismo* (Portuguese *senão,* 'fault, defect, flaw').
90 *pedió,* 'pidió.' *Lusismo* (Portuguese *pediu*). Failure to inflect the stem vowel in the preterite of radical-changing verb is frequent in '1562,' though the correct Castilian forms are also found; the same error is often found in Spanish texts by other sixteenth-century Portuguese writers. See *Don Duardos,* ed. Alonso, n. 46.
93 *diesa,* 'diosa.' A hypercorrection, caused by the frequent correspondence of Portuguese *e* to Spanish *ie* (e.g., *terra*: *tierra*); the usual form both in medieval Portuguese and in early Spanish was *deessa* or *deesa.* See *Don Duardos,* ed. Alonso, n. 133.

bolando mucho de priessa
hecho niño esclarecido. 95

Y fue el capitán principal,
que cercó la fortaleza,
el castillo angelical,
por parte de Portugal
y por bien de su nobleza. 100
Quando Venus no halló
en el cielo el dios d'amor,
sus músicas convertió
en lágrimas, y decendió
del cielo con gran dolor. 105

Vem a deusa Vénus, rainha da música, em busca de seu filho, deus d'amor, e diz:

VENUS No sé a quién preguntar
por el mi hijo Copido,
vuestro dios d'amor, perdido;
y no sé en qué lugar
se me ha desaparecido. 110
¡Oh mi hijo esclarecido!
¿Adónde estás?
Que en mis tetas he sentido
que es cierto que llorarás,
y no serás socorrido. 115

¿En qué calle te perdí,
en qué calles te perdiste?
Oh mi amor, ¿adó fuiste?
¿Qué hará el cielo sin ti?

---

94 *de priessa,* 'de prisa.' *Priessa* was the usual form in medieval and classical Spanish; see Corominas, s.v. *prisa.*
104 *decendió,* 'descendió.' *Decender* is common in early Spanish, alongside *deçir*; Nebrija uses *decendir,* as do some sixteenth-century writers, among them Fray Luis de Granada. See Corominas, s.v. *descender.*
106ff The ultimate source of Venus's search for her lost son is the First Idyl of Moschus, but Vicente surely did not know the Greek text. See Ramalho, pp. 130-159.
112 *adónde,* 'dónde.' The original force of the preposition in *adónde* (and its variant form, *adó*) is lost in sixteenth-century Spanish, so that *adónde* is a synonym of *dónde,* and may be used indifferently to express either place toward which or place in which. See Keniston, 14.731, 14.761.

Oh mi hijo, ¿qué heziste? 120
Bien sé que no te escondiste,
mas, perdido,
no te vi ni tú me viste;
y ansí, desacorrido,
llorarás la madre triste. 125

Y si por tu voluntad
a tu madre has dexado,
y a la tierra abaxado,
es muy alta novedad
y caso muy desviado. 130
El mundo será mudado
en alegría,
o el su Rey es casado.
¡Oh, no sé por vida mía
que diga a tanto cuidado! 135

¿Adónde te hallaré?
¿Adónde me hallarás?
Vida mía, ¿adó estás?
Que sin ti siempre estaré
pensando dónde estarás. 140
Dos mil angustias me das
en buscarte;
tú de niño olvidarm' has,
mas yo no podré olvidarte
como tú me olvidarás. 145

Nunca limpiaré mi cara
de las lágrimas sobradas,
con que mexillas, quexadas,
por esta desdicha amara
a menudo son regadas. 150
Salgan muy apresuradas,
sin recelo,
del coraçón estiladas.
Oh, lágrimas de mi consuelo,
¿quándo seréis consoladas? 155

---

149 *amara*, 'amarga.' The etymological form *amaro* is found only in fifteenth and sixteenth-century poetry, where it may be a Latinism; see Corominas, s.v. *amargo*.
153 *estiladas*, 'destiladas.' See Gillet, III, 104, n. 19.

PEREGRINO Señora Venus, ¿qué havéis?
¿De qué vos andáis quexando?
VENUS Pelegrino, ando buscando
mi hijo; si de él sabéis,
haved dolor de qual ando. 160
PEREGRINO ¿Por qué no andáis cantando,
perdiendo tal dios de amor:
"Nunca fue pena mayor
ni tromento tan estraño
que iguale con el dolor"? 165

ROMERO Pues sois señora de Orfeo, *f. 152 v.*
diesa de la melodía,
cante vuessa señoria:
"¿Dónde estás que no te veo?
¿Qué es de ti, esperança mía?" 170
VENUS Mas ansí, sin alegría,
llorando cantaré yo:
"Tristeza, ¿quién a vos me dio?
Pues no fue la culpa mía,
no ge la merecí, no." 175

PEREGRINO Señora, ¿qué nos daréis,
y qué bien nos haréis vos
a mi y a dambos a dos,
si por nos nuevas sabéis

163-165 See *Júpiter,* n. 412-413.
164 *tromento,* 'tormento.' See *India,* n. 441.
169-170 A song found in the *Cancionero general* (Valencia, 1511), where it is attributed to Rodrigo Dávalos. See Torner, No. 95; *Cancionero llamado Espejo de enamorados,* p. 16.
173-175 The *cabeza* of a *villancico* found, in a somewhat different form, in the *Cancionero musical* (No. 18): "Tristeza, quien a mí vos dió,/ no ge lo mereçía yo."
175 *ge la,* 'se la.' *Ge lo* is found alongside the more frequent *se lo* in texts of the first three decades of the sixteenth century. Keniston (7.514) records no examples after 1530.
178 *dambos a dos,* 'ambos.' See Vicente's *Comedia del viudo,* n. 570.
179 *por nos,* 'por nosotros.' As the object of a preposition, *nos* is almost completely replaced in sixteenth-century Castilian by *nosotros,* though the shorter form is occasionally found, especially in the first decades of the century. See Keniston, 4.12. Vicente may have been influenced by the use of *nós* as a stressed object pronoun in Portuguese.

	de esse sublimado dios?	180
VENUS	¿Dónde está?	
PEREGRINO	¿Qué prometéis?	
VENUS	Prometo de os hazer	
	que no améis a muger	
	que de ella no alcancéis	
	quanto vuesso amor quisier.	185
ROMERO	No quiero yo más valer.	
PEREGRINO	Ni yo más riqueza pido.	
VENUS	Dadme nuevas de Copido;	
	recobraré mi plazer,	
	que está todo en mí perdido.	190
PEREGRINO	El dios d'amor decendió	
	a España, según suena,	
	y él per sí se demovió,	
	porque nunca cosa buena	
	sin amor se concertó.	195
	Entró en un castillo tal,	
	qual hizo Júpiter sólo	
	con los rayos de Apolo	
	por su mano divinal.	
	Entró con paz general	200
	'n el castillo y con razón	
	le assentó en prefeción	
	las armas de Portugal	
	en medio del coraçón.	
	Coraçón, alcaide mayor	205
	del castillo alto y grave,	
	y al niño dios de amor	
	entregó luego la llave,	
	como a su superior.	
	Y obrado este lavor	210
	por parte de Portugal,	
	visitó el Emperador;	

185 *vuesso,* 'vuestro.' See *India,* n. 127.
201 *'n el,* 'en el.' Vicente's Castilian texts offer many examples of the apheresis of the *e-* of *en* (e.g., *nel, nesta*), as well as of the usual Castilian forms (*en el, en esta*). It is a *lusismo* (Portuguese *no, nesta*), common in the Spanish works of other sixteenth-century Portuguese writers. See Teyssier, pp. 367-369.

él fue el correo mayor
y embaxador principal.

Hizo buenas maravillas; 215
renovó los coraçones;
abatió openiones;
hizo amores de renzillas;
de las discordias, canciones;
de los enojos, desseos; 220
de los males, esperanças;
de las iras, concordanças;
y de los respectos feos,
muy graciosas mudanças.

Loado seas, castillo, 225
loado seas, amor,
que sin ti y tu resplandor,
esto osaré dezillo,
no se obra tal lavor.

VENUS Muy ciertas son las señales; 230
ésse es mi hijo amado,
y pues que anduvo ocupado
en obras tan divinales,
tomo a bien el mal passado.

PEREGRINO Él convertió en herreros 235
quatro planetas nombrados,
para hazer hombres mudados
milagrosos fragüeros
con sus martillos dorados.
Es maravilla de ver; 240
no hay quien no se assombre,
que rehunden qualquiera hombre

---

228 *dezillo,* 'decirlo.' Assimilation of the final *-r* of the infinitive to the initial *l-* of a following pronoun is usual in sixteenth-century Spanish, and continued to be used in rhyme in the following century. See Lapesa, *Historia de la lengua,* p. 242.
238 *fragüeros,* 'fraguadores.'
240 *Es maravilla de ver.* For this construction, common in sixteenth-century Castilian, see Keniston, 37.5.
242 *rehunden,* 'refunden.' A hypercorrection, of the same type as *enhadar* for *enfadar* (line 694). Elsewhere in the play Vicente uses the correct Castilian forms; cf. *refundi-*

y buélvenle de nuevo hazer
la fación : ¡ ponelde el nombre !

Si queréis de más altura, *f. 153 r.* 245
si ancho, si delicado,
si viejo, moço tornado,
de la edad y estatura
que les fuere demandado.

Vem um negro cantando na língua de sua terra e diz Vénus:

VENUS Prieto, ¿ vienes de Castilla ? 250
NEGRO Poro que puruguntá bos esso ?
Mi bem lá de Tordesilha ;
que tem bos de ver co'esso,
que eu bai Castilha, que eu bem Castilha ?
VENUS ¿ Y qué nueva hay allá ? 255
NEGRO Nova que uba já maduro ;

---

ción (line 388) ; *refundido* (line 406). *qualquiera hombre.* Apocopation of *cualquiera* before a masculine singular noun was less regular in the sixteenth century than it is today, though the shortened forms tended to predominate. See Keniston, 25.2, 25.236.
244 *ponelde,* 'ponedle.' Juan de Valdés preferred the forms without metathesis, which were to become usual in modern Spanish : "yo, aunque todo se puede dezir, sin condenar ni reprehender nada, todavía tengo por mejor que el verbo vaya por sí y el pronombre por sí, y por esto digo *Al moço malo, ponedle la mesa y embiadlo al mandado*" (pp. 50-51).
Before line 250 There were many Negro slaves in Vicente's Lisbon. See Duffy, *Portuguese Africa,* pp. 133-134. Teyssier studies the characteristics of *a língua de preto* in Vicente and in other sixteenth-century texts, pp. 227-250. He concludes that Vicente makes a real attempt to reproduce, or at least to suggest, the speech of the Negro slaves and, further, that their speech was very similar to the Portuguese creole dialects of today. See also Whinnom.
251f *Poro que puruguntá bos esso,* 'por que perguntais vós isso.' The lines spoken by the Negro are translated into Portuguese by Teyssier, pp. 231-235. In the following notes I shall translate only words and phrases whose meaning may not be immediately apparent.
252 *mi bem,* 'eu venho.'
254 *bai,* 'vou.' Note that the Negro uses the Spanish form *Castilha,* rather than *Castela.*
256 *uba já maduro,* 'as uvas já estão maduras.'

já vindimai turo, turo.
Tordesilha, tanto vinha;
a mi faratai, puro vida minha!
Lá é tera mui seguro. 260

VENUS ¿En viñas te hablo yo?
NEGRO Pos en que, minha condessa?
Que inda que negro sô,
bosso oio é tão trabessa,
tão preta, que me matô. 265
Senhora, quem te frutasse
poro quatro dia nô-más,
e logo morte me matasse,
que más o dia não durasse,
polo vida que boso me dás! 270

[*Canta o negro:*]

"Le bella mal maruvada,
de linde que a mi vê,
vejo-ta trisse, nojara:
dize tu razão puru quê.

---

257 *vindimai turo,* 'vindimaram tudo.'
259 *a mi faratai, puro vida minha,* 'fartei-me, por minha vida.'
260 *tera,* 'terra.' Intervocalic *-rr-* regularly appears as *-r-* in the speech of the Negro; initial *r-* was doubtless pronounced in the same way, though the spelling provides no way of indicating it. Both initial and intervocalic *d* sometimes appear as *r* (e.g., 257 *turo,* 'tudo'; 312 *vontare,* 'vontade'; 484 *riabo,* 'diabo'), though less often than in the passages in *língua de preto* in *O Clérigo da Beira* and *Nau de Amores.*
261 *hablar en.* See *Índia,* n. 157.
264 *oio,* 'ôlho.' Palatal *lh* and *nh* are usually reduced to the semi-vowel [j] in the *língua de preto.* Cf. 293 *seora,* 'senhora'; 482 *moier,* 'mulher.'
271-282 The Negro's song is a parody of the very popular ballad of *La bella mal maridada.* For another Vicentine parody of the same text, see *Inverno,* line 1136ff. The history of the text is discussed by Romeu Figueras, *Cancionero musical,* pp. 362-364. The first four lines of Vicente's text follow closely the earliest known version, that of the *Cancionero de Juan de Molina* (Salamanca, 1527): "La bella malmaridada,/ de las lindas que yo vi,/ véote triste, enojada,/ la verdad dila tú a mí."

A mi cuida que doromia 275
quando ma foram cassá.
Se cordaro a mi jazia,
esse nunca a mi lembrá.
Le bele mal maruvada,
não sei quem casá a mi. 280
Mia marido não vale nada;
mi sabe razão puru quê."

VENUS ¿Cúyo eres, negro coitado?
NEGRO A mi sá negro de crivão,
agora sá vosso cão, 285
vossa cravo murgurado,
cativo como galinha
quando boso água querê,
logo a mi bai trazê,
e más o feixe de lenha. 290

A mi leva boso roupa Alfama.
Quando a mi manta frutai,
mi bai, seora, tomai
esse para bosso cama.
Quando uba maruro já, 295
que a mi furutai cada hora,
a mi bai tomai, senhora,
uba que boso fratá.

275-282 The rest of Vicente's parody diverges from the other known versions. Romeu Figueras notes as a "dato curioso y chocante" that "las glosas de la canción o del romance fueron usadas como canto epitalámico durante un siglo por lo menos" (p. 363). Vicente's use of the song in a play which celebrates the wedding of John III and Catherine of Austria is thus perfectly traditional.
In Portuguese: 'Eu cuido que dormia/ quando me foram casar./ Se eu jazia acordada,/ isso nunca me lembrou./ La bella mal maridada,/ não sei quem me casou./ Meu marido não vale nada,/ eu sei a razão porquê."
283 *¿cúyo eres?*, '¿de quién eres, quién es tu amo?'
284 *a mi sá*, 'eu sou.' *crivão*, 'escrivão.'
286 *cravo murgurado*, 'escravo amargurado.'
289 *a mi bai trazê*, 'eu a irei trazer.'
292 *quando a mi manta frutai*, "quando eu furtar uma manta.'
295-298 'Quando as uvas já estiverem maduras,/ que eu furto cada hora (sempre),/ eu vou tomar, senhora,/ uvas que vos fartarão.'

Se camisa furutá eu,
labrado d'ouro faramosa, 300
mi bai: "Senhora, esse é bossa,
pois que Seoro Deus ma deu."
Se podê furutá rinheiro,
corpo de reos, esse si
nunca guardai para mi, 305
bossa é toro enteiro.

VENUS Niegro, no te entiendo cosa.
¿Eres ya cristiano? Di.
NEGRO Furunando chamá a mi,
e a bos chamá foromosa. 310
VENUS Di ahora el crieleisón.
NEGRO De muto boa vontare.
Pato nosso é muto bom.

Em este passo foi posto um muito fermoso castelo, e abriu-se a porta dele, e sairam de dentro quatro galantes em trajo de caldeireiros, com cada um sua serrana muito louçã pola mão, e eles mui ricamente ataviados, cubertos de estrelas, porque figuram quatro planetas, e elas os gozos d'amor; e cada um deles traz seu martelo muito façanhoso, { *f. 153 v.* } *e todos dourados e prateados, e ũa muito grande e formosa frágua, e o deus Copido por capitão*

299-302 'Se eu furtar uma camisa,/ lavrada de ouro, formosa,/ eu vou [dizer]: "Senhora, essa é vossa,/ pois o senhor Deus ma deu." '

303-304 'Se eu puder furtar dinheiro,/ corpo de Deus, isso sim.'

305 *nunca guardai,* 'nunca o guardarei.'

306 *toro,* 'todo.'

307 *niegro,* 'negro.' A *lusismo,* possibly due to the printer, since Vicente elsewhere uses the correct form. Cf. *supra,* n. 93. *cosa,* 'nada,' is usual in medieval and classical Spanish, though in sixteenth-century prose it is seldom found without a modifier. See Gillet, III, 67, n. 4.

309 *Furunando,* 'Fernando.'

311 *crieleisón,* 'kirie eleisón.' For other deformations of the Greek phrase *Kyrie eleison,* see Gillet, III, 336, n. 20. Here, in a speech assigned to Venus, the form surely has no special popular flavor.

313 *pato nosso,* 'pater noster.' A more nearly complete version of the Lord's Prayer in *língua de preto* is given in *O Clérigo da Beira* (f. 235 v.; ed. Marques Braga, VI, 25).

dele[s]: e estas serranas *trazem cada ũa sua tenaz do teor dos martelos, pera servirem quando lavrar a frágua d'amor. E assi sairam do dito castelo com sua música, e acabando fazem o razoamento seguinte, pera declaração do significado das ditas figuras, e cada planeta fala com sua serrana.*

MERCURIO Vos sois, señora serrana,
primero gozo d'amor, 315
que es mirar al servidor
contino de buena gana,
sin le mostrar desamor.
Y pues os hizo de nada
Copido por su loor, 320
mirad a vuesso servidor
con voluntad namorada.

SERRANA PRIMERA Yo lo haré ansí, señor.

MERCURIO Vos miraréis mucho en hito
los ojos del amador, 325
porque deis gozo al dolor
que se recibe infinito,
y no paguéis con desamor;
ni sea en general
el mirar de este teor, 330
sino a vuesso servidor.

SERRANA PRIMERA Quando yo viere que es tal,
ansí lo haré yo, señor.

JÚPITER Vos sois, serrana hermosa,
segundo gozo d'amor, 335
que es hablar al servidor
mucho blanda y amorosa;
y si queréis ser dichosa,
quered a quien os tiene amor,
que la tema presuntuosa 340
es cruel al servidor.

---

317 *contino,* 'continuamente.' The usual form in sixteenth-century Castilian; after about 1600 the word was used only in an adverbial sense, as it is here. See Corominas, s.v. *continuo.*
322 *namorada,* 'enamorada.' See *Farelos,* n. 63.
330 *teor,* 'tenor.' *Lusismo,* perhaps due to the printer; the word does not appear elsewhere in Vicente's Castilian texts.
337 *mucho,* 'muy.' See *Farelos,* n. 95.

SERRANA SEGUNDA — Quando fuere justa cosa,
ansí lo haré yo, señor.

JÚPITER — Reconociendo el servicio
le daréis plazer mayor, 345
que el mayor gozo de amor
es mirar al beneficio;
que el servicio mal mirado
es dolor más que dolor
al triste que es namorado. 350

SERRANA SEGUNDA — Si yo le viere tal cuidado,
yo lo haré ansí, señor.

[*Fala*] *Saturno à serrana terceira:*

SATURNO — Sois, serrana, sin mentir,
el tercer gozo de amor,
que es mostrar al servidor 355
grande gloria en lo oír,
porque es dulce favor.
Y para el gozo ser mejor
y mucho más estimado,
quanto más en apartado 360
le dad oído mayor.

SERRANA TERCERA — Si no hablare en lo escusado,
ansí lo haré yo, señor.

SATURNO — Que quien escucha de gana,
señal es de grande amor. 365
Por esso, linda serrana,
hazed lo que os digo, hermana,
sin otro ningún rigor.
Y aunque él sea vencedor,
y vos, señora, vencida, 370
por no serdes homecida,
dalde vida al servidor.

SERRANA TERCERA — Se mi honra fuere servida,
yo lo haré ansí, señor.

---

361 *le dad,* 'dadle.' This construction, found occasionally in sixteenth-century Castilian texts, becomes increasingly rare in the latter part of the century. See Keniston, 9.541.
371 *por no serdes,* 'para que no seáis.' For the inflected infinitive, see *Índia,* n. 134.
373 *se,* 'si.' See *Farelos,* n. 99.

[*Fala o Sol à serrana terceira:*]

SOL Vos sois, serrana de flores, 375
el quarto gozo d'amor,
y es que el vuesso servidor
no os sienta otros amores,
porque es engaño mayor.
No le deis competidor; 380
sea vuesso amor senzillo,
porque el otro es desamor.

SERRANA QUARTA Si él sopiere sentillo, *f. 154 r.*
yo lo haré ansí, señor.

CUPIDO Paréceme que es razón, 385
pues reina tan excelente
viene a reinar nuevamente,
que hagamos refundición
en la portuguesa gente.
Hagamos mundo nuevo aquí, 390
pues nuevos reyes son venidos,
por el gran Dios escogidos.
Apregonad por ahí
mis milagros ascondidos.

MERCURIO Quien quisiere renovarse, 395
o hazerse de otra suerte,
venga aquí, que sin la muerte
puede muy bien emendarse:
y no lo hayáis por cosa fuerte.

---

391 *reyes.* The meter demands the monosyllabic form *reis.* Vicente uses both *reis* and *reyes,* though the former predominates. It is probably to be considered a *lusismo,* though it is found in some fifteenth-century Spanish writers, among them Fray Iñigo de Mendoza. See *Don Duardos,* ed. Alonso, n. 811, and Teyssier, pp. 337-338.
393 *apregonad.* 'pregonad.' Both *apregonar* and *empregonar* are also found in Old Spanish, but the simple form *pregonar* seems always to have been the most common. See Corominas, s.v. *pregonar.*
394 *ascondidos,* 'escondidos.' Both forms are found in sixteenth-century Castilian. See Gillet, III, 545, n. 45.
398 *emendarse,* 'enmendarse.' Though *enmendar* is found occasionally in Old Spanish, the usual form until at least the end of the fifteenth century is the etymologically correct *emendar,* which is also often found in texts of the *siglo de oro.* See Corominas, s.v. *enmendar.*

Qualquiera hombre baxuelo 400
que quisiere ser mayor,
y aun el longo ser menor,
véngase aquí sin recelo
a la fragua del amor.

Hombre muy ancho, pesado, 405
como fuere refundido
en la fragua de Cupido,
tornará muy delicado,
y el viejo remocecido.
Negra mucho denegrida, 410
si blanca quisiere ser,
o pera parda muger
moça alva, gentil, garrida,
todo se puede hazer.

NEGRO Faze-me branco, rogo-te, home, 415
asinha, logo, logo, logo!
Mandai logo acendere fogo!
E minha nariz feito bem,
e faze-me beiça delgada te rogo!

JÚPITER ¡Mirad quien començará 420
en un negro tal labor!
NEGRO Quem te manda a vós falá?
A mi falá con deos d'amor,
que farmoso ma fará.
CUPIDO Sí, sí, sí, quantos venieren, 425
negros, moros, y villanos,
mancebos y ancianos,
hazeldos como os pidieren
muy presto, y ande[n] las manos.

El que nació desdichoso 430

---

402 *longo,* 'luengo.' *Lusismo.* Vicente elsewhere uses the correct Castilian form. Juan de Valdés regarded *luengo* as an archaism, though one worth retaining: "*Luengo,* por *largo,* aunque lo usan pocos, yo lo uso de buena gana, y úsalo también el refrán que dize: *De luengas vías, luengas mentiras*" (p. 115).
409 *remocecido,* 'remozado.' Corominas, s.v. *mozo,* gives the date of the first appearance of *remozar* as around 1570, in Fray Luis de León; the older form *remocecer* is found in Nebrija.
419 *beiça,* 'beiço.'

y sin ninguna ventura,
y lo sigue desventura,
hazeldo mucho dichoso
y con ventura segura.
Y el que menos namorado 435
de lo que es quisiere andar,
ahí se puede emendar;
y el hombre desnamorado,
namorado singular.

JÚPITER ¿Cómo quieres tú hazerte? 440
NEGRO Branco como ovo de galinha.
MERCURIO Ora entra y no hayas miedo,
que no has de sentir nada.
NEGRO Fazer nariz mui delgada,
e fermosa minha dedo. 445

Entra o negro na frágua, e andam os martelos todos quatro em seu compasso, e cantam as serranas quatro vezes ao compasso dos martelos esta cantiga seguinte, feita polo autor ao propósito:

SERRANAS El que quisiere apurarse
véngase muy sin temor
a la fragua del amor.

Todo oro que se afina
es de más fina valía, 450
porque tiene mejoría
de quando estava en la mina:
ansí se apura y refina *f. 154 v.*
el hombre y cobra valor
en la fragua del amor. 455

El fuego bivo y ardiente
mejor apura el metal,
y quanto más, mejor sal,

458 *sal*, 'sale.' Such forms without final *-e* (e.g. *diz, faz, sal, quier, tien, vien*) are found in Old Spanish and in Leonese dialects, whence they passed into *sayagués*. Vicente often uses them, as he does here, without regard for their dialectal flavor. He was perhaps influenced by the fact that all of them are monosyllables in Portuguese (*diz, faz, sai, quer, tem, vem*). Elsewhere, he uses the correct Castilian form. See *Don Duardos*, ed. Alonso, n. 150; Teyssier, pp. 374-375.

más claro y más excelente:
ansí el bivir presente 460
se pára mucho mejor
en la fragua del amor.

Quanto persona más alta,
se deve querer más fina,
porque es de más fina mina 465
donde no se espera falta.
Mas tal oro no se esmalta
ni cobra rica color
sin la fragua del amor.

Sai o negro da frágua muito gentil homem branco; porém a fala de negro não se lhe pôde tirar na frágua, e ele diz:

NEGRO Já mão minha branco estai, 470
e aqui perna branco é,
mas a mi falá guiné:
se a mi negro falai,
a mi branco para quê?
Se fala meu é negregado, 475
e não fala portugás,
para que mi martelado?

MERCURIO No podemos hazer más;
lo que pediste te han dado.

NEGRO Da caminha negro tornai: 480
se mi falá namorado
a moier que branco sai,
ele dirá a mi: "Bai, bai!
Tu sá home o sá riabo?"
A negra se a mi falai 485
dirá a mi: "Sá chacorreiro?"
Oiae, seoro ferreiro:
boso meu negro tornai,
como mi saba primeiro.

Vem a Justiça em figura de ũa velha corcovada, torta, muito mal feita, com sua vara quebrada, e diz:

JUSTIÇA Sempre Deus faz cousas boas! 490

---

486 *chacorreiro,* 'chocarreiro.'

Dizei, que tenhais prazer,
isto é cousa de crer
que refundis as pessoas,
e as tornais a fazer?

SOL ¿Quién sois, que ansí estáis polida? 495

JUSTIÇA A Justiça sou chamada.
Ando muito corcovada;
a vara tenho torcida,
e a balança quebrada.

E pois de novo nos vem 500
rainha de tanto honor,
irmã do Emperador,
renovai-me muito bem,
que cada vez vou pior.

CUPIDO ¿Qué pedís o qué buscáis? 505

JUSTIÇA Que me mandês reformar
e de novo endereitar,
que a rainha que esperais
não pode muito tardar.

MERCURIO Vos venís tan maltratada, 510
que tenemos bien que hazer.

CUPIDO Es de fuerça, y ha de ser
la Justicia adereçada,
por lo ál no se perder.

JUSTIÇA Fazei-me estas mãos menores, 515
que não possam apanhar,
e que não possa escutar
esses rogos de senhores,
que me fazem entortar.

MERCURIO Alto, pues, ¡a refundir! 520

JUSTIÇA Ó Jesu, a que[m] me eu dou!

---

495 *polida*, 'pulida.' The question is ironic, as the following lines make clear.

514 *lo ál*, 'lo demás.' Cf. Juan de Valdés: "No digo *ál* adonde tengo que dezir *otra cosa,* aunque se dize: *So el sayal ay ál* y *En ál va el engaño*" (p. 105).

520 *alto*. Cf. Covarrubias, s.v.: "Algunas vezes tiene sinificación de imperativo, como: Alto de ay, Andad de ay; porque los que están echados o sentados para irse se han primero de alçar y levantar de la tierra o del lugar donde están sentados." See also Corominas, s.v.

Apartai-vos, que eis-me. Vou! *f. 155 r.*

JÚPITER Nos tenemos bien que heñir.

JUSTIÇA Sus, que já na frágua estou.

Andam os martelos forjando a Justiça com a dita música, e acabado diz Júpiter a Copido:

JÚPITER Señor, nuestro martillar 525
no nos aprovecha nada,
porque la Justicia dañada,
los que más la han de emendar
la hazen más corcovada.
Ansí que en vano gastamos 530
el carbón y herramienta:
ninguna cosa emendamos,
mas quanto más martillamos,
menos crece la emienda.

CUPIDO Serranas, sacalde vos 535
las escorias bien sacadas
con las tinazas doradas,
que con la ayuda de Dios
ella saldrá sana aosadas.

Tornam os planetas a dar outra calda, e a serrana primeiro gozo d'amor, tira da frágua com as tenazas um par de galinhas e diz Copido:

CUPIDO Esso, esso, norabuena, 540
que es el mal que la fatiga.
¡Ande otra vez la cantiga,
salga ess'otra ave de pena!

Andam outra vez os martelos, e a serrana segundo gozo d'amor, tira da frágua um par de pássaras, e diz Copido:

CUPIDO ¿Qué escoria es essa, serranilla?

SERRANA [SEGUNDA] Son perdizes, mi señor. 545

---

537 *tinazas,* 'tenazas.'

539 *aosadas.* Cf. Covarrubias, s.v.: "Es un término muy usado para assegurar y esperar de cierto una cosa, y vale tanto como: osaría yo apostar." See also Gillet, III, 432, n. 134. For the corresponding Portuguese form, see *Farelos,* n. 43.

CUPIDO Pues aún queda otra peor,
que mucho más la manzilla.

Tornam outra vez a dar outra calda e tiram as serranas terceiro e quatro gozo d'amor duas grandes bolsas de dinheiro da frágua, e diz Copido:

CUPIDO Ess'otra escoria, ¿qué es?
SERRANA [TERCERA] Son dineros de las pechas.
CUPIDO Ora sacalda y veréis 550
maravillas que havéis hechas.

Sai a Justiça da frágua muito fermosa e dereita, e diz:

JUSTIÇA Agora que estou assi
fermosa e bem aparada,
por não ir acorcovada
que remédio será aqui, 555
que inda estou temorizada?
CUPIDO Ios mirar al espejo
de Trajano, mi señora,
y veréis quál vais ahora,
porque hovistes buen consejo. 560
Ios, Justicia, en buen hora.

---

549 *pechas.* Vicente uses the word here not in the usual Castilian sense of 'tributo que se paga al rey,' but in that of Portuguese *peita,* 'bribe.'
552 *assi,* 'assim.' See *Índia,* n. 64.
553 *fermosa,* 'formosa.' See *Índia,* n. 75.
556 *inda,* 'ainda.' See *Índia,* n. 216.
557 *Ios,* 'idos.' The los of final *-d* in the imperative occurs sporadically in sixteenth-century Castilian texts; see Keniston, 30.41. For the corresponding phenomenon in Portuguese, see *Índia,* n. 348.
558 *Trajano.* Cf. *Don Duardos,* lines 1748-1749: "Sed vos Roma, yo Trajano/ para vos." See also Pedro Mexía, *Silva de varia lección,* (Madrid, 1662), part I, chapter vi: "aquel buen Emperador de Roma Trajano, natural de nuestra España, en cuyo tiempo fue mayor el Imperio Romano en tierras, y potencia, que antes, ni despues lo ha sido, y mejor con armas, y justicia administrado, y regido." (The first edition is that of Seville, 1540.)
561 *en buen hora.* The apocopation of *buena* in the phrase *en buen hora* was usual in sixteenth-century Spanish, though the full form *en buena hora* also occurs. See Keniston, 25.225.

Vai-se a Justiça e vem um frade e diz:

FRADE Senhores, fui carpinteiro
da Ribeira de Lixboa,
e muito boa pessoa,
e de mero malhadeiro 565
me fui fazer de coroa.
Cousas m'aquecem a mi,
que o demo anda comigo:
conselhou-me um meu amigo
que fosse frade, e fi-lo assi, 570
de Rui Pírez, Frei Rodrigo.

Eis-me frade: andar em bo-hora!
E fui azemel primeiro,
antes de ser carpinteiro,
e estou assi frade agora, 575
porém fora do mosteiro.

CUPIDO Padre, ¿qué es lo que queréis?

FRADE Queria-me desfazer,
e tornásseis-me a fazer
muito leigo se podeis: 580
que leigo tornasse a ser.

Um fidalgo assi meão, *f. 155 v.*
um Vasco de Fois na altura,
a barba daquela feitura,
não tão denegrida, não, 585
senão assi, castanha escura.
Uns olhos garços cansados,
e o ar de Pero Moniz;
e eu peitarei perdiz
e dous pares de cruzados, 590
se me mudais o matiz.

---

572 *andar em bo-hora!* See *Índia*, n. 122.
583 *Vasco de Fois.* Courtier and contributor to the *Cancioneiro geral.* See Braamcamp Freire, pp. 179-180. Vicente mentions him also in *Inês Pereira*, and in *O Clérigo da Beira*, where Pedreanes, in answer to the question "Sabes quantos anos há/ que Vasco de Fois é nado?," replies "Quando foi a do Selado/ era ele mancebo já,/ mas não era tão barbado" (f. 238 r.; ed. Marques Braga, VI, 40). The battle of Salado took place in 1340.
588 *Pero Moniz.* For this royal official, see Braamcamp Freire, p. 186.
589 *peitarei*, 'pagarei.'

CUPIDO ¿Por qué no queréis ser fraile?
FRADE Porque meu saber não erra:
somos mais frades cá [à] terra
sem conto na Cristandade, 595
sem servirmos nunca em guerra.
E haviam mister refundidos
ao menos três partes deles
em leigos, e arneses neles,
e mui bem aprecebidos: 600
então a Mouros co'eles!

Começai em mi, senhor.
CUPIDO Bien veo vuessa intención;
traedme vos provisión
de vuesso superior, 605
y yo haré lo que es razón.
FRADE Mal fazeis, senhor Copido,
que por ser vosso vassalo
o faço ainda que calo;
mas eu virei aprecebido 610
de feição pera acabá-lo.

Vai-se o frade e vem um pagem, e diz Copido:

CUPIDO ¿Mandáis algo, hermano, acá?
PAJEM Recado do senhor marquês.
CUPIDO ¿Qué manda, hijo? ¿Qué es?
PAJEM Que leveis a frágua lá 615
logo, e que lhe não tardeis.
CUPIDO Dizid a su señoría
que no le haze menester,
ni le quiero deshazer,
porque mi sabedoría 620
otro tal no puede hazer.

Dezid que no le faltó
nunca prefeción ninguna;
que la próspera fortuna
reinava quando él nació, 625
y lo amó dende la cuna.

---

613 *recado do senhor marquês.* Dom Pedro de Meneses, Marquis of Vila Real. See Braamcamp Freire, p. 186.
626 *dende,* 'desde.' *Dende* originally meant 'de allí,' but it soon became confused with *desde*; it is still used with the

Y pues lo hizo Anibal,
cavallero tan famoso,
si yo refundirlo oso,
¿cómo se hará otro tal? 630

Vai-se o pagem, e vem um parvo e diz:

PARVO Manda-me cá Vasco de Fois,
que o mandeis vós forjar.
CUPIDO ¿Para qué hombre tan fino?
PARVO Para que o façais menino,
e eu para o embalar. 635
CUPIDO No sé si es moço, si viejo,
mas no sé dónde le viene
que ninguna cana tiene,
y arrugado el pelejo.
JÚPITER Algunos péinanse allá 640
con peines de vinte y ocho.
PARVO E vinta nove, e tinta ainda.
CUPIDO Este parvo es pevidoso;
por dezir trinta dixo tinta.

Vem outro pagem, e diz Copido:

CUPIDO Devéis vos page de ser 645
del conde de Marialva.
PAJEM Si, e manda-vos dizer

latter meaning in many parts of the Hispanic world. See Corominas, s.v. *ende*.
627 *Anibal,* 'Aníbal.' Cf. Gillet, III, 571, n. 310: "This proper name, *esdrújulo* in Latin, has now the *acento grave,* but was *agudo* until the end of the seventeenth century."
637 *dónde,* 'de dónde.' Though *dónde* in this sense may be a *lusismo,* the word is found in Old Spanish and is not rare in fifteenth-century texts. See *Don Duardos,* ed. Alonso, n. 579.
639 *pelejo,* 'pellejo.' See Teyssier, pp. 369-370.
642 *vinta nove,* 'vinte e nove.' For *vinta,* see Williams 133.2. The pun on *tinta*: *trinta* is a reference to Vasco's practice of dying his beard.
643 *pevidoso,* here, 'one who has a speech defect, especially one who has difficulty in pronouncing the sound *r*.' *Lusismo.* See Teyssier, p. 398.
646 *del conde de Marialva.* Dom Francisco Coutinho. See Braamcamp Freire, p. 260. Vicente refers to him in similarly unflattering terms in *O Clérigo da Beira* (f. 238 r.; ed Marques Braga, VI, 39). To the question how long the count will live, Pedreanes replies: "Mau é isso de saber,/ que ele não é flor de malva,/ que apodrece sem chover./

se o podereis fazer
mancebo no corpo e na alma.
e que lhe não refundais 650
o dinheiro que ele tem,
mas nele forjeis tão bem,
que apanhe muito mais
e não dé nada a ninguém.

Torna o frade com um saco de carvão, e diz: f. 156 r.

FRADE Toda-las cousas do mundo 655
estão na boa diligência.
CUPIDO ¿Qué manda su reverencia?
FRADE Senhor Copido, eu me fundo
não curar da con[s]ciência.
Avorrece-me a coroa, 660
o capelo e o cordão,
o hábito e a feição,
e a béspora e a noa,
e a missa e o sermão.

E o sino e o badalo, 665
e o silêncio e deceplina,
e o frade que nos matina;
no espertador não falo,
que a todos nos amofina.
Parece-me bem bailar 670
e andar nũa folia,
ir a cada romaria
com mancebos a folgar:
isto é o que eu queria.

Parece-me bem jugar, 675
parece-me bem dizer:

Com todas sųas feridas/ e muito enferma canseira,/ contratou-se de maneira/ que Deus lhe deve três vidas/ e esta é inda a primeira."

654 *dé*, 'dê.' In '1562': *dee*. The rimes of the early *cancioneiros* show that the first and third singular of the present subjunctive of *dar* had an open vowel in Old Portuguese; it subsequently became closed by analogy with the second singular. See Williams, 182.2.

658 *eu me fundo*. See *Índia*, n. 333.

663 *béspora*, 'véspera.'

666 *deceplina*, 'disciplina.' For the pretonic *e*, see *Índia*, n. 163.

"Vai chamar minha molher,
que me faça de jantar."
Isto, eramá, é viver!

JÚPITER ¿De qué faición o idade — 680
queréis vos que os hagamos?

FRADE Esperai, assi vejamos:
eu direi minha vontade,
pois já em al não estamos.

Conheceis o marichal? — 685
Assi, daquela feição,
idade e desposição,
assi nobre e liberal,
e gasta[s]se todo carvão.

CUPIDO ¿Traéis licencia, Fray Fonil? — 690

FRADE Trago, senhor, a bastante,
assinada mui galante
pera mi e sete mil,
que virão daqui avante.

Mete-se o frade na frágua, e depois de refondido com a dita música, diz Copido:

CUPIDO Vámonos, no enhademos, — 695
cantando a nuesso plazer,
y nuestra fragua llevemos,
que lo que está por hazer
otro día lo haremos.

Co[m] esta música se vão, e fenece a Frágua.

---

679 *eramá.* See *Índia,* n. 9.
680 *faición o idade,* 'faccion[es] o edad.' The *lusismo idade* is demanded by the rime with *vontade* in line 683, but note that Vicente elsewhere does not hesitate to use rimes which are good only if one of the two words is replaced by its equivalent in the other language; see Teyssier, pp. 310-323. *Idade* may be a printer's error, rather than a lapse on the part of the poet.
685 *o marichal.* Dom Alvaro Coutinho. See Braamcamp Freire, p. 83.
690 *Fray Fonil.* Vicente often makes fun of the friars and frequently has other characters address them by comically disrespectful names. Here *fonil,* 'a large wooden funnel,' may suggest that Frei Rodrigo is a drunkard. See Teyssier, pp. 491-495.
695 *no enhademos,* 'no enfademos.' Vicente never uses the correct Castilian form. See Teyssier, p. 371.

Cortes de Júpiter

Cortes de Júpiter

A tragicomédia seguinte foi feita ao { *f. 165 r.* } *muito alto e poderoso Rei Dom Manuel, o primeiro em Portugal deste nome, à partida da ilustríssima senhora ifante dona Breatiz, duquesa de Sabóia, da qual sua invenção é que o senhor Deus, querendo fazer mercê à dita senhora, mandou sua Providência por messageira a Júpiter, rei dos elementos, que fizesse cortes em que se concertassem planetas e sinos em favor de sua viagem. Foi representada nos Paços da Ribeira na cidade de Lisboa. Era de M.D.XXI.*

Entrou logo a Providência em figura de princesa, com espera e cetro na mão, e diz:

PROVIDÊNCIA Eu, Providência chamada,
provedora do presente,
no porvir anticipada,
sam por Deus ora enviada
polas orações da gente. 5
Rogam per toda Sabóia
e nos reinos onde estais,
por esta deusa de Tróia,
por esta divina jóia,
que agora lhe enviais. 10

É de tantos e de tantas
o meu Deus tão requerido,
dos anjos, santos e santas,
e todos com prezes tantas,

Before line 1 The date of the first performance is incorrectly given in the *Copilaçam* as *M.D.xjx,* perhaps simply a printer's error for *M.D.xxj.* The play was presented on Sunday, August 4, 1521; see Garcia de Resende, "Hida da Infante Dona Beatriz pera Saboya," in his *Chronica,* p. 326. *sinos,* 'signos.' See *Frágua,* n. 5.

Before line 1 *espera,* 'esfera.' The usual form in medieval and classical Portuguese, as in older Spanish; see Gillet, III, 661, n. 450.

4 *sam,* 'sou.' See *Farelos,* n. 27.

5 *polas,* 'pelas.' See *Índia,* n. 76.

14 *prezes,* here apparently used to mean 'resolução' or perhaps 'presteza,' i.e., 'skill (in argument), eloquence.' See Morais, s.v. *prez.*

que não têm conto sabido. 15
Reis, rainhas, e donzelas,
e muitos, por esta estrela,
rogam a seu senhor delas,
nosso Deus, que vá com ela
coma estrela antr'as estrelas. 20

Sobre a qual todos pastores
leixam sem pasto as manadas,
e se fazem oradores,
em oferta dando flores
e suas pobres soldadas. 25
Bispos, frades, e beguinos,
e monjas de Jesu Christo,
até moços e meninos
de joelhos pedem isto,
humilhados e continos: 30

Que ele muito a seu prazer
a leve a salvamento;
e pera isto haver de ser,
Júpiter há-de fazer
cortes logo em um momento, 35
porque Deus me deu a mi
que o fizesse rei do mar,
e dos ventos outrossi,
e dos sinos. Venha aqui
pera logo começar! 40

Vem Júpiter e diz:

JÚPITER Eis-me aqui, alta senhora.
Que quer vossa magestade?
PROVIDÊNCIA Nobre rei, venhais em bo-hora!
Cumpre que façais ness'ora
cortes com solenidade. 45
JÚPITER Sobre quê, divina jóia?
PROVIDÊNCIA Porque vai ũa princesa,

---

20 *coma,* 'como.' See *Índia,* n. 71; *antre,* 'entre.'
21 *todos pastores,* 'todos os pastores.' See *Farelos,* n. 12.
33 *pera,* 'para.' See *Índia,* note preceding line 1.
38 *outrossi,* 'outrossim.' See *Índia,* n. 64.
43 *em bo-hora.* See *Índia,* n. 122
47 *ũa,* 'uma.' See *Índia,* note preceding line 1.

alta ifante portuguesa,
duquesa pera Sabóia.

JÚPITER Por muito seu bem será 50
e vida do coração.
PROVIDÊNCIA O Senhor a levará;
tanto prazer lhe dará
como lhe deu perfeição.
Sobi a vossa exaltação, 55
e mandai chamar o mar,
e mandai pôr em prisão
os ventos de Meredião, *f. 165 v.*
que empedem seu navegar.

E venha a Lũa dourada, 60
o Sol e Vénus, causando
que a linda desposada
não caminhe esta jornada
com saudade sospirando.
Manda Deus que vá folgando 65
per esses mares de Tróia;
fazei-lhe o mar muito brando
e não se catará quando
se verá dentro em Sabóia.

A hora do partir se vem; 70
fazei cortes logo ess'ora.
JÚPITER Elas se farão mui bem,
pois que Nosso Senhor tem
cuidado dessa senhora.
PROVIDÊNCIA Eu vou prover logo ess'ora 75
naquela casa dozena
dos males, que é malfeitora,
ainda que tudo adora
aquilo que Deus ordena.

---

58 *os ventos de Meredião,* 'the south winds.' Cf. *Inverno,* line 711: "¡ Riésguese Meredión!"
60 *Lũa,* 'Lua.' The usual form in medieval and classical Portuguese.
66 *per,* 'por.' See *Farelos,* n. 14.
76-77 *naquela casa dozena/ dos males, que é malfeitora,* 'the Zodiac.' The Old Portuguese forms *onzeno* and *dozeno* have been replaced in the modern language by the learned forms *undécimo* and *duodécimo;* note, however, that ordinal numbers above ten are rarely used today.

Vai-se a Providência e entram os quatro ventos em figura de trombeteiros, e diz Júpiter:

JÚPITER I logo dizer ao mar — 80
que faço cortes agora,
e que eu o mando chamar.
SUL Cumpre-nos bem de ventar
pera ele saltar cá fora.

Tocam os ventos suas trombetas & vem o mar muito forioso, & diz a Júpiter:

MAR Par Deus, grande farnesia — 85
me dão vossas forças belas,
que muito bem merecia
mandardes messajaria
polas vossas sete estrelas,

Ou por um rio dos meus, — 90
ou polo meu maior pego,
ou polos Montes Perineus,
e não por quatro sandeus,
que são contra meu sossego.
JÚPITER Muito bravo vem o mar! — 95
MAR Vós não sois minha senhora
a Lũa que m'há-de mandar.
JÚPITER Eu te farei amansar
pola tua superiora.

Ide, ventos, à mui bela — 100
Lũa, Diana fermosa;
dizei que a mais bela que ela
está pera ir à vela
destes reinos, poderosa.
Venha às cortes aqui — 105
o Sol, e Vénus, e ela,
e tu, mar, não te vás d'hi.

Before line 85 *forioso,* 'furioso.' See *Farelos,* n. 20.
85 *Par Deus,* 'por Deus.' See *Farelos,* n. 125. *farnesia,* 'frenesi.' Cf. Morais, s.v., who cites this passage. For the related adjective *farnétego* 'frenético,' cf. *Inverno,* line 1168.
88 *messajaria,* 'mensagem.' Cf. Morais, s.v.
94 *contra meu sossego.* For the omission of the definite article before a possessive pronoun, see *Índia,* note preceding line 1. Cf. *supra,* line 18: 'rogam a seu senhor."
107 *hi,* 'ali.' See *infra,* n. 314.

MAR Venha a senhora de mi,
que eu me entenderei com ela.

JÚPITER Tudo se há-de concertar 110
nestas cortes que fazemos;
o céu e a terra e o mar
e os ventos se hão-d'amansar,
pera ser o que queremos.

Vêm o Sol e a Lũa bailando ao som das trombetas dos ventos, e com eles Vénus, e diz o Sol:

SOL Oh caso pera espantar! 115
Que é isto, Jupiter?
A que nos mandais chamar?
Quer-se o orbe renovar,
ou torna-se o mundo a fazer?

JÚPITER Mas é um caso profundo 120
e de tanta preminência
que Deus, com rosto jocundo
como se fizesse um mundo,
manda poer diligência.
Vai a serena e altiva, 125
cuja graça persevera, *f. 166 r.*
contra todo o mal esquiva,
filha do que muito viva,
neta do que não morrera.

Polo qual vós, clara Lũa, 130
concertai vossas marés,
porque em tudo esta é ũa,
que no Oriente nenhũa
tal com'esta não pôs pés.
Primeiramente vos digo, 135
ventos, sereis avisados
que vão as naus sem perigo.

SUL Eu sou Sul, falai comigo.

NORTE Senhor, eu sam Norte, eu.

---

116 *Jupiter.* For the accentuation, demanded by the rhyme and indicated in '1562' by the spelling *Jupiteer*, see Teyssier, pp. 312-313.
121 *preminência,* 'preeminência.'
124 *poer,* 'pôr.' See *Farelos*, n. 491.

[NORDESTE] Eu sam Nordeste, eu sim, 140
e digo que o Sul é sandeu.
SUL Tal siso tens tu com'eu:
falas como vento em fim!
JÚPITER Tu, Norte, terás cuidado,
e Noroeste outro tal, 145
de ventar e com recado.
NORTE O Sul há mester atado
cos doudos no esprital.

NORDESTE Si, senhor, e o Sudueste,
[e] ele, Sueste, também; 150
vente Norte, e Nornoroeste,
porque a viagem preste;
e não vente outrem ninguém.
VÉNUS Oh, quem fora agora o mar!
LUA Nunca ele foi tão ditoso. 155
SOL Mais ditoso se há-d'achar,
quando a vir, o seu esposo.

E dirá, como a olhar,
namorado com rezão:
"Niña, erguédeme los ojos, 160
que a mi namorado m'hão."

---

146 *com recado,* 'com prudência.' Cf. *Índia,* n. 423.
148 *esprital,* 'hospital.' *Espital* is found in Old Portuguese (e.g., in *Cantigas d'escarnho e de mal dizer,* No. 169, line 17) and is common in sixteenth-century Spanish (ee Gillet, III, 780, note 513). The form used here by Vicente doubtless represents a blend of *espital* and *esprito,* 'espíritu.' For the latter, see *Índia,* n. 452.
159 *rezão,* 'razão.' See *Índia,* n. 292.
160 The full text of this *villancico* is given in the *Cancionero musical,* No. 72; the fact that '1562' gives only the *cabeza* suggests that Vicente used the existing *glosa* without modification. The text as given in the *Cancionero* is as follows: "*Niña, erguídeme los ojos,/ que a mí enamorado m'an.* [I] No los alçéis desdeñosos,/ syno ledos y amorosos,/ que mis tormentos penosos/ en verlos descansarán./ [II] De los muertos hazés bivos/ y de los libres cativos./ No me los alçés esquivos,/ qu'en vellos me matarán."
161 *m'hão.* In '1562' *mam,* perhaps a printer's error for *man* (i.e., *m'han*) rather than a *lusismo* attributable to the author himself. The combination of Portuguese and Spanish forms is, however, common in Vicente's popular songs; cf. my edition of his *Poesía,* p. 14. *namorado.* See *Farelos,* n. 63.

Este vilancete foi cantado a três vozes [por] o Sol e Lũa e Vénus, e acabado diz Júpiter:

Pera esta viagem ser
aquela que Deus ordena,
vós, Lũa, haveis de fazer
ao mar obedecer 165
a esta frota serena.

SOL Mande primeiro, senhor,
que não seja retrogada
Vénus, pois sois seu maior,
e Deus, que é superior, 170
favorece a desposada.

JÚPITER Partirá esta alta esposa
no ponto de preamar
com sua frota lustrosa
na conjunção mais ditosa 175
que lhe podermos guisar.

E ao desferir das velas
faremos que vá também
com todas suas donzelas,
que hajam saudades delas, 180
e elas não de ninguém.
E por mais solenidade,
e sua alteza folgar,
sairão desta cidade
toda a geralidade 185
dos nobres per esse mar.

Não com velas nem com remos,
mas todos feitos pescados
da feição que aqui diremos;
que em tal caso os estremos 190
em estremo são louvados.
Os cónegos da Sé em bo-hora
em figura de toninhas

---

168 *retrogada.* A popular form of *retrógrado,* defined by Morais, s.v., as "que marcha ou parece marchar contra a ordem dos signos" (i.e., the astrological signs of the zodiac).
190 *estremos,* 'excessos, exageros.' The word is not, of course, used here in a pejorative sense; cf. *Comedia del viudo,* lines 960-964: "Amparemos y honremos/ huérfanas tan preciosas,/ que en las cosas virtuosas/ los estremos."

irão com esta senhora
até bem de foz em fora 195
por essas ondas marinhas.

SOL E também até Cascais
irão os vereadores,
feitos rodovalhos tais, *f. 166 v.*
e deles darão mil ais, 200
e deles dirão amores.

VÉNUS Também irão frades alguns
do termo e da cidade.

LUA Mas não ficarão nenhuns!
Serão ruivos a metade; 205
os outros serão atuns.

VÉNUS E todo-los corretores
em figura de robalos.

SOL Juizes e ouvidores,
deles peixes voadores, 210
e deles peixes cavalos.

LUA Como irão os estudantes?

JÚPITER Feitos barbos de Monção,
e deles em rãs cantantes,
dizendo per consoantes: 215
"Quem nos dera aqui o Durão!"

Os da Moeda irão tornados
em garoupas de Guiné,
das moréas espantados,
preguntando aos pescados 220

200-201 *deles . . . deles,* 'alguns deles . . . , outros.' See *Farelos,* n. 491, and cf. *Inverno,* lines 1271-1272.
205 *ruivos.* Cf. Morais, s.v.: "Nome vulgar dos peixes do género *Trigla* Lin., família dos triglídeos, na costa de Portugal."
207 *todo-los,* 'todos os.' Cf. *infra*, n. 229.
216 *Durão.* Carolina Michaëlis de Vasconcelos suggests that the reference may be to the "mestre de música dos infantes," but this is pure conjecture, since we have no records of a court musician who bore this name. Cf. *Notas Vicentinas,* p. 400.
217 *os da Moeda,* 'os empregados da Casa da Moeda.'
219 *moréas,* 'moréias.' See *Índia,* n. 27. Further examples in *Júpiter* include *balea,* 'baleia,' in line 507, and *veo,* 'veio,' before line 520.

cada um que peixe é.
VÉNUS Sairão as regateiras
em cardume de sardinhas,
nadando muito ligeiras,
desviadas das carreiras, 225
por não topar coas toninhas.

SOL Irão certos bacharées
em forma de tubarões.
JÚPITER Esses apó-las galés,
e irão almotacés 230
convertidos em cações.
VÉNUS Jorge de Vasco Goncelos
num esquife de cortiça
irá alfenando os cabelos,
por devisa dous novelos; 235
a letra dirá "Oh iça!"

LUA Sabeis vós quem irá bem
em figura de balea?
Gil Vaz da Cunha; porém
encalhará em Belém 240
e dirá: "Eis-me na area."
Dona Isabel, sua molher,
faremos raia num salto
e cantará ao pratel:
"Eu me era dona Isabel, 245
agora raia do alto."

---

229 *apó-las,* 'após as.' The loss of final *-s* in combination with the older forms of the object pronouns (*lo, la, los, las* for *o, a, os, as*), now found only after verb forms (e.g., *tens* + *o* becomes *tem-lo, compramos* + *os* becomes *compramo-los*), was subject to fewer restrictions in sixteenth-century usage; cf. *supra,* line 207, "todo-los corretores." See Williams, 143, 3, D.
230 *almotacés.* Cf. Morais, s.v.: "Ant. Funcionário municipal encarregado de fiscalizar os pesos e medidas e de taxar o preço dos géneros; competia-lhe ainda a distribuição dos mantimentos em época de escassez."
232 *Jorge de Vasco Goncelos.* See *Índia,* n. 19.
234 *alfenando.* Cf. Morais, s.v. *alfenar*:"*Ant.* tingir, colorir com a alfena, ou com as folhas, bagas, ou pós dela."
239 *Gil Vaz da Cunha.* For biographical information on this courtier and others mentioned in the following lines, see Braamcamp Freire, pp. 145-148.

Irão molheres solteiras
todas nuas, trosquiadas,
bem rapadas as moleiras,
carregadas de peneiras, 250
em senhas sibas sentadas.

SOL Irão todo-los cantores:
contras-altas, carapaus;
os tiples, alcapetores;
enxarrocos, os tenores; 255
contrabaxas, bacalhaus.

Com eles Pero do Porto
em figura de çafio,
meo congro deste rio,
cantando mui sem conforto: 260
"Yo me soy Pero Çafío."

JÚPITER Agora cumpre atentar
como poemos as mãos,
porque é rezão d'ordenar
como a vão acompanhar 265
o príncipe e seus irmãos.

LUA Em que figuras irão?

VÉNUS Aves me parecem a mi,
que em peixes não é rezão:
em aves doutra feição. 270

JÚPITER Não hão-d'ir senão assi:

O príncipe nosso senhor
irá em quatro rocins
marinhos, em um andor
do ouro que milhor for 275
em toda a terra dos Chins,
e um sobrecéu per cima, *f. 167 r.*
de esmeraldas e robis,

---

251 *senhas.* See *Farelos,* n. 216.
254 *alcapetores.* Morais defines *alcapetor* simply as "certa espécie de peixe" and cites only this passage from *Cortes de Júpiter* as an example of its use.
255 *enxarrocos.* Cf. Morais, s.v.: "Nome vulgar dos peixes do género *Zeus, Z. faber* Lin."
258 *çafio,* 'safio.'
268 *mi,* 'mim.' See *India,* n. 357.
271 *assi,* 'assim.' See *India,* n. 64.
272 *o príncipe nosso senhor.* The future King John III.

lavrado d'obra de lima,
que não possam dar estima 280
a lavores tão sotis.

Sua figura será
um Alexandre segundo,
que sem grifos sobirá
onde bem devisará 285
toda-las cousas do mundo.

VÉNUS E Gracia de Resende,
feito peixe tamboril;
e inda que tudo entende,
irá dizendo por ende: 290
"Quem me dera um arrabil!"

JÚPITER O mui precioso ifante,
dom Luís esclarecido,
irá muito triunfante,
senhor da vida galante, 295
em cirnes alvos sobido.

---

283 Correas explains that to call someone an Alexander is to say that he is "liberal i manífiko" (*Vocabulario,* p. 623).
287 *Gracia,* 'Garcia.' Metathesis of *r* is common in Portuguese; see Teyssier, pp. 351-356. Garcia de Resende, court poet and chronicler, compiled the *Cancioneiro geral* of 1516, often called the *Cancioneiro de Resende* to distinguish it from the Spanish *Cancionero general* (1511) of Hernando del Castillo. His weight was a frequent target of witticisms from his contemporaries who called him "o redondo do Resende," "barril," "odre de vinho," and "melão de Agosto." See *Dicionário das literaturas,* pp. 685-686.
289 *inda,* 'ainda.' See *Índia,* n. 216.
290 *por ende,* 'por ali.' See Corominas, s.v. *ende.*
291 *arrabil.* Cf. Morais, s.v.: "Instrumento de cordas, usado pelos Árabes; rabeca mourisca. *Ant.* Pequena rabeca pastoril." Viterbo, s.v.: "Instrumento pastoril de cordas e arco, semelhante a uma rabeca pequena."
293 *Dom Luís.* Duke of Beja (1506-1555), younger brother of John III.
296 *cirnes,* 'cisnes.' Morais lists *cirne* as an archaic form of *cisne.* Garcia de Resende, *Dom João II,* p. 178, tells of the *momos* of 1490 in which the king played the role of "[o] cavalleiro do Cirne," and was preceded, on his entry into the hall, by "hum muyto grande e fermoso Cirne, com as penas brancas e douradas." Vicente uses the same form in Spanish in the *Auto de las gitanas* where one of the ladies of the court is called "huerta de la hermozura,/ cirne de la mar salada" (lines 215-216).

E irá João de Saldanha
no mar muito afadigado,
feito arenque d'Alemanha,
dizendo: "Es cosa estraña 300
ser castellano y pescado."

O precioso Cardeal
irá sobre homens marinhos,
em um carro triunfal,
padre santo natural 305
per mui naturais caminhos.

SOL Dom Fernando, ifante belo,
fermoso, bem assombrado,
irá posto em um castelo,
que será prazer de vê-lo, 310
sobre sereas armado.

LUA Diogo Fernandes irá,
porque é comendador,
em um peixe que hi não há;
porém dele se fará, 315
prazendo a Nosso Senhor.

VÉNUS Sobre três liões marinhos
o ifante dom Anrique
irá em cama d'arminhos
brincando com dous anginhos, 320
que não é razão que fique.

SOL E na sua dianteira
Tristão da Cunha irá
em congro da Pederneira,

---

302 *o precioso Cardeal.* Dom Afonso (1509-1540), son of Manuel and Mary, cardinal and archbishop of Lisbon.
307 *Dom Fernando.* Duke of Guarda (1507-1534), third son of King Manuel and Queen Mary.
308 *fermoso,* 'formoso.' See *Índia,* n. 75.
314 *hi não há,* 'não há.' Sixteenth-century Portuguese used *ha hi* alongside *há. Hi* (from Latin IBI) was still an independent word; it might precede or follow *há* or be separated from it by another word, as it is here. See Teyssier, pp. 381-383.
318 *Dom Anrique.* Son of Manuel and Mary (1512-1580), cardinal and inquisitor general, he became king after the death of Sebastian at the battle of Alcázarquivir in 1578.

bradando "aparta carreira!" 325
tanto que enrouquecerá.
A mui preciosa senhora,
ifante dona Isabel,
irá como superiora,
estrela clara da aurora, 330
nũa galé sem batel,

Com seis remos de marfim,
e o céu todo por vela;
e levará à toa ali
todo o mundo após de si, 335
e irá adorando a ela.

VÉNUS E o estribeiro mor,
convertido em peixe mu,
irá por corregedor
das baleas e senhor 340
de "Par Deus, grão peixe és tu!"

JÚPITER Madama dona Maria
irá sobre querubins
nũa roupa d'alegria,
por aia Santa Luzia, 345
e por guardas serafins.

LUA Joana do Taco no mar,
em grão centola tornada,
irá rija, sem tardar,
dizendo: "Cumple aguijar, 350
que de prissa va ell armada."

JÚPITER Também é bem de ordenar
que as damas que ficam cá,
que a vão acompanhar
vinte léguas polo mar. *f. 167 v.* 355

---

328 *Dona Isabel.* Oldest daughter of Manuel and Mary (1503-1539), who married the Emperor Charles V in 1526.
342 *Dona Maria.* Daughter of King Manuel and his third wife, Queen Leanor, born June 8, 1521, and hence less than two months old when the play was first performed. See Braamcamp Freire, pp. 146-147.
351 *ell armada.* Vicente occasionally uses the old form of the definite article *ell* before nouns, both masculine and feminine, which begin with a vowel. Many sixteenth-century Castilian writers did the same. See Gillet, III, 245, n. 113; Keniston, 18. 126 ff.

VÉNUS Senhor, muito bem será.
JÚPITER O conselho que há mister,
em que figura irão?
Diga aqui seu parecer
cada um como entender, 360
e tomar-se-á concrusão.

E por ir de todo ornada
a dama há-de levar
cada ũa sua criada,
e que vá deferençada 365
no vestido e no lugar.
E não digamos aqui
nenhum nome de molher
nem dama; mas tomem d'hi
cada ũa pera si 370
o que milhor lhe vier.

Digo que ũa irá assentada
sobre três garças sobida,
como rosa ataviada,
toda de seda amorada, 375
pois dá namorada vida.

Irá bem sua criada
metida nũa gamela,
e a cabeça rapada,
ũa touca esfarrapada, 380
e ũa gorra amarela.
E irá junto da vela
onde o arcebispo vai;
cantará rouca, singela:
"Não me quis casar meu pai: 385
ora folgai!"

---

361 *concrusão,* 'conclusão.' Vicente uses this classical and medieval form of the word several times, apparently without any stylistic distinction. For the vacillation between forms in consonant + *l* and those in consonant + *r,* characteristic of sixteenth-century Portuguese, see Teyssier, pp. 358-359.
371 *milhor,* 'melhor.' See *Índia,* n. 82.
375 *amorada,* 'côr de amora, vermelha.' Note the pun.
385-386 A variant of this song is cited by Romeu Figueras, p. 118, n. 116.

SOL Sobre fermosa salvagem
outra dama irá também
de cremesim d'avantagem
por alegrar a viagem, 390
mas não já outrem ninguém.
Irá cantando porém,
que bem lhe parecerá:
"aquel cavallero, madre,
¿si me havrá 395
con tanta mala vida como há?"

E a sua moça irá
em trusquia num sendeiro,
com um saínho de liteiro,
descoberto o alvará. 400
E sabeis que cantará
lá defronte de Cascais?
"A que horas me mandais
aos olivais?"

VÉNUS Sobre três garças reais 405
irá outra linda dama,
com graças especiais,
e não desejando mais
senão de cruel ter fama.
Cantará com mal tamanho 410
o triste seu servidor:
"Nunca fue pena mayor
ni tromento tan estraño."

---

389 *cremesim*, 'carmesim.' *d'avantagem*. Cf. Morais, s.v. *avantagem*: '*De avantagem*, loc. adv.: mais, melhor.' The whole phrase *de cremesim d'avantagem* thus means 'dressed in the finest crimson [cloth].'
394-396 A variant form, which substitutes "si morirá" for "si me haverá," is found in the *Cancionero musical*, No. 350.
403-404 Cf. Gonzalo Correas, *Arte de la lengua española castellana (1625)*, ed. Emilio Alarcos García (Madrid: Consejo Superior de Investigaciones Científicas, 1954), p. 446: "Envíame mi madre/ por agua sola:/ ¡mirad a qué hora!"
412-413 The same song is cited in *Frágua*, lines 163 ff. Cf. *Cancionero musical*, No. 1. The remaining lines of the *estribillo* are "que iguale con el dolor/ que resçibo del engaño."
413 *tromento*, 'tormento.' See *Índia*, n. 441.

A moça irá dianteira
num zambuco de Cochim, 415
por piloto um beleguim,
e por toldo ũa joeira,
muito negra a cabeleira,
cantando mui de verdade
"Estes meus cabellos, madre, 420
dos a dos me los lleva el aire."

LUA Irá outra linda estrela
sobre carreta de estrelas,
vestida toda amarela,
porque desesperem dela 425
como das outras donzelas.
Irá mui cara e altiva;
cantar-lhe-á um desditoso:
"De vos y de mí quexoso,
de vos porque sois esquiva." 430

Sua moça sem mais moço
irá cos olhos na gente,
trosquiada, muito rente,
cos toucados ò pescoço; *f. 168 r.*
cantará com alvoroço 435
e alteração consigo:
"enganado andais, amigo,
comigo;
dias há que vo-lo digo."

JÚPITER Sobre sátiros do mar 440
irá outra fresca rosa
dentro de um lindo pumar,
ouvindo as aves cantar,

420-421 The song must once have been very popular; these verses are cited by Luis Milán in *El cortesano* and by Gonzalo Correas. See Romeu Figueras, p. 96.
424 *amarela*. Cf. Covarrubias, s.v. *amarillo*: "Entre las colores se tiene por la más infelice, por ser la de la muerte, y de la larga y peligrosa enfermedad y la color de los enamorados." For yellow as the color of despair, and for green as that of hope (cf. *infra*, lines 460-461), see Kenyon.
429-430 Cf. *Cancionero musical*, No. 17. The *estribillo* continues thus: "de mí, porque nunca biva/ si mi mal deziros oso."
434 *ò*, 'ao.' See *Índia*, n. 202.

vestida muito custosa.
Cantarão a esta fermosa 445
a calhandra e o rous[s]inol:
"Gentil dama valerosa
y donzella, por cuyo amor."

A moça irá num alguidar;
e vestido um alquicé, 450
o alguidar por lavar
e ela por pentear,
perguntando por Guiné.
Cantará batendo o pé:
"Sem mais mando nem mais rogo 455
aqui me tendes, levai-me logo."

SOL Outra de grão fermosura
irá em nuvem de bonança
em um brial sem custura;
a cor será verde escura, 460
porque dá triste esperança.
E com esperança perdida
cantará seu namorado:
"Al dolor de mi cuidado,
y en tus manos, la mi vida, 465
me encomiendo, condenado."

Su[a] aia em corvos marinhos
irá antre uns almadraques,
e nos marinhos caminhos,
fazendo a todos focinhos, 470
porque cospem dos seus traques.

---

444 *vestida muito custosa.* For the adverbial use of adjectives in sixteenth-century Portuguese and Castilian, see Epiphânio da Silva Dias, p. 65, and Keniston, 25.410-411, 35.39.

457 *grão fermosura.* After some hesitation, I have transcribed the *gram* of '1562' as *grão* rather than as *grã*. The apocopated form of *grande* was originally the same in both masculine and feminine; *grã* arose by analogy with paradigms like *são*: *sã, vão*: *vã*. See Williams, 124.4.A. Williams gives no date for the introduction of the analogical form; Salgado Júnior, in his edition of Camões, p. 946, asserts that "a sutileza duma distinção entre *grão* e *grã*" appeared after the sixteenth century.

464-466 A variant is given in *Cancionero musical,* No. 40.

Levará mil tarramaques
de pez, por mais alegria:
cantará cos atabaques:
"Se disseram, digam, alma mía." 475

LUA As outras damas irão
à malmaíça vestidas;
segundo sua tenção,
assi as cores tomarão
diferentes e escolhidas. 480
Em carros d'ouro metidas,
sobre seiscentos golfinhos,
e mil sátiros marinhos,
com harpas d'ouro compridas,
tangendo polos caminhos. 485

VÉNUS E irão suas criadas
num lagar d'azeite todas,
sem crenchas, descabeladas,
como salvagens pasmadas
de tão altíssimas vodas. 490
E sairão às janelas
com senhas tochas de palha
debrũadas amarelas:
se não olharem par'elas,
não lhes dará ne[m] migalha. 495

JÚPITER Acompanhá-la-á esta gente
assi em cima à frol do mar,

---

475 Cf. *Cancionero musical,* No. 193, where the text is given as follows: "*Si lo dizen, digan,/ alma mía;/ si lo dizen, digan./* Dizen que vos quiero/ y por vos me muero./ Dichoso es verdadero, *alma mía.*" (*Dichoso* is doubtless an error for *dicho.*)

477 *à mal maíça.* Morais, s.v. *maíça,* says only that the word is used in the expression *andar com alguém a mal maíça,* 'andar de rixa com alguém,' but this can hardly be the meaning here.

488 *crenchas,* 'tresses,' or perhaps 'part (in hair).' See Corominas, who cites this passage, s.v.

490 *vodas,* 'bodas.' Both forms were usual in sixteenth-century Portuguese; both are found in the *Copilaçam.*

493 *debrũadas,* 'debruadas.' Cf. the noun *debrum,* 'hem, border.'

497 *frol,* 'flor.' Both forms existed in medieval Portuguese; both are used by Vicente, though *flor* is the more common. See Teyssier, p. 361.

por servir a excelente
nova estrela d'Oriente;
tornar-s'ão de Gibraltar. 500
E a desposada bela,
bela e bem aventurada,
verá tudo da janela
da nau; e o mar verá a ela,
e será dele adorada. 505

SOL Será bem que desd'o estreito
vão em cima de baleas,
havendo à tal festa respeito,
cantando todas a eito
cento e trinta mil sereas. 510
Diante do seu navio *f. 168 v.*
cantarão estas que digo:
"por el río me llevad, amigo,
y llevádeme por el río."

JÚPITER Deus Mars, que é das batalhas, 515
desd'o estreito adiante,
pera segurar a ifante
que não vá a lume de palhas,
venha aqui mui triunfante.

Cantaram todas estas figuras em chacota a cantiga de "Llevádeme por el río"; e os ventos foram chamar o planeta Mars, o qual veo com seus sinos, s[cilicet] Câncer, Leo e Capricórnio, e diz Mars:

MARS Humilho-me a vós, sagrado 520
Júpiter. Que me mandais?
Eis-me aqui a vosso mandado.
JÚPITER Vós sejais mui bem chegado
a estas cortes reais.
Manda el-Rei de Portugal, 525
senhor do Mar Oceano,
sua filha natural
per conjunção divinal
pelo mar Meoterrano.

MARS Já sei que quereis dizer; 530

---

529 [*o*] *mar Meoterrano*, 'Medioterrâneo.' In '1562' *meoterreno*, but the rime demands *-ano*.

direis que tem adversairos.
Descansai e havei prazer,
que pera seu grão poder
podem pouco seus contrairos.
Leva gente muito fina, 535
poderosa artelharia,
e a nau Santa Caterina,
que vai per graça divina
coa proa na Alexandria.

E mais eu tenho cuidado 540
deste reino Lusitano;
Deus me tem dito e mandado
que lho tenha bem guardado,
porque o quer fazer Romano.
Que nas batalhas passadas 545
que Castela o quis tentar,
levaram tantas pancadas,
que depois de bem levadas,
não ousaram mais tornar.

E assi nas partes d'além 550
sempre foi favorecido,
e na Índia também;
ou digam se viu alguém
reino em fama tão luzido.
Pequeno e mui grandioso, 555
pouca gente e muito feito,
forte e mui vitorioso,
mui ousado e furioso
em todo o que toma a peito.

Cavaleiros de vontade, 560
gente sem rebolaria,
fidalgos que amam verdade,

---

531 *adversairos,* 'adversários.' See *India,* n. 90.
536 *artelharia,* 'artilheria.' The usual form in classical Portuguese. The word originally was applied to any sort of arms, but was already sometimes used in its modern sense of "mounted guns as distinct from small arms" in the fifteenth century (*e.g.,* by the Marquis of Santillana); Vicente probably uses it in this way. See Gillet, III, 136, n. 68.
550 *nas partes d'além.* Cf. Morais, s.v. *além*: "*Ant.* Possessões portuguesas ultramarinas, especialmente na África: 'Foi morrer nas partes (ou nos lugares) de além.' "

a nenhũa adversidade
mostram nunca covardia.
São estremo nos amores, 565
amadores do seu rei
e grandes seus servidores;
com favores, sem favores,
sempre têm dereita lei.

Assi, senhor, que agora 570
não se trate aqui de guerra,
porque vai esta senhora,
em tal ponto e em tal hora,
que seu é o mar e a terra.
Mas deveis, senhor, mandar 575
os planetas musicais
ao encantado lugar,
e a poder de seu cantar
tragam cá a Moura Tais.

JÚPITER Pera tal caso há mister 580
Diana e Vénus que cante. *f. 169 r.*
MARS E a Moura há-de trazer
três cousas que vos disser
pera do estreito avante:
um anel seu, encantado, 585
e um didal de condão,
e o precioso treçado
que foi no campo tomado
depois de morto Roldão.

O terçado, pera vencer; 590
o didal é tão facundo,
que tudo lhe fará trazer;
o anel, pera saber
o que se faz polo mundo.
Quantas festas maginar, 595
até cousas invisíveis,
todas verá polo mar;

---

587 *treçado*, 'terçado.' The latter form occurs in line 590.
591 *facundo*. The precise sense of this word is not clear. Vicente seems to use it as a general term of approval in both Spanish and Portuguese. See *Amadís*, ed. Waldron, n. 34.
595 *maginar*, 'imaginar.'

farà os peixes cantar,
e cousas mais impossíveis.

Desencantemo-la ora, 600
e pera mais a forçar,
havemos-lhe de cantar
a história desta senhora,
como vai longe a morar.
E ficará por vitória 605
polo mundo adiante
pera sempre por sua glória
este romance em memória
da partida desta ifante.

Romance

Niña era la ifanta, 610
doña Breatiz se dezía,
nieta del buen rey Hernando,
el mejor rey de Castilla,
hija del rey don Manuel
y reina doña María, 615
reyes de tanta bondad
que tales dos no havía.
Niña la casó su padre,
muy hermosa a maravilla,
con el duque de Saboya, 620
que bien le pertenecía;
señor de muchos señores,
más que rey es su valía.
Ya se parte la ifanta,
la ifanta se partía 625
de la muy leal ciudad
que Lixbona se dezía;
la riqueza que llevava
vale toda Alexandría,
sus naves muy alterosas, 630
sin cuento la artellaría.
Va por el mar de Levante,
tal que temblava Turquía.

---

631 *artellaría,* 'artillería.' The usual form in older Spanish was *artellería*; the form used by Vicente, with pretonic *-a-*, is a *lusismo,* perhaps to be attributed to the printer. See Teyssier, p. 370.

Con ella va el arçobispo,
señor de la cleresía; 635
van condes y cavalleros
de muy notable osadía;
lleva damas muy hermosas,
hijasdalgo y de valía.
¡Dios los lleve a salvamiento 640
como su madre querría!

Este romance cantam os planetas e sinos a quatro vozes, pera com as palavras dele e música descencantarem a Moura Tais de seu encantamento, a qual entra com o terçado e anel e didal de condão que Mars disse que ela tinha em seu poder, e diz:

MOURA Mi no xaber qué exto extar,
mi no xaber qué exto xer,
mi no xaber ónde andar.
Halá xaber divinar, 645
lo que extar Halá xaber.
Halá xaber qué es aquexto;
Halá xaber e yo no.
Halá xaber máx que yo.
Halá digirme qué ex exto. 650

Júpiter, ¿qué a mí mandar?
Dox mil añox extar cantada: *f. 169 v.*
¿agora dónde llevar?
Agora otro mundo extar,
agora no xaber nada. 655
¿Por qué tirarme de caxa?
¿Por qué de inferno tirarme,

642ff The *moura's* speech is basically Spanish, not Portuguese, though there are a few *lusismos* (e.g., *inferno* [657], *mãi* [667], *tudo* [675]). It is characterized by substitution of *x* for *s*, *b* for *v*, and *j* or *g* for *z* and for intervocalic *-s-*. The replacements are not perfectly systematic; thus, *casa* appears as *caxa* in line 656, rather than the expected *caja* (cf. *coja*, 'cosa' in 663). Other features include the use of the infinitive as the only verbal form, and the replacement of *ser* by *estar* (642, 660, 667). It will be observed that the *moura's* speech shares many features with that of the Negro in the *Frágua de Amor*, lines 251 ff. For a fuller analysis of her language, see Teyssier, pp. 251-254.
645 *divinar*, 'adivinar.' For a similar case of apheresis, cf. *cantada*, 'encantada,' in line 652.

de compañía de Axa,
mi hija, nieta de Braxa,
reina que extar del Algarbe? 660

JÚPITER Presentai isso à senhora
ifante e nova duquesa.
MOURA ¡Gran coja mandar agora!
Señora, assí mi morir mora,
Júpiter darbox gran empresa, 665
que exte dedal, ¡Halá quebir!,
extar de mãi de Mahomad.
Señora, quanto box pedir,
él fager lugo venir:
Halá xaber exte verdad. 670

Exte anel da condón;
perguntalde box a él,
y él dar a box razón
de quantox xacretos xon:
tudo box xaber por él. 675
JÚPITER Amigos, isto é feito,
vão-se as cortes acabando
por seu estilo dereito.
Cante-se o que no estreito
as sereas hão-d'ir cantando. 680

Tornaram todos a cantar a modo de chacota "Por el río me llevade," e com ela se foram e acabam as cortes.

---

666 *Halá quebir,* 'God is great' (Arabic).
669 *lugo,* 'luego.'
672 *perguntalde,* preguntadle.' A perfectly normal form in Vicente's Castilian, not an example of Moorish jargon. For the metathesis of *r,* see *Frágua,* n. 43; for the ending-*lde,* see *Frágua,* n. 244.
674 *xacretos,* 'secretos.'

O Triunfo do Inverno

O Triunfo do Inverno

A tragicomédia que se segue é chamada { *f. 174 v.* }
Triunfo do Inverno. *Foi representada ao muito alto e excelente príncipe el-rei Dom João, o terceiro deste nome em Portugal, na sua cidade de Lixboa, ao parto da devotíssima e muito esclarecida rainha Dona Caterina, nossa senhora.*

É repartida em duas partes.

Figuras da primeira parte: O Autor, Inverno, Brisco, João Guijarro, Velha, Piloto, Marinheiro, quatro grumetes, s[*cilicet*] *Martinho, Gregório, Gonçalo, Afonso, duas sereas.*

AUTOR Em Portugal vi eu já
em cada casa pandeiro
e gaita em cada palheiro;
e de vinte anos acá
não há hi gaita nem gaiteiro. 5
A cada porta um terreiro,
cada aldea dez folias,
cada casa atabaqueiro;
e agora Geremias
é nosso tamburileiro. 10

Só em Barquerena havia
tambor em cada moinho,
e no mais triste ratinho
se enxergava ũa alegria
que agora não tem caminho. 15
Se olhardes as cantigas
do prazer acostumado,

Before line 1 The initial rubric, as often in the *Copilaçam,* is inaccurate. Only three *grumetes* appear in the play (cf. line 599); Martinho is not mentioned again. Conversely, there are not two but three mermaids, if we accept the stage direction preceding line 880.

5 *há hi,* 'há.' See *Júpiter,* n. 314.

7 *aldea,* 'aldeia.' See *Índia,* n. 27.

8 *atabaqueiro,* 'drummer.' Cf. Morais, s.v.

10 *nosso tamburileiro.* For the omission of the definite article before a possessive adjective, see *Índia,* note preceding line 1.

14 *ũa,* 'uma.' See *Índia,* note preceding line 1.

todas têm som lamentado,
carregado de fadigas,
longe do tempo passado. 20

O de então era cantar
e bailar coma há-de ser:
o cantar pera folgar,
o bailar pera prazer,
que agora é mau d'achar. 25
Não ca[n]tavam de terreiro
"Terra frida, déismelo
no me neguéis mi consuelo,"
que fez um judeu d'Aveiro
pola muerte de su avuelo. 30

É de feira em concrusão,
e bailam-na cada dia
porque saia a melodia
tal qual fica o coração
ao revés do que soía. 35
Mas aqueles que folgavam
nas vilas e nas aldeas
quando as festas se ajuntavam,
cantigas de mil raleas
deste compasso cantavam. 40

---

22 *coma,* 'como.' See *Índia,* n. 71.
23 *pera,* 'para.' See *Índia,* note preceding line 1.
27 "Terra frida, déismelo." Both *frida,* 'fría,' and *déismelo,* 'dadmelo,' are characteristic Judeo-Spanish forms; cf. my introduction to "The Festival Plays," p. 50. It is likely that *déismelo* should be pronounced as a *palabra aguda,* like *Jupiter* in *Cortes de Júpiter,* line 116; see my note on that passage and Teyssier, p. 314. It is not, however, necessary to agree with him that the rhyme with *consuelo* is merely "une 'rime pour l'oeil.'" Both words may be stressed on the last syllable; such displacements of the tonic accent are frequent in Spanish folksongs; Vicente's own "En la huerta nace la rosa" (*Auto de los cuatro tiempos,* lines 181 ff.) may offer an example. If we accent the words in this way, however, we shall no longer have two metrically equivalent lines; I have therefore refrained from making the change in my text, despite the frequency of anisosyllabic verses in Spanish traditional poetry.
30 *pola,* 'pela.' See *Índia,* n. 76.
31 *concrusão,* 'conclusão.' See *Júpiter,* n. 361.

Cantando:

No penedo João Preto
e no penedo.

Quais foram os perros — *f. 175 r.*
que mataram os lobos
que comeram as cabras — 45
que roeram o bacelo
que posera João Preto
no penedo?

[*Falando:*]

Se neste tempo de glória
nacera a infanta sagrada — 50
como fora festejada
sòmente pola vitória
da rainha alumiada!
Já tudo leixam passar,
tudo leixam por fazer — 55
sem pessoa preguntar
a este mesmo pesar
que foi daquele prazer.

Porém coa ajuda dos céus
imaginei ũa festa — 60
à nossa Júlia modesta,
nacida per mão de Deus,
a qual festa será esta.
Quando vi de tal feição
tão frio o tempo moderno, — 65
fiz um triunfo d'inverno;
despois será o do verão,

---

54 *leixam*, 'deixam.' See *Índia*, n. 10.
61 *à nossa Júlia modesta*. Some scholars see this as a reference to Lisbon, called by the Romans *Felicitas Julia* in honor of Julius Caesar. I agree with A. da Costa Ramalho that it is a reference to Princess Isabel, whose birth the play was written to celebrate; see "'À Nossa Júlia Modesta,'" in his *Estudos sobre a Época do Renascimento*, pp. 150-158.
67 *despois*, 'depois.' The usual form in medieval and classical Portuguese; *verão*, 'primavera e primeira parte do verão, época do bom tempo.' See Corominas, s.v. *verano*.

nos quais foi meu pensamento
fazer a farsa distinta.
Por não gastar tanta tinta 70
neste primeiro argumento,
e porque milhor se sinta,
o Inverno vem salvagem,
castellano en su dezir:
porque quem quiser fingir, 75
na castelhana linguagem
achará quanto pedir.

(Argumento da figura primeira do triunfo do Inverno:)

INVIERNO Sepan todos a barrisco
que yo me soy Juan de la Greña,
estragador de la leña 80
y sembrador del pedrisco,
cozinero de las patas,
assador mayor de patos,
alcahuete de los gatos,
y partero de las gatas, 85

oxeador de las cigüeñas,
destierro de golondrinas,
boz de las aguas marinas,
agravio de viejas dueñas,
dios de los fríos vapores, 90
y señor de los ñublados,
peligro de los ganados,
tormiento de los pastores.

Soy portero de los vientos,
pastor de las tempestades, 95
ayo de las frialdades,
ira de los elementos,
maestresala de la luna,
de los hielos corretor,

---

72 *milhor*, 'melhor.' See *Índia*, n. 82.
91 *ñublados*, 'nublados.' Palatalization of *n* is a characteristic feature of *sayagués*; see Teyssier, pp. 68-70. Winter's speech is not, however, marked by the use of other *sayagués* forms (though *a barrisco* in line 78 might be considered one; see Teyssier, p. 37).
93 *tormiento*, 'tormento.' See *Índia*, n. 441.

y soy capitán mayor 100
de la marina fortuna.

Aunque veáis mi figura
hecha un salvage bruto,
yo cubro el aire de luto
y las sierras de blancura. 105
Quito las sombras graciosas
debaxo de los castaños,
y hago a los ermitaños
encovar como raposas.

Hago mustios los perales, 110
los bosques frescos, medoños,
y alegres los madroños,
y llorosos los rosales.
Hago sonar las campanas
muy lexos con mis primores, 115
y callar los ruiseñores,
y los grillos y las ranas.

Hago a buenos y a roínes
cerrar ventanas y puertas *f. 175 v.*
y hago llorar las huertas 120
la muerte de los jardines.
Las viñas hago marchitas,
y los arroyos riberas ;
hago lagunas las eras,
y cisternas las ermitas. 125

Y porque alabarme es sospecho
no me quiero más loar,
porque el mucho blasonar
nunca hizo grande hecho.
¡ Salgan los vientos y el frío ! 130
Pues mi potencia me sobra,
es bien que muestre por obra
el primer triunfo mío.

Afuera, afuera, calores,
y locuras del Verano, 135
y traiga el viento solano
otros misterios mayores.
Y será de tal manera :

que se hielen las riberas,
los tanques y las carreras 140
y pozos, que el sol no quiera.

Luego el cierço regañado
traya nieves y ñublados,
que ni valgan abrigados
ni corrales al ganado. 145
Los pastores con desmayo
erizan ya los cabellos.
Aqui viene el uno de ellos,
que llaman Brisco Pelayo.

[*Entra*] *Brisco, cantando.*

BRISCO ¡Quién m'ahora ca mi sayo, 150
cuitado,
quién m'ahora ca mi sayo!

Falando:

Bendito seas, Verano,
y el padre que te engendró,
aquel, aquel, digo yo 155
que Dios hizo por su mano.
Mas Invierno, yo juraría
por la crisma del baptizo,
que Satañe se lo hizo
sin saber lo que hazía. 160

Cantando:

El moço y la moça
van en romería:
tómales la noche
'n aquella montina.
¡cuitado, 165
quién m'ahora ca mi sayo!

---

143 *traya,* 'traiga.' See *Índia,* n. 164.
152 *Quién m'ahora ca mi sayo,* '¡quién me diera ahora acá mi sayo!' Vicente uses the same line, though not as part of a song, in *Auto de los cuatro tiempos,* line 179. See Margit Frenk Alatorre, "*Quien maora ca mi sayo.*"
159 *Satañe,* 'Satanás.'
164 *'n aquella,* 'en aquella.' See *Frágua,* n. 201.

Falando:

Oh Verano, ¿qué es de ti?
Amparo de los pastores,
sácame de estos temblores,
si has manzilla de mí, 170
que este Invierno determina,
a según veo tratarme,
que sólo por acabarme
ha tomado esta contina.

Cantando:

Tómales la noche 175
'n aquella montina;
la moça cantava,
el moço dezía:
¡Cuitado,
quién m'ahora ca mi sayo! 180

INVIERNO Pues del ganado te alexas
y temblas con cuitas tantas,
dime, pastor, ¿por qué cantas?
Ya cantas, ¿de qué te quexas?
Porque mira, hermano mío, 185
quien canta no tien tormiento.
BRISCO No te oigo con el viento,
ni te entiendo con el frío.

INVIERNO ¿Cantas o lloras, vaquero?
No tienes orejas, creo. 190
BRISCO Con la niebla no te veo.
¡Derreñiego del tempero!
Ya no sé lo que me hablo.
¡Ay, que me fino, cuitado!
Si no fuera desposado, 195
muriera con el diablo.

---

172 *a según,* 'según.' See *Índia,* n. 99.
182 *temblas,* 'tiemblas.' See *Índia,* n. 143.
186 *tien,* 'tiene.' Probably a *lusismo* (Portuguese *tem*) though *tien* is found in *sayagués* and may be used here to give a rustic flavor to Winter's speech. Note, however, that Vicente often uses it with no special stylistic value; cf. *Farelos,* line 132. See Teyssier, pp. 374-375.
192 *derreñiego,* 'derreniego.' See *Índia,* n. 161.

Mas la mi beços de mona, *f. 176 r.*
hija de Giraldo Gil,
si me muero antes d'abril,
¡cuitada de la soplona! 200
Que a según le cayó en suerte
condición de mataperros,
comerá trezientos puerros
con ravia de la mi muerte.

Digo yo a la boz que suena, 205
no sé si es aquí, si allí,
que el Invierno es tan roín
que no tiene cosa buena.

INVIERNO Blasfemas de mí, pastor,
como si yo fuesse el infierno. 210

BRISCO Si tú eres el Invierno,
aun te tengo por peor.

¡Mal gozo veas de ti!
¿Para qué es perseverar?

INVIERNO Prosigue el tu cantar, 215
y déxame hazer a mí.

BRISCO Tú te pensarás que el canto
no sirve sino al plazer;
pues yo te hago saber
que a los más tristes es planto. 220

INVIERNO ¿Por qué no buscas abrigo
de este cierço, hombre cuitado?

---

197 *la mi,* 'mi.' The use of the definite article before a possessive adjective was dying out in the sixteenth century. See Keniston, 19.33.

203 *trezientos,* 'trescientos.' Not a *lusismo,* but the usual form in older Spanish (e.g., in Nebrija). See Corominas, s.v. *tres.*

217-220 Brisco's speech recalls two well-known motifs of Hispanic folksongs: "El que me oyera cantar/ pensará que estoy alegre;/ yo soy como el pajarito,/ que canta cuando se muere" (Torner, No. 98), and "Quem canta seu mal espanta,/ quem chora seu mal aumenta;/ eu canto para espalhar/ uma dor que me atormenta" (*ibid.,* No. 199). Chaves offers "Quem canta seus males (ou 'maus fados') (ou 'fados') espanta, quem chora mais os aumenta" (p. 331).

220 *planto,* 'llanto.' The usual form in medieval Spanish; Juan de Valdés preferred it to *llanto* (p. 81).

BRISCO Porque el mal perseverado
muchos males tien consigo.
INVIERNO ¿ No hay remedio en el corral ? 225
BRISCO Do al diabro el dolor,
quando el remedio es peor
que no el daño principal.

Mi corral está agua hecho,
y el agua hecha regelo, 230
el regelo sin provecho
¡ mal te haga Dios del cielo !
Que si remedio hoviera,
ya lo hoviera topado ;
pero el mal que es perlongado, 235
quando algún remedio espera,
es ya de desesperado.

INVIERNO Con todo tu querellar,
quanto hablas todo es rosas,
y dizes tan buenas cosas 240
que huelgo de te escuchar.
Si tú sabes repastar
'n esta sierra tu manada
como tú sabes hablar,
bien te puedes alabar 245
que mereces la soldada.

BRISCO Con todas essas razones,
mala pascua te dé Dios.
INVIERNO Y a ti de dos en dos
pierdas cabras y cabrones. 250
BRISCO ¿ Tú quieres pullas comigo ?

---

226 *do,* 'doy.' See *Frágua,* n. 58. *diabro,* 'diablo ;' a *sayagués* form ; see Teyssier, p. 34.
231 *regelo,* 'hielo.' *Lusismo.* See Teyssier, p. 399.
235 *perlongado,* 'prolongado.' Perhaps a *lusismo* (*perlongar,* 'to delay unduly'), but Vicente may also have been influenced by the extensive use of the prefix *per-* in *sayagués.* See Teyssier, pp. 57-58 ; Weber de Kurlat.
249 *de dos en dos,* 'en abundancia.' See Gillet, III, 699, n. 13.
251 *pullas.* For this rustic exchange of abusive remarks, see Gillet, IV, 40-45. *comigo,* 'conmigo.' Not a *lusismo* ; *comigo* is found alongside *conmigo* in sixteenth-century Castilian texts, though the latter is somewhat more common. See Keniston, 6.16.

Pues estémonos a ellas;
que yo echaré tantas de ellas,
como hay granos de trigo.

INVIERNO Veamos, comiença pues, 255
que yo te responderé.
BRISCO ¿Sabes quántas pullas sé?:
como hay de horas en el mes.
INVIERNO No cures de más razones;
veamos qué pullas son. 260
BRISCO Plega al mártir Sant'Antón
que piojos y ratones
te pongan en tentación.

INVIERNO Aun te veas, pastor,
de amores tan maltratado 265
que la sierra y el ganado
se te convierta en dolor.
BRISCO Los ojos y el coraçón
te trayan tales amores
que den a ti la passión, 270
y a otro los favores.

INVIERNO Mas quiera Dios que tú seas
querido de una donzella,
y estando tú bien con ella *f. 176 v.*
te la casen, y tú veas 275
que es por su voluntad de ella.
BRISCO Tú tengas hado tan fuerte
que ames zagala tal
que te quiera tanto mal
como quieres a la muerte. 280

INVIERNO Dios te dé tan fuerte plaga,
pues contra mí te sostienes,
que por linda amiga penes,
y tantas burlas te haga
como de cabellos tienes. 285
BRISCO Y tú por ley de mugeres
te vengan tan fuertes daños,
que te paguen sus engaños
los servicios que hizieres.

INVIERNO Muger ames en porfía 290

que sueñes con gran querella
todas las noches con ella
sin poderla ver un día.
BRISCO Tú ames de coraçón
zagala de gran beldad, 295
y sea de tierna edad
y fuerte la condición.

INVIERNO Tal gozo veas de ti
que quieras bien a muger
que no vea otro plazer 300
que verte partir de sí
y te muestre gran querer.
BRISCO Pues no quieres concluir,
del amor seas llagado
por dama de tal estado 305
que no ge lo oses dezir
y mueras de enamorado.

INVIERNO Por muger tengas enojos,
pues aguzas tus sentidos
contra mí, 310
que tenga hermosos ojos
y cerrados los oídos
para ti.
BRISCO Zagala vayas mirar
por quien tan perdido seas 315
que jamás nunca la veas
ni la puedas olvidar.

INVIERNO Tal moça servir te vea
que te dé crudas fatigas;
y quando tu mal le digas, 320
ninguna cosa te crea.
BRISCO Por muger casada penes,
d'amores muerto perdido,
y pensando que la tienes
se quexe de ti al marido, 325
y que te quiebre las sienes.

INVIERNO Tengas amiga hermosa
que la quieras muy querida,

---

306 *ge lo*, 'se lo.' See *Frágua*, n. 175.

y te ame como a su vida,
y sea dulce y graciosa; 330
y que se venga a finar,
y tú de presente allí,
y al tiempo del espirar
ponga los ojos en ti
para jamás te mirar. 335

No hay más pullas, pastor.

BRISCO Cuido que más me quedaron.

INVIERNO No, que en ésta se acabaron
quinze dolores d'amor,
que a muchos maltrataron. 340

BRISCO Ansí biva la fortuna
como tú sabes d'amores;
que sus casos de dolores
no tienen cuenta ninguna.

(Argumento da figura terceira:)

BRISCO Acá viene Juan Guijarro, 345
muy perdido a maravilla,
que gastó con Torobilla
con que no compró çamarro.
Hízole muy cruda guerra *f. 177 r.*
todo el verano el amor, 350
y agora, el pecador,
esta frialdad lo atierra.

[*Entra*] *Juan Guijarro, cantando:*

JUAN ¿Por dó passaré la sierra,
gentil serrana morena?

Falando:

Gran remedio es para'l frío 355
al que viste poca lana
bailar rezio de mañana
al son de este cantar mío;
y si mi espirito no yerra,

---

337 *cuido,* 'pienso, juzgo.'
353 *dó,* 'dónde.'
359 *espirito.* The verse is a syllable too long; we should therefore pronounce *esprito,* a form often found in '1562.' See *India,* n. 452.

a según quedé en faldetas, 360
si no diesse çapatetas
caería muerto en tierra.

Cantando:

¿Por dó passaré la sierra,
gentil serrana morena?

—Tu ru ru ru lá 365
¿quién la passará?
Tu ru ru ru rú
no la passes tú.
—Tu ru ru ru ré,
yo la passaré. 370
Di, serrana, por tu fe,
si naciste en esta tierra
¿por dó passaré la sierra,
gentil serrana morena?

Falando:

Tódalas cosas a ratos 375
tienen su remedio cierto:
para pulgas, el desierto;
para ratones, los gatos;
para la muerte, enterrar;
para el rico, mal bivir; 380
para el amor, el dormir;
y para'l frío, bailar.

Cantando:

—Ti ri ri ri rí,
queda tú aquí.
—Tu ru ru ru rú, 385
¿qué me quieres tú?
—To ro ro ro ró,
que yo sola estó.

---

360 *en faldetas,* 'al frío' [?]. See Gillet, III, 204, n. 14.
375 *tódalas,* 'todas las.' *Lusismo* (sixteenth-century Portuguese *tôdalas*). It may be simply a printer's error; Teyssier (p. 403) notes only one other example in Vicente's Castilian texts. For the corresponding Portuguese structure, see *Júpiter,* n. 229.
388 *estó,* 'estoy.' See *Frágua,* n. 58.

—Serrana, no puedo, no,
que otro amor me da guerra. 390
¿Cómo passaré la sierra,
gentil serrana morena?

Falando:

Ell amor ha d'ir al infierno,
esto es ya canto llano,
porque me hizo en verano 395
olvidarme del invierno.
Mi vida no fue acordada;
quando serví, ella morío;
que el amor no mata frío,
ni paga nunca soldada. 400

BRISCO Oh bien vengas, Juan Guijarro!
JUAN Mejor estás tú, hermano,
que guardaste del verano
con que compraste çamarro;
y no yo, que gasté en flores 405
mi soldada, sin más tiento,
y agora me toma el viento
la cuenta de mis amores.

El cierço me toma cuentas
de mis cuidados vacíos; 410
de mis sospiros, los fríos;
de mi querer, las tormentas;
los aires, de mi bonança;
las nieves, de mi franqueza;
los nublos, de mi firmeza; 415
la hambre, de mi esperança.

---

393 *ell amor.* See *Júpiter*, n. 351.
398 *morío,* 'murió.' Vicente here conjugates *morir* like a Portuguese verb of the third conjugation, doubtless deliberately for the sake of the rhyme with *frío*; for an analogous case, see Teyssier, p. 317.
413 *bonança.* Cf. Covarrubias, s.v.: "La serenidad del tiempo quando se sossiega y amansa en el mar la tempestad y está quieta. Por similitud llamamos bonança el tiempo de la prosperidad, quando todas las cosas suceden a gusto y la fortuna va pujante con prosperidad y viento en popa."
416 *la hambre.* Cf. Keniston, 18.122: "During much of the sixteenth century initial *h-*, derived from Latin *f-*, was an aspirate, particularly in the south of Spain. Feminine nouns beginning with *ha-* therefore took the feminine article."

BRISCO ¿No tienes tú otro hato,
çamarrón o çamarrilla?
JUAN Ni capote ni capilla,
ni tengo más de un çapato. 420
Yo saqué en Santintín
este sayo en hora mala
sólo para la zagala
verme y pagarse de mí.

Y comprélle una sortija, 425
y una saya verde escura;
por do sé que la locura
es muy mala sevandija.
Yo te juro, Alberto amigo,
que el que sigue tras zagalas *f. 177 v.* 430
terná tantas hadas malas
como yo traigo comigo.

Que juro al cuerpo de mí,
que gasté en agujetas
mis cabras blancas y prietas, 435
y agora ándome ansí
sin çamarro, sin çurrón,
perdido, manguispanado:
el diablo llevó el cayado,
y su madre el mi çurrón. 440

BRISCO Mal estás, carillo mío,

425 *comprélle,* 'compréle.' Perhaps a *lusismo* (Portuguese *comprei-lhe*), which may be due to the printer. It is possible, however, that the *ll* is purely graphic; cf. the use of *ll* for the sound *l* in sixteenth-century Portuguese orthography, e.g., in *elle, bello,* today *ele, belo. Lle* for *le* occurs only here and in line 954, beside countless examples of the correct forms in this and the other plays. See Teyssier, p. 369.
428 *sevandija,* 'sabandija (bicho vil y despreciable).' *Lusismo.* See Corominas, s.v. *sabandija.*
431 *terná,* 'tendrá.' Sixteenth-century Castilian still vacillated between the forms with metathesis which were usual in Old Spanish (*porná, terná, verná*) and the modern forms which were destined to replace them.
433 *juro al cuerpo de mí.* Probably a distortion of *cuerpo de nos,* itself a euphemism for *cuerpo de Dios.* See Gillet, III, 344, n. 130.
441 *carillo,* 'amigo.' Though this word is not really *saya-*

que este i[n]vierno es harto crudo.
JUAN Pues que yo no fui sesudo,
¿qué culpa me tiene el frío?
Dame el tu çamarro, a ver, 445
y callentarme he un poco.
BRISCO Harto es el hombre de loco
que da lo que ha menester.

JUAN Di, por vida de tu hermana,
¿cómo seré rico? ¡Di! 450
BRISCO Si tú aprendieras de mí,
no bailaras tan sin gana.
Ora ñota y ño seas loco:
¿quieres tú enriquecer?
Dezirte he mi parecer: 455
gana mucho y gasta poco.

(Argumento da figura quarta:)

INVIERNO Pastores, acullá asoma
una vieja sin sentido
que quiere un moço marido;
y él dize que la toma, 460
y sacóle este partido:
que si esta sierra passar
assí lloviendo y nevando,

---

gués, it is frequently used by Encina and Fernández. Covarrubias, s.v., calls it "vocablo aldeano, pero muy propio, y usado en la antigua lengua castellana." See Teyssier, p. 41; Lihani.

446 *callentarme he.* Not a *sayagués* form; the palatalization of the *l* is caused by the following diphthongue of the rhizotonic forms. See Gillet, III, 470, n. 272; Teyssier, p. 69.

447ff Juan's attitude may see a little less callous if we remember that it is solidly based on folk tradition. Cf. the following proverbs, all cited from Chaves: "Quem não trabalha não come" (p. 356); "Quem muito gasta e pouco tem, a pedir tem" (p. 349); "Quem pouco tem e isso dá, cedo se arrependerá" (p. 360); "Quem dá o que tem, a pedir vem" (p. 335); "Quem dá o seu antes de morrer, aparelhe-se a bem sofrer" (p. 335); "Nem no inverno nem no verão, largues o teu gabão" (p. 270); "Quem não tem calças no inverno, não fies dele dinheiro" (p. 354).

460ff Cf. Camões's *voltas* based on the *mote* "Descalça vai pela neve:/ assi faz quem Amor serve" (*Obra completa,* p. 458).

462 *passar,* 'passare.' See *Frágua,* n. 70.

luego la quiere tomar;
y ella por se casar 465
viene descalça cantando.

[Entra a] Velha, cantando:

VELHA Assi andando, amor, andando,
assi andando m'ora irei.

Fala[n]do:

Mando-vos eu a vós chover
e nevar e saraivar, 470
pois pera haver de casar
não se pode hi al fazer.
Jesu! Que neve tamanha!
Nunca hei daqui de sair.
Muitos haviam de rir, 475
se soubessem a artimanha
que em tal tempo me fez vir.

BRISCO ¿Adó vais, vieja honrada?,
que no hay acá camino.
VELHA Eu não vou senão a tino 480
per esta serra nevada.
É tamanha a frialdade
que levo nas ilhargadas,
e as gengibas inchadas,
que haveríeis piedade 485
se me vísseis as queixadas.

JUAN Vos, madre vieja, ¿a qué vais?
VELHA É mui longo de contar;
porém, por desabafar,
direi um pouco e nô-mais. 490
Eu desejo ser casada
com um mancebo solteiro,

---

467 *assi,* 'assim.' See *India,* n. 64.
467-468 A *pliego suelto* cited by Margit Frenk Alatorre in the prologue to her edition of the *Cancionero de galanes,* p. xlvii, has the following *letrilla*: "Ansi andando/ el mundo se va acauando/ andando asi/ nunca tan trocado le vi."
472 *al,* 'outra coisa.' See *India,* n. 27.
481 *per,* 'por.' See *Júpiter,* n. 186.
490 *e nô-mais,* 'e não mais.' See *India,* n. 184.

filho do priol d'Aveiro,
e eu sua namorada,
e o moço çapateiro. 495

Ora fui-lhe eu falar nisso.
Dixe eu: "Fernando amigo,
s'havés de casar comigo,
agora é o tempo disso,
que vai abaixando o trigo." 500
Dixe ele: "Brásia Caiada,
praz-me, pois que vós querés,
com condição que passés
aquela serra nevada
sem levar nada nos pés. 505

E fosse isto logo agora, *f. 178 r.*
que triunfa a invernada."
Fui eu contente e pagada
coa muita da bo-hora.

BRISCO Hiziérades por bolar, 510
si os imbiara al cielo.

VELHA É um mancebo tão belo,
que iria polo cob[r]ar
nua per este regelo.

Não cuideis, que é desse geito. 515
Vedes vós um alemão?

---

493 *priol,* 'prior, superior de convento em algumas ordens monásticas.'
497 *dixe eu,* 'disse eu.' See *Índia,* n. 17.
498 *havés,* 'haveis.' In the sixteenth century, the second person plural ending *-edes* of Old Portuguese had not yet taken its definitive modern form *-eis*; the latter existed alongside *-és* and *-ês.* There was apparently no social or stylistic distinction among the three forms. See Teyssier, pp. 173-174. The existence of forms with both open *é* and closed *ê* seems to be guaranteed by rimes. Note, however, that rimes of an open with a closed vowel are not rare in Portuguese; see Mattoso Câmara, pp. 160-162. Cf. *Farelos,* n. 30-31.
511 *imbiara,* 'enviara.' A *lusismo,* perhaps to be attributed to the printer, suggested by such cases as Portuguese *inteiro*: Spanish *entero,* Portuguese *inveja*: Spanish *envidia.* Note that in Modern Portuguese initial *em-* and *en-* followed by another consonant are often pronounced [ĩ] in popular speech, though careful speakers prefer [ẽ].

Assi é ele, tão dereito,
um mancebo tão bem feito,
que é ũa consolação.
Ora verde-lo jugar 520
cos pranches pela do vento!
Bengò Deus e o anjo bento:
parece que anda no ar!

BRISCO Si él es tal, juri a mí
que sois vos bien corcobada. 525
VELHA Encolhi coa geada,
mas não sam eu feita assi:
vedes-m'aqui estirada.
BRISCO Ya sois tan vieja arrugada
que no sé lo que me diga. 530
VELHA Hi há velha rapariga,
e manceba velhentada.

BRISCO ¿No sentís que sois ya tierra?
VELHA Não dizedes vós verdade,
que se eu fosse velha terra, 535
não passaria eu a serra
per tamanha frialdade.
Vistes vós quanto embaraço!
BRISCO Mejor fuera romería.
VELHA Não há hi tal obra pia 540
como a que eu pera mi faço.

Ouvides vós, Juan Guaitero?
Ide assoviar ò gado
e não tenhades cuidado
do meu Fernão çapateiro. 545

---

522 *bengò*, a contracted form of *benga-o*, 'benza-o' (spelled *bengoo* in '1562'). This archaic form of the present subjunctive of *benzer* appears only here in '1562'; Teyssier is doubtless right in considering it a deliberate attempt to give a rustic flavor to the speech of the *velha* (p. 194).
527 *sam*, 'sou.' See *Farelos*, n. 27.
533 Cf. the proverbs "Velho namorado, cedo enterrado" and "Velho recencasado, reza-lhe por finado" (Chaves, p. 422).
534 *dizedes*, 'dizeis.' See *Índia*, n. 3.
541 *mi*, 'mim.' See *Índia*, n. 64.
543 *ò*, 'ao.' See *Índia*, n. 202.

Hui, amara! Eu estou brincando!
Quero-me ir, que perco tempo.
Jesu! Que neve e que vento!
G'eu vou tarameleando.

Cantando:

Assi andando, amor, andando, 550
assi andando m'ora irei.

[*Falando:*]

Ora pois, mando-vos eu,
Dona Neve amargurada,
que hei-d'alongar a passada,
e hei-de fazer o meu. 555
Jesu! Jesu! Eis-me. Vou.
Amara de mi! G'eu jaço!
Quem me tirará o braço
e a perna que atolou?

Acorrede-me, pastores, 560
ajudade-m' ora alçar.

BRISCO Mirá quien quiere casar
y negociar amores.

VELHA Inda eu sou molher bem tesa;
e cair não é maravilha; 565
porque empecei na fraldilha,
que coa pressa
não lhe fiz, má-hora, a presa,
nem me lembrou a mantilha.

Porque diz o exemplo antigo: 570
quando te dão o porquinho,
vai logo co baracinho.

---

546 *estou brincando.* See *Índia,* note preceding line 1.
549 *g'eu,* 'já eu.'
557 *amara,* 'amarga.' See *Frágua,* n. 149.
562 *mirá,* 'mirad.' See *Frágua,* n. 557.
564 *inda,* 'ainda.' See *Índia,* n. 216.
571-572 Cf. Correas, *Vocabulario,* p. 447: "Kuando te dieren la kochinilla, akorre kon la sogilla. Otros dizen: 'Kuando te dieren la vakilla . . . ,' otros: ' . . . la kabrilla . . . '." Chaves, p. 317: "Quando te derem o porquinho, acode logo com o baracinho. Quando te derem a vaca, vem logo com a corda."

Ora eu cá assi o digo;
e mais, quem inda s'atreve
com' eu, que o posso fazer, 575
que assi case eu com prazer,
que vou cada vez mais leve.

Vai-se cantando

Polo canaval da neve
não há hi amor que me leve.

INVIERNO Pastores, íos del frío, 580
acogeos all aldea,
porque quiero que se vea
el segundo triunfo mío *f. 178 v.*
sobre la mar de Guinea.

Vam-se [os pastores] cantando:

BRISCO ¡Quién m'ahora ca mi sayo. 585
cuitado,!
quién m'ahora ca mi sayo!

JUAN ¿Por dó passaré la sierra,
gentil serrana morena?

(Argumento das figuras do segundo triunfo:)

INVIERNO El mi triunfo segundo 590
son tormentas en la mar,
que luego quiero tratar,
las más fuertes que en el mundo
natureza pudo dar.
Y antes de començadas 595
verná un piloto boçal

---

578 *canaval*, archaic form of 'canavial.' See *Inês Pereira*, ed. Révah, n. 650. For the song, cf. *Inês Pereira*, lines 647-651: "Canas do amor, canas,/ canas do amor./ Polo longo de um rio,/ canaval vi florido,/ canas do amor."
594 *natureza*, 'naturaleza.' See *Frágua*, n. 42.
596 *un piloto boçal*. Cf. Duffy, *Shipwreck*, pp. 71-72: "The charge of arrogance—and incompetence—is hurled more frequently against the pilot than against any other member of the ship's company . . . More than any other man on board, the pilot was responsible for the ship and the lives of those who sailed in it. He was the most conspicuous figure to blame for any wreck; even though a ship was leaking and overloaded, he was assumed to be able to bring her to safety . . . Possibly because of the personal responsi-

y un marinero, aosadas,
buen maestro especial,

y tres grumetes bobazos,
todos cinco navegando, 600
el piloto inorando,
el marinero carpazos
oiréis que le va dando.
[*O piloto apita.*]

PILOTO Pi pi pi pii.
GRUMETE Adés!
PILOTO Esta nau vai emproada, 605
se a tendes bem olhada.
MARINHEIRO Mas antes é ò revés!

Porque o paiol d'avante.
não leva biscouto já,
nem há senão o de cá 610
que comam daqui avante.
A nau vai bem arrumada:
Deus a leve a salvamento!
Em al tende vós o tento,
que isso não releva nada. 615

Levais viagem gentil,

---

bility for the ship and the presence of so many 'second-guessers' the pilot chose to be arrogant and aloof, and thus, in the eyes of his critics, compounded stupidity with false pride."

597 *aosadas.* See *Frágua,* n. 539.

599 *grumetes.* Cf. Boxer, *Tragic History,* p. 9, n. 3: "They were apprentice seamen, not necessarily boys, though most of them were probably in their teens. They did all the hardest work aboard the ship and slept on the deck at the waist, between the mainmast and the foremast . . . At the end of the last century the word 'grummet' still survived in south-east England with the meaning of 'awkward boy.' "

601 *inorando,* 'ignorando.' See *Júpiter,* note preceding line 1.

602 *carpazos.* The meaning is unclear; perhaps a misprint for *çarpazo,* though Corominas, s.v. *zarpa,* rejects this hypothesis and suggests that it may be derived from Portuguese *carpir* or *carmear,* in the sense 'surrar, fustigar, maltratar com pancadas.'

604 *adés.* '1562' places a question mark after this word, which Marques Braga tentatively translates 'Estás aí? Que queres?' I should prefer to relate it to Catalan *adés,* 'agora mesmo'; Italian *adesso,* 'agora.' See Corominas, s.v. *adieso.*

não vades com ventos largos
cair nos baxos dos pargos
nessa costa do Brasil.
[*O piloto apita.*]
PILOTO Pi pi pi pi pii. 620
Não há aqui nenhum grumete?
TOD[OS OS GRUMETES] Que manda vossa mercêa?
PILOTO O nosso vento escassea:
caça poja do traquete.

GREGÓRIO E quem é aqui o traquete? 625
O traque sei eu que é,
mas o quete não sei eu
inda agora onde ele s'é
AFONSO Samicas é o lançol
que vai naquela picota. 630
PILOTO Caçai eramá a escota,
que vai o vento co sol.

Apito:

Pii pi pi pi pi.
GREGÓRIO Tanto monta assoviar
coma aquilo que s'é li. 635
PILOTO Não sabeis ali caçar?
GONÇALO E cães tendes vós aqui?
Vês, vês, tu, tu, tu!
AFONSO Gonçalo, vai polo forão.
GONÇALO Vá Grigório.
GREGÓRIO Mas vai tu, 640

---

618 *baxos*, 'baixos,' here in the sense of 'shoals.'
619 Cf. Boxer, *Tragic History*, p. 7: 'Most seamen thought that the first half of March was about the best time [to set out on the voyage to India], but in practice the ships often left in the second half of March or in the first half of April. Departures later in April, or even early in May, were not unknown, but the ships involved almost invariably made *arribadas*, or abortive voyages, being compelled either to return to Lisbon or to 'winter' in Brazil. Delayed departures were chiefly due to administrative and financial difficulties at Lisbon, such as a shortage of ready money when most needed, and trouble in collecting crew."
622 *mercêa*. A rustic form of *mercê*. See Teyssier, pp. 152-153.
624 *caça*, 'colhe, ata (velas, cabos, etc.).' Lines 636 ff. are built on a pun involving this verb and its homonym *caçar*, 'to hunt.'

e eu chamarei o cão
do piloto : tu, tu, tu.

Vês, vês ! Raiva te tome !
E como há o vosso cão nome, piloto ?

PILOTO Vosso pai torto ! 645
Milhor matais vós a fome.
Não vai nesta nau grumete,
que valha um só caracol :
à vela chamam lançol,
e picota ao traquete. 650

MARINHEIRO Vós sois, piloto, a picota.
Se nosso caminho é em Leste,
e o vento é Noroeste,
pera que é caçar a escota ?
Eu não vos posso entender. 655

PILOTO Onde vos fazeis aqui ? *f. 179 r.*

MARINHEIRO E vós preguntais a mi
o que deveis de saber ?
Sois piloto d'Alcouchete
pera o Rio das Inguias, 660
e navegar nestas vias
quer cabeça e capecete.

[*O piloto apita.*]

PILOTO Pi pi pii — pi pi pii.

---

647 Cf. Boxer, *Tragic History*, pp. 9-10: "The Crown *regimentos* stressed that only experienced mariners should be entered as sailors for the India voyage, but these have never been too plentiful in Portugal. As early as the first decade of the sixteenth century, a captain found that his rustic crew could not distinguish between starboard and larboard until he tied a bunch of onions to one side of the ship and a bunch of garlic to the other. Those makeshift seamen who survived a couple of India voyages presumably became 'old salts,' but complaints abounded in the years 1570-1650 that tailors, cobblers, lackeys, ploughmen and 'ignorant boys' of all kinds were freely shipped as deep-sea mariners."
656 *Onde vos fazeis aqui?* 'What do you reckon our position to be?'
660 *Rio das Inguias.* Today Ribeira das Enguias, in the Ribatejo (Marques Braga's note).
662 *capecete.* 'capacete,' literally 'helmet,' but here used, as often, as a synonym for *cabeça* in a figurative sense. Cf. Morais, s.v. *capacete.*

GREGÓRIO Mando-vos eu assoviar?
Que não hei hoje de falar, 665
ou siquais me irei per hi.
MARINHEIRO Tomastes vós hoje a altura
por saberdes onde estais?
PILOTO Co Rio dos Bôs Sinais
me faço a Deus e à ventura, 670

ou na auguada da Boa Paz,
ou seremos tanto avante
como o Rio do Infante,
segundo o tempo aqui faz,
ou co Cabo das Correntes. 675
MARINHEIRO Isso é ou lobo ou rã,
ou feixe de lenha ou arméu de lã!
Isto fazem aderentes!

Quem vos houve a pilotagem
pera a Índia desta nau? 680
Porque um piloto de pau
sabe mais na marinhagem.
PILOTO Fernão Vaz, verdade é
que me acho eu cá reboto,
porque nunca fui piloto 685
senão lá pera Guiné.

MARINHEIRO Esta é ũa errada
que mil erros traz consigo:
ofício de tanto perigo
dar-se a quem não sabe nada. 690
Este ladrão do dinheiro
faz estes maus terremotos;
que eu sei mais que dez pilotos
e sempre sou marinheiro.

Ũa cousa juro eu, 695
que os que são sabedores
nunca metem rogadores

669ff The pilot obviously has no idea of the true location of the ship, since he mentions four different places on the east coast of Africa in no particular order. See the map reproduced from Linschoten's *Itinerario* (1595) in Boxer, *Tragic History*, facing p. 8.
684 *reboto*, 'embotado, rude.'

nem peitam nada do seu.
Se agora se acertar
tormenta como acontece, 700
piloto, a mi me parece
que havia a nau de suar.

(Argumento da tormenta seguinte, do segundo triunfo do Inverno:)

INVIERNO Yo quiero sobre la mar
demostrar mi poderío;
pues la tierra gusta el frío, 705
tormentas quiero ordenar.
Haré cantar las serenas,
y peligrar a las naves,
y haré gritar las aves,
y bolar a las arenas. 710

¡Riésguese Meredión!

---

705 The sense is not clear. Aubrey F. G. Bell, *Estudos vicentinos* (Lisbon, 1940), p. 179, proposes emending *gusta* to *gasta*. I prefer to keep the reading of '1562,' taking *gustar* in the sense of 'catar, probar.' The subject is *tierra*. For the construction, see Corominas, s.v. *gustar*. The whole sentence seems to mean "Since the earth has already had a taste of cold, I want to go a step further and show what I can do in the way of a storm."
707 *serenas*, 'sirenas.' The usual form in Old Spanish, found also in the *siglo de oro*, and still alive in many dialects. Corominas, s.v. *sirena*, explains the form with pretonic *e* as "una etimología popular bastante natural (por el canto dulce y apacible de la sirena)." Like the wild man, the mermaid was popularly supposed to sing in bad weather. In the *Bestiaire* of Philippe de Thaun we find: "Serena en mer hante/ Cuntre tempeste chante/ E plure en bel tens." In the mid-thirteenth century, another French poet writes: "Tot ausi com la serene/ Qui chante quant il fet torment,/ Chante je quant plus ai painne/ Por cuidier que allegement/ Me veigne." (Both examples from Mulertt, pp. 74-75.) Bartholomaeus Anglicus, Book XVII, chapter lxxxx, "De la serena & de sus propiedades," says: "La serena es un monstruo marino que del ombliguo arriba ha la figura de una virgen muy hermosa & del ombliguo abajo ha la forma de un pez. Esta bestia se goza mucho en la tempestad & quando haze buen tiempo & sereno se duele."
711 *riésguese*, 'rásguese.' *Resgar* is found in Old Spanish (*Libro de buen amor*) and in Portuguese dialects. See Corominas, s.v. *rasgar*. For *Meredión*, see *Júpiter*, n. 58.

Salgan las furias ventales
con tormentas generales
y brava rebulución;
y diçan de las estrellas, 715
y suban de las honduras
nuves negras muy escuras,
y mil fuegos salgan de ellas.

Ansí, ansí, temporales,
que ahora triunfo yo. 720
¡Oh qué rayo que cayó
entre aquellos robledales!
Grandes bozes da la mar
de temor de esta tormenta;
terrible será el afrenta, 725
que terná quien navegar.

MARINHEIRO Ó nosso piloto mor!
Eu vejo vir por d'avante
tão temeroso sembrante
que não pode ser pior, 730
e aquele afozilar
fere fogo mui vermelho.
Tomai lá vosso conselho,
que eu não quero mais falar.

PILOTO Pera que é recear 735
o que inda não é nada?
Aquilo é trovoada *f. 179 v.*
e não há cá de chegar.

MARINHEIRO O bom piloto d'afrenta
ou grande senhor de mando 740
na bonança há-d'ir cuidando
os perigos da tormenta
que fortuna anda ordenando.

Não cuideis que é mar da Mina.

---

714 *rebulución,* 'revolución.'
715 *diçan,* 'bajen.' *Deçir* is usual in Old Spanish; see Corominas, s.v. *descender*. The *i* of *diçan* is doubtless due to analogy with the rhizotonic forms of *dezir*.
725 *el afrenta,* 'la afrenta.' The use of *el* before feminine nouns beginning with unstressed *a-* is the prevailing practice in sixteenth-century Castilian, though *la* is also found. See Keniston, 18.123.

	Isto é noite fechada,	745
	e a Lũa mercolina,	
	e a costa indiabrada,	
	e a nau má de bolina.	
PILOTO	À verdade g'este vento	
	entra mui indiabrado.	750
MARINHEIRO	Vós, piloto, sois a azado	
	pera perder logo o tento,	
	E mais noite tão escura.	
PILOTO	Que quereis vós, Fernão Vaz?	
	No mal que o inverno faz	755
	tenho eu culpa per ventura?	
MARINHEIRO	Quê? E vós chorais ant'ora?!	
PILOTO	Ó Virgem da Luz Senhora!	
	São Jorge! São Nicolau!	
MARINHEIRO	Acudi eramá à nau	760
	e leixai os santos agora!	
	Siquer mandai amainar	
	a meio masto essa vela,	
	e à mezena colhê-la	
	e ũa vez segurar,	765

---

746 *Lũa,* 'Lua.' See *Júpiter,* n. 60. *mercolina.* Ventura, p. 96, explains that "quando a Lua andar perto do Sol como Mercúrio, as noites serão escuras por falta da sua luz."
747 *indiabrada,* 'endiabrada.'
749 *g'este,* 'já este.'
759ff Cf. Boxer, *Tragic History,* p. 19: "[The missionaries' letters] also comment sometimes on . . . the want of religious devotion, save in times of storm and stress when outward manifestations of contrition seldom left anything to be desired. 'If you want to learn how to pray, go to sea,' was a proverbial expression by 1564, and the tendency of passengers and crew to invoke hysterically the aid of the Saints and the Virgin Mary in time of crisis, instead of making more practical efforts to save the ship, is a feature of most narratives in the *História Tragico-Marítima,* and was remarked by many foreign observers. On such occasions it was the practice for those in peril to make vows of alms or other benefactions to their favorite shrine or saint if they reached their destination in safety. The purser's standing-orders enjoined him to remind such devout penitents of the great hospital of All Saints at Lisbon, where their thank-offerings would be put to good practical use in relieving the sick."

[*O piloto apita.*]

PILOTO Pii pii pii.

GRUMETES Adés!

PILOTO Amaina, amaina a mezena.

GREGÓRIO Praz?

AFONSO Hão?

GREGÓRIO Mezena?

PILOTO Amainai essa mezena.

GREGÓRIO Que amainemos a mezena? 780

PILOTO Acudi ali todos três.

GREGÓRIO E eu também irei lá?

AFONSO E eu irei lá também?

PILOTO Ó pesar de Santarém!
O demo vos trouxe cá! 785

GREGÓRIO O demo vos trouxe cá
e a nós outros também.

PILOTO Vai, fideputa, Fernando.

GREGÓRIO Sabeis como me eu irei?
Per hi fora esfoziando. 790

PILOTO Amainai! Aque del-Rei!
Que nos imos alagando!

GONÇALO Per u puxaremos nós?
Grigório, puxa per hi.

GREGÓRIO Afonso, tir-te tu d'hi, 795

766ff In this scene, as often in the *Copilaçam*, the assigning of speeches to the several characters is unsatisfactory. This line is marked "Gru;" after some hesitation, I have assigned it to the three cabin boys speaking in chorus. In line 793, the same abbreviation is used for a speech which must clearly be addressed by one of the boys to another; I have arbitrarily assigned it to Gonçalo.
791 *Aque del-Rei!* Cf. Morais: "*Àque d'el-rei,* dizia o vulgo erradamente por *aqui d'el-rei: acudam aqui da parte d'el-rei,* é a sentença por inteiro."
792 *imos,* 'vamos.' This analogical form is used by a number of sixteenth-century writers, among them Camões. It is found in Old Spanish, and occasionally also in texts of the *siglo de oro*. See Rosenblat, p. 301.
793 *per,* 'por.' See *Farelos,* n. 14. *u,* 'onde.' By the beginning of the sixteenth century, *u,* the usual form in medieval Portuguese, was found only in popular or rustic speech; see Teyssier, pp. 484-485.
795 *tirte.* Cf. *Auto de la Sibila Cassandra,* line 166. The same imperative form is often found in Castilian texts of

e darei aqui dous nós.
PILOTO Fernão Vaz, acudi ali,
que vai a nau çoçobrando.
Ó Virgem de Monserrate,
livra-nos deste rebate 800
polo teu precioso mando.

Grumetes!
GRUMETES Bofá mei migo!
PILOTO Dou ò demo a grumetada!
Amaina o papafigo!
GREGÓRIO Vamo-nos polo abrigo; 805
dai ò demo a comiada!
Sabés que vento aqui faz?
GONÇALO Já aquesta é farrapada.
AFONSO Acodi ali, Fernão Vaz.
GREGÓRIO Acodi ali, Fernão Vaz, 810
que já vai toda quebrada
a tranca do guaroupaz.

AFONSO Havemos nós de nadar!
MARINHEIRO Que dizes, tolo, que dizes?
AFONSO Digo que havéis d'ir pescar 815
dos cranguejos cos narizes,
que andam per fundo do mar.
MARINHEIRO Jesu! Jesu! Santiago!
Ó Virge[m] Maria da Luz,
eu te prometo ũa cruz, 820
e um tríbulo e um bago.

PILOTO Ó Senhora da Batalha,
nas tuas santos mãos me meto.
GREGÓRIO Ó Virge[m] Maria do Loreta,
se escapulo eu te prometo 825
ũa cárrega de palha

---

the early sixteenth century. See Gillet, III, 548, n. 88; Keniston, 30.4, 29.342, 43.31. For the corresponding phenomenon in Portuguese, see *Farelos,* n. 451.
798 *çoçobrando,* 'soçobrando.'
802 *bofá,* 'a boa fé.' See *Farelos,* n. 86. *mei migo,* 'meu amigo.' Another rustic form; see Teyssier, pp. 155-156.
816 *dos cranguejos,* 'alguns caranguejos.' For the partitive construction, see *Farelos,* n. 491.
823 I have arbitrarily assigned this speech, marked "Gru" in the *Copilaçam,* to Gregório.

	polo santo dia de Deus.	
PILOTO	Ei-lo pricioso santo	
	Frei Pero Gonçalves bento,	
	empara-nos de tanto vento	830
	co teu precioso manto.	
	Senhor, *solibra nos a malo.*	
MARINHEIRO	Dêmos à bomba, piloto:	*f. 180 r.*
	dai ò demo Frei Gonçalo,	
	e são Frei Pero minhoto.	835
PILOTO	É o bem-aventurado	
	Frei Pero Gonçalves bento.	
GREGÓRIO	Santo que anda com tal vento,	
	não é ele senão pecado,	
	polos santos evangelhos!	840
MARINHEIRO	Vós, piloto, esmoreceis,	
	e mais, mui pouco sabeis	
	reger vossos aparelhos.	
	[*O piloto apita.*]	
PILOTO	Pi pi pii.	
GRUMETES	Adés?	
PILOTO	Ea, filho, alijar	845

828ff I have reassigned two speeches which seem to me inappropriate to the characters who speak them in the *Copilaçam*. There lines 828-829 are assigned to the *marinheiro*; lines 833-835 to *Gri*, that is, Gregório.
829 *Frei Pero Gonçalves.* Cf. Carolina Michaëlis de Vasconcellos, p. 440: "Dominicano de Amarante (falecido em 1259, festejado a dez de Janeiro), em cujo prepotente poder sobre raios e fogos de toda a espécie o povo tem fé, que manifesta, p. ex., atribuindo-lhe os fogos de Sant'Elmo." See also Duffy, *Shipwreck*, p. 110: "The most faithful portent of good or evil was found in the corposant. If the blue flames of St. Elmo appeared two or more times high on the mast, it was a sign of good fortune ahead; if it appeared but once, and low on the mast, then it was a certain augury of destruction. So great was the devotion of the Portuguese sailors to their saint that if priests on board tried to point out that the flames were the result of natural causes, the mariners threatened to take up arms and assault them."
830 *empara-nos*, 'ampara-nos.' *Emparar* is found in Old Spanish (*Poema de Mio Cid, Berceo*); see Corominas, s.v. *parar*. For the development of the Portuguese form, see Williams, 111, 2.
832 *solibra nos a malo*, 'sed libera nos a malo' (Matthew 6.13).

	quanto vai nesse convés,	
	que vai a nau a través.	
	Deitai as arcas ao mar!	
MARINHEIRO	Feito, feito, bem será.	
	Aqui, grumetes, aqui,	850
	vá ò mar esta arca, vá.	
GREGÓRIO	Não j'essa arca, ta ta ta,	
	que vai o meu pentem hi.	
PILOTO	A minha mesma não fique!	
	Ó Fernão Vaz, que faremos?	855
MARINHEIRO	É per força que arribemos	
	na volta de Moçambique.	
PILOTO	Arriba todo arribado:	
	Fernão Vaz, não sei que faça.	
MARINHEIRO	Ó Virgem Maria da Graça!	860
	Ei-lo masto já quebrado.	
AFONSO	Quebrou a tranca d'ametade,	
	e faz aqui ũa escurana.	
GONÇALO	Ora chamai a São Frade	
	que vos ponha outra de cana.	865
PILOTO	Fernão Vaz, que será aqui?	
MARINHEIRO	Oh arrenego de mi!	
	Se piloto aqui viera,	
	já esta nau estevera	
	a salvamento em Cochim.	870

848ff Cf. Boxer, *Tragic History,* p. 18: "Virtually all deck-space above the holds was the perquisite of some officer or member of the crew, who could sell it to the highest bidder. These men were also allowed *caixas de liberdade,* or 'liberty-chests,' of a standard measurement, in which they were permitted to bring home cinnamon (otherwise a royal monopoly) and certain other goods partly duty-free. The value and number of these *caixas de liberdade* were graduated in a sliding scale according to rank from captain-major to cabin-boy, the former originally being allowed four chests each and the latter one chest between three."
863 *escurana,* 'escuridade.' Morais lists it as an archaic form with the same meaning as *escuridão.*
864 *São Frade.* Here Vicente combines two of his favorite comic devices, the invocation of saints with humorously inappropriate names and ridicule of the friars. See *Índia,* n. 304; *Frágua,* n. 689.

(Argumento das três figuras que entram no fim do segundo triunfo do Inverno:)

INVIERNO Porque no pueda faltar
a mi triunfo cosa alguna,
la cumbre de la fortuna
quiero luego demostrar.
Veréis cantar las serenas, 875
que es señal de grande afrenta,
y cantan haziendo cuenta
que todas bonanças buenas
son después de la tormenta.

Vêm três Sereas cantando este vilancete:

SIRENAS Por más que la vida pene 880
no se pierda el esperança,
porque la desconfiança
sola la muerte la tiene.

Si fortuna dolorida
tuviere quien bien la sienta, 885
sentirá que toda afrenta
se remedia con la vida;
Y pues doble gloria tiene
después del mal la bonança,
no se pierda el esperança 890
en quanto muerte no viene.

INVIERNO Reinas mías, por agora
no curéis más de cantar,
porque os quiero llevar
al señor y a la señora 895
rey y reina de la mar.
Estos solos, sin temor
de mi terror tan profundo,
conquistan la mar del mundo,
y mata su resplandor 900
las tormentas que yo fundo.

Son sus naves tan poderosas

---

872 *cosa alguna,* 'nada.' See *Frágua,* n. 307.
873 *fortuna,* 'tempestad.' See *Índia,* n. 112.
902 The verse is a syllable too long. Vicente elsewhere uses the form *podrosas.* Both suggest a characteristically Portu-

con la gracia de su zelo,
que aunque se hunda el cielo
con tormentas peligrosas, 905
van y vienen sin recelo.
Y estos por excelencia
son reyes de las serenas,
y todas las cosas buenas
les hazen obediencia. 910

Y daros he presentadas
en poder de sus poderes
ansí, peces y mugeres,
serenas bien empleadas. *f. 180 v.*
Y poderos heis loar 915
que servís dos resplandores,
dos cosas para adorar,
dando gracias y loores
al que los quiso criar.
¿Ya entendéis estas cuentas? 920
Dezid si os plaze o no.

Respondem as sereas cantando:

SIRENAS Ha a a: ha a a: ha a a.
INVIERNO Pues dezís que sois contentas,
y yo muy contento so.

A El-Rei:

Pues que soy Invierno yo, 925
y vos la serenidad,
delante tal claridad
mi fuerça se consumió.
Empero quiero deziros
lo que se ve y no se entiende: 930
que nadie sabe sentiros,
y para saber serviros
en la tierra no se aprende.

Y porque va enflaquesciendo
mi fuerça delante vos, 935

---

guese pronunciation of Castilian. See *Don Duardos,* ed. Alonso, n. 232.
923 *so,* 'soy.' See *Frágua,* n. 58.

para dezir lo que entiendo,
señores, dígalo Dios,
que yo ya voy pereciendo,
y ansí quasi en vida
os trayo a empresentar 940
el briço para briçar
la reina rezién nacida,
y éstas para cantar.

Vos, serenas, cantaréis,
por memoria y enxalçamiento 945
de su vida y nacimiento,
este romance que oiréis.

Romance

Dios del cielo, rey del mundo,
por siempre seas loado,
que mostraste tus grandezas 950
en todo quanto has criado:
heziste reinos distintos,
cada uno en su grado;
dístelle muy justos reyes
cada rey en su reinado; 955
también diste a Portugal,
de moros siendo ocupado,
el rey don Alonso Henríquez,
que se le huvo ganado.
Este santo cavallero, 960
del tu poder ayudado,
venció cinco reyes moros
juntos en campo aplazado;
tus cinco llagas le diste
en pago de su cuidado, 965
que las dexasse por armas
a su reino señalado.
¡Recuérdate, Portugal,
quanto Dios te tiene honrado!

---

945 *enxalçamiento,* 'ensalzamiento, exaltación.' See *Don Duardos,* ed. Alonso, n. 3.
954 *dístelle,* 'disteles.' *Le* for *les* is common in medieval and classical Spanish; it is still occasionally found in literary texts and is often heard in popular speech. For the corresponding phenomenon in Portuguese, see *Índia,* n. 292.
960ff A reference to the battle of Ourique (1139).

Diote las tierras del sol 970
per comercio a tu mandado;
los jardines de la tierra
tienes bien señoreado;
los pumares de Oriente
te dan su fruto preciado; 975
sus paraísos terrenales
cerraste con tu candado.
¡Loa al que te dio la llave
de lo mejor que ha criado!
Todas las islas innotas 980
a ti solo ha revelado.
De quinze reyes que has tenido,
ninguno te ha desmedrado,
mas de mejor en mejor
te tienen acrecentado; 985
todas tus reinas passadas
santamente han acabado.
Si a Dios diste loores
por quantos bienes te ha dado,
dale gracias nuevamente, 990
pues de nuevo te ha mirado:
diote el rey don Juan,
tercero de este ditado,
y de su reina preciosa,
porque seas más liado, 995
dos hijas primeramente, *f. 181 r.*
todo por Dios ordenado;
como quien sabe lo bueno,
ansí te lo ha guisado.
Bien sabes, reino dichoso, 1000
las infantas que te ha dado,
unas para emperatrizes,
otras reinas, que has criado;
los más reyes de la cristi[a]ndad
de su progenie han manado, 1005
y otro[s]sí emperadores
proceden de su costado.
Tu príncipe natural,

---

996 *dos hijas.* Dona Maria, born October 15, 1527, married Philip II; Dona Isabel, born in April, 1529, died in infancy.
1009 *tu príncipe natural.* D. Afonso, born February 24, 1526, heir to the throne of Portugal. Braamcamp Freire (p. 256)

Dios te le tiene guardado,
y nacerá en tus manos 1010
a su tiempo limitado.
Cantad esto, mis serenas,
y sea muy bien cantado.

Este romance cantaram as sereas, e acabado diz o Inverno:

INVIERNO Serenas, por mi amor
que no cantéis más os pido. 1015
Porque el Verano es venido,
mi enemigo mayor
y capitán de Cupido.
Esperallo no me cale;
vos os podréis quedar, 1020
y acoger a la mar,
si la tierra no os vale.

(Esta segunda parte da Tragicomédia trata do triunfo do Verão, o qual entra cantando:)

VERANO Del rosal vengo, mi madre,
vengo del rosale.

Falando:

¡Afuera, afuera, ñublados, 1025
ñeblinas y ventisqueros!
Reverdeen los oteros,
los valles, priscos y prados.
Sea el frío rebentado,
salgan los frescos vapores; 1030
píntese el campo de flores,
alégrese lo sembrado.

---

points out that this referece to him in Vicente's play is our only evidence that his death occurred before April 1529.

1019 *esperallo,* 'esperarlo.' See *Frágua,* n. 228; *no me cale,* 'no me conviene.' See Corominas, s.v. *caler*.

1023 *rosal,* 'rosaleda.' The use of the word in this sense is not a *lusismo*. Cf. Covarrubias, s.v. *rosa*: "Rosal, la mata donde nacen las rosas."

1025-1032 These lines are repeated, with very slight variations, from *Auto de los cuatro tiempos,* lines 185-192.

1027 *reverdeen,* 'reverdezcan.'

Cantando:

A riberas d'aquel vado
viera estar rosal granado:
vengo del rosale. 1035

Falando:

Buélvase la hermosura
a cada cosa en su grado:
a las flores su blancura,
a la tierra su verdura,
que el bravo tiempo ha robado. 1040
Bendito el triunfo mío
que da claridad al cielo,
y no es menos mi zelo
de lo que es mi señorío.

Cantando:

A riberas d'aquel río 1045
viera estar rosal florido:
vengo del rosale.

Falando:

El dios de los amadores
me dio su poder y llaves,
que mande cantar las aves 1050
los salmos de sus amores.
Y las damas sin piedad
sepan que soy yo venido,
y que me manda Cupido
que no goze mi amistad 1055
coraçón desgradecido.

Cantando:

Viera estar rosal florido,
cogí rosas con sospiro:
vengo del rosale.

1053 *soy yo venido*. The use of *ser* with the past participle of intransitive verbs to form the perfect tenses survives in sixteenth-century Castilian, but becomes increasingly rare in the latter part of the century. See Keniston, 33.82.

Del rosal vengo, mi madre, 1060
vengo del rosale.

Falando:

La sierra de Sintra viene,
que estava triste del frío,
gozar del triunfo mío,
que a su gracia conviene. 1065
Es la sierra más hermosa
que yo siento en esta vida; *f. 181 v.*
es como dama polida,
brava, dulce y graciosa,
namorada y engrandecida. 1070

Bosque de cosas reales,
marinera y pescadora,
montera y gran caçadora,
reina de los animales;
muy esquiva y alterosa, 1075
balisa de navegantes,
sierra que a sus caminantes
no cansa ninguna cosa.

Refrigerio en los calores,
de saludades minero, 1080
contemplación de amores,
la señora a que yo más quiero
y con quien ando d'amores.

[*Vem a Serra de Sintra, e diz:*]

SERRA Oh Verão, Verão, Verão!
Verão os que bem te olharem 1085

1070 *namorada*, 'enamorada.' See *Farelos*, n. 63.
1076 *balisa*, 'baliza.' Corominas, s.v. *baliza*, considers the Castilian form to be a borrowing from Portuguese *balisa*, and gives the date of its first recorded appearance in Spanish as 1673. Vicente's use of the term is thus perhaps to be considered a *lusismo*.
1080 *saludades*, 'soledades' (pesar y melancolía que se sienten por la ausencia, muerte o pérdida de alguna persona o cosa). This Castilianized form of Portuguese *saudade* is used by Vicente also in *Floresta de Enganos*; elsewhere he uses the correct Castilian form *soledad*. See Teyssier, pp. 400-402.

teus mistérios quantos são;
e se bem te contemplarem,
como a deus te adorarão.

VERANO Si el amor que tengo a ti,
dama de noble criança, 1090
otro tal tienes a mí,
dambos tenemos aquí
santa bienaventurança.

SERRA Meu senhor, tu saberás
que co poder que em mi tens, 1095
se me alegras quando vens,
matas-me quando te vás,
e em suidades me manténs.

E em quanto lá estás,
sendo eu certa que hás-de vir, 1100
suidade me faz sentir
dúvidas se tornarás,
ou se o céu pode mentir.

VERANO Discreta dama serena,
del bien se sigue el amor, 1105
del amor se sigue pena,
de la pena amor mayor,
del mayor, mayor cadena.

Mas después que vi los males
de esta sin piedad dolencia, 1110
supe por experiencia
que sus dolores mortales
son en quanto tura ausencia;
que ésta me haze pensar,
siendo firme tu edificio 1115
que te ha de llevar la mar
y sacarte de tu quicio,
por me hazer desesperar.

SERRA A suidade na molher

1092 *dambos,* 'ambos.'
1098 *suidades,* 'saudades.' Vicente uses *suidade* only in *Triunfo do Inverno*; elsewhere he uses *saudade.* Both these forms, as well as *soidade,* are frequently found in sixteenth-century texts. See Teyssier, p. 400.
1113 *tura,* 'dura.' See Corominas, s.v. *durar.*

mata o coração e alma, 1120
porque momento não acalma
a tormenta que tever;
que tu, se te vás de mi,
verás outras fermosuras;
falas e ouves doçuras, 1125
mas eu não vejo sem ti
senão cousas muito escuras.

(Argumento da figura terceira do triunfo do Verão:)

VERANO Aquel maestro herrero
tiene la muger hornera,
y quieren — lo que Dios no quiera — 1130
que siempre sea genero.
Tiénenme amenazado
porque los hago sudar;
yo téngolos de escuchar,
que es casal muy concertado. 1135

FORNEIRA Marido mal maridado,
dos mores ladrões que eu vi,
vejo-te mal empregado,
mas peor vejo eu a mi.
Que se fora tecedeira 1140
casada com tecelão,
no inverno e no verão
sempre andara a lançadeira.
Ajuntou-nos o pecado,
e pois isto é assi, 1145
marido desmazelado,
mau pesar vej'eu de ti.

FERREIRO Sem vergonha de ninguém
essas são as falas tuas;

1124 *fermosuras,* 'formosuras.' See *Índia,* n. 75.
1129 Cf. the proverb "No inverno forneira, no verão taberneira" (Chaves, p. 276).
1131 *genero,* 'enero.' *Lusismo* (Portuguese *janeiro*).
1135 *casal,* 'pareja.' *Lusismo*; see Teyssier, p. 390; Corominas, s.v. *casa.*
1136ff For another parody of this popular *romance,* cf. *Frágua,* lines 271-282.
1147 *mau pesar vej' eu.* See *Índia,* n. 67.

porém, se no forno suas, *f. 182 r.* 1150
eu na frágua também.
Tu, velha bem maridada,
das mais bravas que eu vi,
vejo-te mal castigada,
porque eu hei medo de ti. 1155

FORNEIRA Custado me houvera um olho,
e foras tu tal, aosadas,
que me encheras de pancadas
e não foras João Piolho.
No verão não ganhas nada, 1160
coa calma vens-te a mim,
e despois que sou casada
nunca me deste um chapim.

FERREIRO Eu sou de marca meã,
não me quero derreter; 1165
em ti há que dar e ter,
como em boi da Golegã.
Hurca, mal entoqueixada,
farnétega maior que eu vi,
quando te vês encalmada, 1170
porque te tornas a mi?

FORNEIRA Chouricinho engargueijado,
forunço de gata prenhe,
não sei, marido coitado,
se te venda, se te empenhe. 1175
Pois não prestas pera nada
quero-me quitar de ti;
que a bela mal empregada
se pode dizer por mi.

FERREIRO Se foras Deus verdadeiro, 1180
tu fezeras à bofé
pipas as torres da Sé,
e o ano todo Janeiro.
Vinhateira tresnoutada,
mau verão se meta em ti! 1185
Nunca vejas invernada,
nem a calma se chegue a mi!

1169 *farnétega,* 'frenética.' See *Júpiter,* n. 85.

SERRA Que má cousa são vilãos
e a gente popular!
Que não sabem desejar 1190
senão uns desejos vãos
que não são terra nem mar.
De nenhum bem dizem bem,
nem o sabem conhecer;
mormuram sem entender, 1195
e ainda o peor que têm,
que seu dano é seu prazer.

Ũa forneira pelada
e um ferreiro pelado
terem coração ousado 1200
com língua escomungada
falar no Verão sagrado!
FORNEIRA Olhai, Maria Mangona,
se eu dou volta ao breviairo,
vereis vós o campanairo 1205
casado coa atafona.

FERREIRO Verdade diz minha molher.
Que bem achais ao Verão?
SERRA Eu to deria, vilão,
mas não podes comprender 1210
seus triunfos quantos são.
FORNEIRA Os seus triunfos benditos,
pois quereis cousas benditas,
são de pulgas infinitas
e mosquitos infinitos. 1215

Pera moscas deligente,
emparo de gafanhões,
remédio pera rascões
que dormem sempre chãmente,
e furtam nesses favais, 1220
e mantêm-se polas vinhas
que não poseram seus pais;
e quanto às camarinhas,
sem elas vive Cascais.

Sua fruita desejada 1225

1204 *breviairo*. 'breviário.' See *Índia*, n. 90.

bem parece e é danosa;
é como a dama fermosa,
galante, muito avisada,
mas não menos perigosa.

FERREIRO Verdade diz minha molher. 1230

FORNEIRA Sabeis pera que ele é bo?
Pera bichas e serpentes,
e fazer suar as gentes
e encher barbas de pó,
e de febres Alentejo 1235
e de maleitas Tomar, *f. 182 v.*
e calmarias no mar;
e quantas ovelhas vejo,
todas as faz trosquiar.

FERREIRO Verdade diz minha molher. 1240

SERRA Meu senhor, *contra verbosos*
noli contendere verbis.

FORNEIRA *Qui semetipsum laudat*
despicit honore suum.
Não me havés vós de vencer 1245
enquanto Deus me der siso.

1231 *bo,* 'bom.' See *Farelos,* n. 77.
1239 *trosquiar,* 'tosquiar.' See Corominas, s.v. *esquilar.* Here Vicente is doubtless playing on the colloquial use of the word, 'to trim, skin, fleece (someone) in a deal.'
1241-1242 The source of the Latin quotation is the *Disticha Catonis,* Bk. I, No. 10: "Contra verbosos noli contendere verbis:/ sermo datur cunctis, animi sapientia paucis," that is, "Do not argue with talkative people: speech is given to all, wisdom to few." See Ramalho, p. 164.
1243-1244 "Whoever praises himself despises his own honor." The Latin is incorrect. Either *semet* or *se ipsum* alone might replace *semetipsum*; *honore* is perhaps a printer's error for *honorem.* The source of the quotation, if it is a quotation, has not been identified. See Ramalho, pp. 165-166. Carolina Michaëlis de Vasconcellos's observation (*Notas Vicentinas,* pp. 292-293) that "um refrã latino, em bôca de uma forneira, descida da Serra de Sintra, afim de maldizer o Verão, talvez seja a única incoerência lingüística cometida por Gil Vicente" seems to me to miss the point. Vicente assigns the Latin phrase to his *forneira* precisely because of its incongruity, for comic effect. See Ramalho, pp. 130-132. Cf. the following proverb, cited by Chaves (p. 366): "Quem se gaba suja-se que nunca mais se lava (ou 'sempre se suja e não mais se lava')."

FERREIRO Verdade diz minha molher.
SERRA Se o nosso asno soube ler,
não é muito que saibais isso.

VERANO Desputar no es cosa honesta 1250
con horneras ni herreros,
porque bien caro les cuesta
en mi tiempo sus dineros,
trabajados por la siesta.
Dexemos baxa requesta, 1255
bolvamos en otra banda,
porque mi triunfo manda
que le hagan todos fiesta
como el caso lo demanda.

Que en mi tiempo fue alumbrada 1260
la reina vuestra señora,
en la más hermosa hora
que del cielo me fue dada.
Queríala visitar,
mas ¿qué le presentaré? 1265
Vos me havéis de endereçar
un presente singular,
que sin vergüença le dé.
SERRA Eu tenho muitos tisouros
que lhe poderão ser dados, 1270
mas ficaram encantados,
deles de tempo de mouros,
deles dos antepassados.

VERANO Baxo presente sería
presentarle yo dineros, 1275
con que compran cadaldía
cosas viles mil grosseros,
y es común su valía;
y más sería esso ansí
echar agua en la mar yo. 1280
SERRA Pois tu que lhe dês a mi:

1272-1273 *deles . . . deles,* 'some . . . others.' See *Farelos,* n. 491, and cf. *Júpiter,* lines 200-201.
1276 *cadaldía,* 'todos los días.' The expression survived only in rustic speech in Vicente's day, though he seems to have been unaware of the fact. See *Don Duardos,* ed. Alonso, n. 131.

eu de sua alteza sou,
e por sua estou aqui.

FERREIRO Dezia eu, senhora Serra,
s'isto bem vos parecer, 1285
que lhe deis minha molher
pera tirar naus em terra.

FORNEIRA Vamo-nos ora, marido
deste sol, deste bochorno,
e acolhamo-nos ò forno, 1290
que já o pão será cozido.

FERREIRO Vai má-hora devagar!
Ah, corpo de Deus contigo!

FORNEIRA Se tu não podes andar,
quem te mete vir comigo? 1295

SERRA E pois que cousa será
que lhe empresentasses ora?

VERANO Cierto para tal señora
de ventura se hallará
dádiva merecedora. 1300

(Argumento das figuras da fim do triunfo do Verão:)

SERRA Um filho de um rei passado
dos gentios portugueses
tenho eu muito guardado,
há mil anos e três meses
per um mágico encantado. 1305
E este tem um jardim
do paraíso terreal,
que Salamão mandou aqui
a um rei de Portugal;
e tem-no seu filho ali. 1310

Este será bo presente,

1282 Cf. Braamcamp Freire, p. 256, n. 682: "A vila de Sintra com todo seu têrmo entrara no apanágio de D. Caterina de Áustria."
Before line 1301 *da fim*. Latin *finis* was both masculine and feminine; the feminine form is found in medieval Spanish and Portuguese and, though less often, in later writers in both languages (e.g., Camões, Cervantes).

e eu irei por ele asinha,
porque é pera a rainha
justo e conveniente.
O qual príncipe virá 1315
em pessoa aqui com ele,
que sabe as virtudes dele, *f. 183 r.*
e como e quem o trouxe cá,
e quanto se monta nele.

E virá acompanhado 1320
dessas cachopas sintrãs
e de mancebos de gado,
louçãos e elas louçãs,
com seu cantar costumado.

VERANO Y el jardín presentado, 1325
por no engendrar hastío,
fenezca el triunfo mío,
aunque no sea acabado.

Assí que, por no enhadar,
quedarán para tratar 1330
del triunfo que me cabe
cosas grandes de notar;
pero el quándo no se sabe.

Entram quatro mancebos e quatro moças, todos muito bem ataviados, em folia, dizendo esta cantiga:

Quem diz que não é este
São João o verde? 1335

[*Entra o Infante e diz:*]

INFANTE Toda-las cousas criadas
têm seu fim determinado,
delas per tempo alongado,
delas mais abreviadas,
delas per curso meado. 1340

1329 *enhadar*. See *Frágua*, n. 695.
Before 1336 It is very likely that the prince made his entrance accompanied by a pageant-wagon or float representing the garden. Such a pageant, representing the garden of love, was used in the *momos* presented at the court of King Manuel after Vespers on December 25, 1500. See Shergold, pp. 131-132.

Assi que esteve guardado
este bel jardim da vida,
e pera desencantado
foi o seu curso acabado
quando a bela foi nacida. 1345

O qual à Rainha convém,
e é por esta rezão:
jardim se toma por João;
também os rosais que tem,
por El-Rei se tomarão. 1350
Por suas virtudes, flores;
polo seu bo zelo, a rama;
os jazmi[n]s, por seus primores;
os olores, pola fama;
por sua graça, as colores. 1355

A rede com que é cercado
se toma por rei prudente;
assi que pròpriamente
este jardim foi criado
para este mesmo presente. 1360
O castanho se prantou
no paraíso terreal,
e a por quem se tomou
não é menos, mas igual,
à que Deus ali formou. 1365

VERANO Infante, devéis saber
que las flores más reales,
los jardines y rosales,
son hijos del mi poder,
nietos de mis temporales. 1370

INFANTE Se por este dizes, pecas;
porque essas flores que fazes,
tu as fazes e desfazes,
tu as floreces e secas.

E o santo jardim de Deus 1375
florece sem fenecer;
que o ser e logo não ser

1347 *rezão,* 'razão.' See *Índia,* n. 292.
1355 *colores,* 'cores.' The usual form in the older language, it survives in such set phrases as *sob color de.*

é obra de fracos céus
que não têm fixo poder.
Que quantas frescuras dás, 1380
e quanto tu e o mundo tens,
é jogo de tu que vás,
e jogo de tu que vens:
isto bem o entenderás.

E com esta concrusão 1385
vamo-lo empresentar,
porque se devem de dar
as cousas a cujas são.

Vão apresentar o jardim a El-Rei, e diz o Ifante:

Reis de todo mal imigos,
dinos de fama imortal, 1390
este jardim perenal,
já de tempos muito antigos,
se encantou em Portugal.
O seu nome principal
jardim de virtudes é; 1395
e segundo nossa fé, *f. 183 v.*
vem-vos muito natural.
E lográ-lo-eis nô-menos
horas e noites e dias,
dos que há que logra Elias 1400
o jardim que nós perdemos.

Os Sintrãos em folia com o príncipe se vão [*cantando a cantiga seguinte,*] *que é a fim da susodita tragicomédia.*

Cantiga

Vento bueno nos há-de levar:
garrido é o vendaval!

1400 *Elias.* Elijah is here treated as a *figura Christi,* an interpretation already implicit in the New Testament where he is seen as prefiguring John the Baptist who in turn prefigures Christ. For the tradition of figural interpretation, see Auerbach, "Figura."

1402-1403 M. F. Alatorre cites the following variant by Mateo Flecha from Fuenllana's *Libro de música para vihuela, intitulado Orphenica Lyra* (Sevilla, 1554): "Pues lo vento nos ha de levar,/ ¡garrido vendaval!" (*Lírica popular,* p. 155).

Textual Notes

Auto da Índia

Before line 1: católica] cacholica
74: estará] estara
101: en] em
201: Moça] cria[da]
204: Moça] cria[da]
219: á] a
304: San Pablo] sam palo
320: Sansón] san Son
329: estáis] estes
366: Dous] tres
369: dous] tres
484: f. 198r] f. 191r
496: destroçados] destrocados
508: louvada] louvado

Quem Tem Farelos?

64: se] si
65: ò] ho
197: Ordo[nho] passo (marginal note)
203: Aires] Escu[deiro]
208: Aires] Escu[deiro]
213: Aires] Escu[deiro]
219: abrid] abrit
338: enfiar] em fiar
348: Cantan] cantam
433: ò] o

Cortes de Júpiter

Before line 1: messageira] messagenra
planetas] planeras
M.D.XXI] M.D.xjx
113: se] te
146: com] con
153: outrem ninguém] outren nyngem
450: alquicé] alquiece
468: uns] hus

495: nem migalha] nemigalha
500: Gibraltar] Gibaltar
529: Meoterrano] meoterreno

Frágua de Amor

52: tamañas] tamanñas
268: matasse] matesse
Before line 314: serranas] serenas
423: A mi] y mi
Before line 446: serranas] serenas
572: Eis-me] Exme
594: cá à] ca
596: em] en

Triunfo do Inverno

1: em] en
31: feira] teyra
33: a] aa
65: o] oo
Before line 78: *primeira*] j
82: patas] papas
149: Brisco] prisco
158: crisma] crizna
349: repeated in '1562'
401: bien] hien
475: haviam] auian
503: com] con
561: ora] mora
Before line 578: vai-se] vamse
818: Santiago] Sautiago
823: santas] sctãs
826: cárrega] carregua
926: claridad] elaridad
1212: os] Oo
1241: senhor] fenhor
1243: *laudat*] ldudat
1283: sua] sue
1292: devagar] devaguar
1321: cachopas] cochopas
1324: com] con

Select Bibliography

The bibliography lists all works cited in the notes. A few other works that I have found useful in preparing this edition are also included.

ALATORRE, MARGIT FRENK. "Dignificación de la lírica popular en el siglo de oro," *Anuario de Letras,* II (1962), 27-54.

ALATORRE, MARGIT FRENK. "Glosas de tipo popular en la antigua lírica," *Nueva Revista de Filología Hispánica,* XII (1958), 301-334.

ALATORRE, MARGIT FRENK (EDITOR). *Lírica hispánica de tipo popular: edad media y renacimiento.* Mexico City: Universidad Nacional Autónoma de México, 1966.

ALATORRE, MARGIT FRENK. *"Quien maora ca mi sayo," Nueva Revista de Filología Hispánica,* XI (1957), 386-391.

ALATORRE, MARGIT FRENK. "Sobre los textos poéticos en Juan Vásquez, Mudarra y Narváez," *Nueva Revista de Filología Hispánica,* VI (1952), 33-56.

ALONSO, DÁMASO. *Poesía de la edad media y poesía de tipo tradicional.* Buenos Aires: Losada, 1942.

ALVAR, MANUEL. *Endechas judeo-españolas.* Granada: Universidad de Granada, 1953.

ANDRADA, ERNESTO DE CAMPOS DE. See Gil Vicente, *Quem Tem Farelos?.*

ARES MONTES, JOSÉ. *Góngora y la poesía portuguesa del siglo XVII.* Madrid: Gredos, 1956.

ASENSIO, EUGENIO. "De los momos cortesanos a los autos caballerescos de Gil Vicente," *Anais do Primeiro Congresso Brasileiro de Língua Falada no Teatro.* Rio de Janeiro: Ministério da Educação e Cultura, 1958. Pp. 163-172.

ASENSIO, EUGENIO. "España en la épica filipina; al margen de un libro de H. Cidade," *Revista de Filología Española,* XXXIII (1949), 66-109.

ASENSIO, EUGENIO. "Gil Vicente y las cantigas paralelísticas 'restauradas.' ¿Folklore o poesía original?," in his *Poética y realidad en el cancionero peninsular de la Edad Media.* Second edition, Madrid: Gredos, 1970. Pp. 134-176.

ASENSIO, EUGENIO. "Inés de Castro de la crónica al mito," *Boletim de Filologia,* XXI (1965), 337-358.

ASENSIO, EUGENIO. "Las fuentes de las 'Barcas' de Gil Vicente: Lógica intelectual e imaginación dramática," *Bulletin d'Histoire du Théâtre Portugais,* IV (1953), 207-237.

AUERBACH, ERICH. "Figura," in his *Scenes from the Drama of European Literature.* New York: Meridian Books, Pp. 11-76.

AUERBACH, ERICH. *Mimesis: The Representation of Reality in Western Literature.* Trans. Willard R. Trask. Princeton: Princeton University Press, 1953.

BARBER, C. L. *Shakespeare's Festive Comedy. A Study of*

Dramatic Form and its Relation to Social Custom. Cleveland and New York: The World Publishing Company, 1963.

BARTHOLOMAEUS ANGLICUS. *El libro de proprietatibus rerum.* Trans. Fray Vicente de Burgos. Toulouse: Henrique Meyer, 1494.

BATAILLON, MARCEL. *'La Célestine' selon Fernando de Rojas.* Paris: Didier, 1961.

BATAILLON, MARCEL. *La vie de Lazarillo de Tormès.* Traduction de A. Morel-Fatio. Introduction de M. Bataillon. Paris: Aubier, 1958.

BELL, AUBREY F. G. *Estudos Vicentinos.* Tradução do inglês por A. A. Dória, revista e emendada pelo autor. Lisbon: Imprensa Nacional, 1940.

BERNHEIMER, RICHARD. *Wild Men in the Middle Ages. A Study in Art, Sentiment, and Demonology.* Cambridge, Mass.: Harvard University Press, 1952.

A Book of Masques: In Honour of Allardyce Nicoll. Cambridge: Cambridge University Press, 1967.

BOWERS, FREDSON. "Textual Criticism," in James Thorpe (ed.), *The Aims and Methods of Scholarship in Modern Languages and Literatures.* New York: Modern Language Association of America, 1963. Pp. 23-42.

BOWRA, C. M. "The Songs of Gil Vicente," *Atlante,* I (1953), 3-21; reprinted in his *Inspiration and Poetry.* London: Macmillan, 1955. Pp. 90-111.

BOXER, C. R. *The Portuguese Seaborne Empire 1415-1825.* London: Hutchinson, 1969.

BOXER, C. R. (EDITOR).*The Tragic History of the Sea 1589-1622: Narratives of the Shipwrecks of the Portuguese East Indiamen* São Thomé *(1589),* Santo Alberto *(1593),* São João Baptista *(1622), and the Journeys of the Survivors in South East Africa.* Cambridge: Cambridge University Press, 1959.

BRAUDEL, FERNAND. *El Mediterráneo y el mundo mediterráneo en la época de Felipe II.* Trans. Mario Monteforte Toledo and Wenceslao Roces. Mexico City: Fondo de Cultura Económica, 1953.

CÂMARA JÚNIOR, J. MATTOSO. *Para o estudo da fonêmica portuguêsa.* Rio de Janeiro: Organização Simões, 1953.

CAMÕES, LUÍS DE. *Obra Completa,* ed. Antônio Salgado Júnior. Rio de Janeiro: Aguilar, 1963.

Cancionero de galanes y otros rarísimos cancionerillos góticos. Ed. Margit Frenk Alatorre. Valencia: Castalia, 1952.

Cancionero de Juan de Molina (Salamanca, 1527). Ed. Eugenio Asensio. Valencia: Castalia, 1952.

Cancionero llamado Espejo de enamorados, Ed. Antonio Rodríguez-Moñino. Valencia: Castalia, 1951.

Cancionero llamado Flor de enamorados (Barcelona 1562). Ed. Antonio Rodríguez-Moñino and Daniel Devoto. Valencia: Castalia, 1954.

Cancionero musical de Palacio (siglos XV-XVI). Ed. José Romeu Figueras. 2 volumes. Barcelona: Consejo Superior de Investigaciones Científicas, 1965.

Cantigas d'escarnho e de mal dizer dos cancioneiros medievais galego-portugueses. Ed. M. Rodrigues Lapa. [Vigo]: Galaxia, 1965.

CARVALHO, JOSÉ G. HERCULANO DE. "Nota sobre o vocalismo antigo português: valor dos grafemas *e* e *o* em sílaba átona," *Revista Portuguesa de Filologia*, XII (1962), 17-39.

CHAVES, PEDRO. *Rifoneiro Português*. Second edition. Oporto: Domingos Barreira, n. d. [1945].

COROMINAS, J. *Diccionario crítico etimológico de la lengua castellana*. 4 volumes. Madrid: Gredos, 1954-1957.

CORREAS, GONZALO. *Arte de la lengua española castellana (1625)*. Ed. Emilio Alarcos García. Madrid: Consejo Superior de Investigaciones Científicas, 1954.

CORREAS, GONZALO. *Vocabulario de refranes y refranes proverbiales (1627)*. Texte établi, annoté et présenté par Louis Combet. Bordeaux: Feret et Fils, 1967.

COVARRUBIAS, SEBASTIÁN DE. *Tesoro de la lengua castellana o española*. Ed. Martín de Riquer. Barcelona: Horta, 1943.

CRAWFORD, J. P. WICKERSHAM. *Spanish Drama before Lope de Vega. A Revised Edition*. Philadelphia: University of Pennsylvania Press, 1937.

CROSBY, JAMES O. (EDITOR). *Política de Dios, govierno de Christo*. By Francisco de Quevedo Villegas. Madrid: Castalia, 1966.

CUNHA, CELSO FERREIRA DA. "Regularidade e irregularidade na versificação do primeiro *Auto das Barcas* de Gil Vicente," *Studia Philologica: Homenaje ofrecido a Dámaso Alonso*, I. Madrid: Gredos, 1960. Pp. 459-479.

CUNNINGHAM, DOLORA. "The Jonsonian Masque as a Literary Form," *ELH, A Journal of English Literary History*, XXII (1955), reprinted in Jonas A. Barish (ed). *Ben Jonson: A Collection of Critical Essays*. Englewood Cliffs, N.J.: Prentice-Hall, 1963. Pp. 160-174.

CURTIUS, ERNST ROBERT. *European Literature and the Latin Middle Ages*. Trans. Willard R. Trask. New York: Pantheon Books, 1953.

DEYERMOND, ALAN D. "El hombre salvaje en la novela sentimental," *Filología*, X (1964), 97-111.

DIAS, AUGUSTO EPIPHÂNIO DA SILVA. *Syntaxe Histórica Portuguesa*. Third edition. Lisbon: Livraria Clássica A. M. Teixeira, 1954.

Dicionário das Literaturas Portuguesa, Galega e Brasileira. Ed. Jacinto do Prado Coelho. Oporto: Livraria Figueirinhas, n. d. [1960].

DUFFY, JAMES. *Portuguese Africa*. Cambridge, Massachusetts: Harvard University Press, 1959.

DUFFY, JAMES. *Shipwreck and Empire: Being an Account of Portuguese Maritime Disasters in a Century of Decline*. Cambridge, Mass.: Harvard University Press, 1955.

EMPSON, WILLIAM. *Some Versions of Pastoral.* Norfolk, Connecticut: New Directions, 1960.

EWBANK, INGA-STINA. " 'These Pretty Devices': A Study of Masques in Plays," in *A Book of Masques: In Honour of Allardyce Nicoll.* Pp. 405-448.

FREIRE, ANSELMO BRAAMCAMP. *Vida e Obras de Gil Vicente.* Lisbon: Edição da Revista 'Ocidente,' 1944.

FRYE, NORTHROP. *Anatomy of Criticism: Four Essays.* Princeton, N. J.: Princeton University Press, 1957.

GALLOP, RODNEY. *Portugal: A Book of Folk-ways.* Cambridge: Cambridge University Press, 1961.

GILLET, JOSEPH E. (EDITOR). *Propalladia and Other Works of Bartolomé de Torres Naharro.* Volumes I-III. Bryn Mawr, Pennsylvania, 1943-1951. Volume IV. Philadelphia: University of Pennsylvania Press, 1961.

GILLET, JOSEPH E. "Spanish *fantasía* for *presunción,*" in *Studia philologica et litteraria in honorem L. Spitzer,* ed. A. G. Hatcher and K. L. Selig. Bern: Francke, 1958. Pp. 211-225.

GLASER, EDWARD. *Estudios hispano-portugueses. Relaciones literarias del siglo de oro.* Valencia: Castalia, 1957.

GÓIS, DAMIÃO DE. *Crónica do Felicíssimo Rei D. Manuel. Nova edição conforme à primeira de 1566.* Four volumes. Coimbra: Por ordem da Universidade, 1949-1955.

GOSSMAN, LIONEL. *Men and Masks, a Study of Molière.* Baltimore: The Johns Hopkins Press, 1963.

HART, THOMAS R. "The Dramatic Unity of Gil Vicente's *Comédia de Rubena,*" *Bulletin of Hispanic Studies,* XLVI (1969), 97-108.

HART, THOMAS R. "La estructura dramática del *Auto de Inês Pereira,*" *Nueva Revista de Filología Hispánica,* XVIII (1965-66), 160-165.

HART, THOMAS R. "Notes on Sixteenth-Century Portuguese Pronunciation," *Word,* XI (1955), 404-415.

HAZLITT, W. CAREW (EDITOR). *Remains of the Early Popular Poetry of England.* London: John Russell Smith, 1886.

HIRSCH, E. D., JR. *Validity in Interpretation.* New Haven: Yale University Press, 1967.

HUIZINGA, J(OHAN). *The Waning of the Middle Ages.* Trans. F. Hopman. Garden City, N. Y.: Doubleday and Company, 1954.

JONSON, BEN. [*Works*], ed. C. H. Herford, Percy and Evelyn Simpson. Volume VII. Oxford: Oxford University Press, 1941.

KEATES, LAURENCE. *The Court Theatre of Gil Vicente.* Lisbon, 1962.

KENISTON, HAYWARD. *The Syntax of Castilian Prose: The Sixteenth Century.* Chicago: University of Chicago Press, 1937. (References are to chapter, section and subsection.)

KENYON, HERBERT A. "Color Symbolism in Early Spanish Ballads," *Romanic Review,* VI (1915), 327-340.

LAPESA, RAFAEL. *Historia de la lengua española.* Second edition. Madrid: Escelicer, n. d.

LAPESA, RAFAEL. "La lengua de la poesía épica en los cantares de gesta y en el romancero viejo," *Anuario de Letras,* IV (1964), 5-24.

LE GENTIL, PIERRE. *La poésie lyrique espagnole et portugaise à la fin du moyen âge.* Volume I. *Les thèmes et les genres.* Rennes: Plihon, 1949.

LIDA DE MALKIEL, MARÍA ROSA. "El fanfarrón en el teatro del Renacimiento," *Romance Philology,* XI (1957-1958), 268-291, reprinted in her *Estudios de literatura española y comparada.* Buenos Aires: Eudeba (Editorial Universitaria de Buenos Aires), 1966, pp. 173-202.

LIDA DE MALKIEL, MARÍA ROSA. *La originalidad artística de 'La Celestina.'* Buenos Aires: Eudeba (Editorial Universitaria de Buenos Aires), 1962.

LIHANI, JOHN. "The Meaning of Spanish *carillo,*" *Modern Philology,* LIV (1956), 73-79.

MARSDEN, C. A. "Entrées et fêtes espagnoles au XVIe siècle," in *Les fêtes de la Renaissance.* II. *Fêtes et cérémonies au temps de Charles Quint.* Ed. Jean Jacquot. Paris: Centre National de la Recherche Scientifique, 1960. Pp. 389-411.

MARQUES, A. H. DE OLIVEIRA. *A Sociedade Medieval Portuguesa: Aspectos de Vida Quotidiana.* Lisbon: Livraria Sá da Costa, 1964.

MEIER, HARRI. "Zum Artikelgebrauch bei Possessivpronomina im Portugiesischen," in *Syntactica und Stylistica: Festschrift für Ernst Gamillscheg,* ed. Günter Reichenkron. Tübingen: Max Niemeyer, 1957. Pp. 373-386.

MENÉNDEZ PELAYO, MARCELINO. *Antología de poetas líricos castellanos.* Santander: Consejo Superior de Investigaciones Científicas, 1944. III, 347-395.

MENÉNDEZ PIDAL, RAMÓN. *Manual de gramática histórica española.* Sixth edition. Madrid: Espasa-Calpe, 1941.

MEXÍA, PEDRO. *Silva de varia lección.* Madrid: Joseph Fernández de Buendía, 1662.

MICHAËLIS DE VASCONCELOS, CAROLINA. *Notas Vicentinas.* Lisbon: Edição da Revista 'Ocidente,' 1949.

MONTAIGLON, ANATOLE DE. *Recueil de poésies françaises des XVe et XVIe* siècles. Thirteen volumes. Paris: P. Jannet, 1855-1878.

MORAIS SILVA, ANTÓNIO DE. *Grande Dicionário da Língua Portuguesa,* 10th ed. prepared by A. Moreno, Cardoso Júnior, and J. P. Machado. 12 volumes. Lisbon: Editorial Confluência, 1949-1959.

MULERTT, WERNER. "Der 'wilde Mann' in Frankreich," *Zeitschrift für französische Sprache und Literatur,* LVI (1932), 69-88.

NORTON, F. J. *Printing in Spain 1501-1520*. Cambridge: Cambridge University Press, 1966.

ORGEL, STEPHEN. *The Jonsonian Masque*. Cambridge, Mass.: Harvard University Press, 1965.

PARKER, A. A. "An Age of Gold: Expansion and Scholarship in Spain," in Denys Hay (ed.), *The Age of the Renaissance*. London: Thames and Hudson, 1967. Pp. 221-248.

PARKER, A. A. *The Approach to the Spanish Drama of the Golden Age*. London: The Hispanic and Luso-Brazilian Councils, 1957.

PARKER, A. A. (EDITOR). *No hay más fortuna que Dios*, by Don Pedro Calderón de la Barca. Manchester: Manchester University Press, 1949.

Pequeno Dicionário Brasileiro da Língua Portuguêsa. Tenth edition. Ed. Aurélio Buarque de Hollanda Ferreira. Rio de Janeiro: Editôra Civilização Brasileira, 1960.

PRATT, ÓSCAR DE. *Gil Vicente. Notas e Comentários*. Lisbon: Livraria Clássica, 1931.

RABY, F. J. E. *A History of Secular Latin Poetry in the Middle Ages*. Second edition. Oxford: Oxford University Press, 1957.

RAMALHO, AMÉRICO DA COSTA. *Estudos sobre a Época do Renascimento*. Coimbra: Instituto de Alta Cultura, 1969.

RECKERT, STEPHEN. "El verdadero texto de la *Copilaçam* vicentina de 1562," *Studia Philologica: Homenaje ofrecido a Dámaso Alonso*, III. Madrid: Gredos, 1963. Pp. 53-68.

RESENDE, GARCIA DE. *Chronica dos Valerosos e Insignes Feitos del Rey Dom Joam II . . . com Outras Obras que Adiante se Seguem, e Vay Acrescentada a sua Miscellania*. Coimbra: Na Real Officina da Universidade, 1798.

RÉVAH, I. S. "La 'comédia' dans l'œuvre de Gil Vicente," *Bulletin d'Histoire du Théâtre Portugais*, II (1951), 1-39.

RÉVAH, I. S. "Gil Vicente a-t-il été le fondateur du théâtre portugais?," *Bulletin d'Histoire du Théâtre Portugais*, I (1950), 153-185.

RÉVAH, I. S. *Recherches sur les œuvres de Gil Vicente*. See Gil Vicente, *Auto da Barca do Inferno, Auto de Inês Pereira*.

RICARD, ROBERT. "La dualité de la civilisation hispanique et l'histoire religieuse du Portugal," *Revue historique*, CCXVI (1956), 1-17.

RILEY, E. C. *Cervantes's Theory of the Novel*. Oxford: Oxford University Press, 1964.

ROMEU FIGUERAS. See *Cancionero musical de Palacio*.

ROSENBLAT, ÁNGEL. "Notas de morfología dialectal," in Aurelio M. Espinosa, *Estudios sobre el español de Nuevo Méjico*. Buenos Aires: Facultad de Filosofía y Letras de la Universidad de Buenos Aires, Instituto de Filología, 1946. Volume II, pp. 105-316.

SARAIVA, ANTÓNIO JOSÉ. *História da Cultura em Portugal.* Volume II. Lisbon: Jornal do Fôro, 1953.

SARAIVA, ANTÓNIO JOSÉ, & RITA, MARIA TERESA. "Diálogo sobre a actualidade crítica de Gil Vicente entre um historiador e uma joven autora teatral," *Vértice,* XXV, No. 264-266 (Sept.-Nov. 1965), 715-724.

SCHULTZ-GORA, O. "Der wilde Mann in der provenzalischen Literatur," *Zeitschrift für romanische Philologie,* XLIV (1924), 129-131.

SHERGOLD, N. D. *A History of the Spanish Stage from Medieval Times until the End of the Seventeenth Century.* Oxford: Oxford University Press, 1967.

SILVEIRA, SOUSA DA (EDITOR). *Textos Quinhentistas.* Rio de Janeiro: Imprensa Nacional, 1945.

SLETSJÖE, LEIF. *O Elemento Cénico em Gil Vicente.* Lisbon: Casa Portuguesa, 1965.

SOLDEVILA, F. *Historia de España.* Second edition. Barcelona: Ediciones Ariel, 1962.

SOUSA, FREI LUÍS DE. *Anais de D. João III.* Ed. M. Rodrigues Lapa. 2 volumes. Lisbon: Livraria Sá da Costa, 1951.

SPITZER, LEO. "Dos observaciones sintáctico-estilísticas a las *Coplas* de Manrique," *Nueva Revista de Filología Hispánica,* IV (1950), 1-24.

STEGAGNO PICCHIO, LUCIANA. *Ricerche sul teatro portoghese.* Rome: Edizioni dell'Ateneo, 1969.

STEGAGNO PICCHIO, LUCIANA. "Sui testi saiaghesi di Gil Vicente," in *Studi di letteratura spagnola,* ed. Carmelo Samonà. Rome: Facoltà di Magistero e Facoltà di Lettere dell'Università di Roma, 1964. Pp. 231-241.

STEVENS, JOHN. *Music and Poetry in the Early Tudor Court.* London: Methuen, 1961.

TAVANI. See Gil Vicente, *Comédia de Rubena.*

TAYLOR, JAMES L. *A Portuguese-English Dictionary.* Stanford, California: Stanford University Press, 1958.

TEYSSIER, PAUL. *La langue de Gil Vicente.* Paris: C. Klincksieck, 1959.

TOMLINS, JACK E. "Una nota sobre la clasificación de los dramas de Gil Vicente," *Duquesne Hispanic Review,* III (1964), 115-131, and IV (1965), 1-16.

TORNER, EDUARDO M. *Lírica hispánica: relaciones entre lo popular y lo culto.* Madrid: Castalia, 1966.

TORRES NAHARRO, BARTOLOMÉ DE. See Gillet, Joseph E.

VALDÉS, JUAN DE. *Diálogo de la lengua.* Edición y notas de J. F. Montesinos. Madrid: Espasa-Calpe, 1946.

VAREY, J. E. "L'auditoire du *Salón Dorado* de l'*Alcázar* de Madrid au XVIIe siècle," in Jean Jacquot, Elie Konigson, and Marcel Oddon, editors, *Dramaturgie et Société: Rapports entre l'œuvre théâtrale, son interprétation et son public aux XVIe et XVIIe siècles.* Paris: Centre National de la Recherche Scientifique, 1968. I, 77-91.

VAREY, J. E. "La campagne dans le théâtre espagnol au XVIIe siècle," in Jean Jacquot, Elie Konigson, and Marcel Oddon, editors, *Dramaturgie et Société: Rapports entre l'œuvre théâtrale, son interprétation et son public aux XVIe et XVIIe siècles.* Paris: Centre National de la Recherche Scientifique, 1968. I, 47-76.

VASCONCELLOS, JORGE FERREIRA DE. *Comedia Eufrosina.* Texto de la edición príncipe de 1555 con las variantes de 1561 y 1566. Edición, prólogo y notas de Eugenio Asensio. Madrid: Consejo Superior de Investigaciones Científicas, 1951.

VÁZQUEZ CUESTA, PILAR, & MENDES DA LUZ, MARIA ALBERTINA. *Gramática portuguesa.* Second edition. Madrid: Gredos, 1961.

VENTURA, AUGUSTA FARIA GERSÃO. *Estudos Vicentinos. I. Astronomia-Astrologia.* Coimbra, 1937.

VICENTE, GIL. *Auto da Alma* in Sousa da Silveira, ed., *Textos Quinhentistas.*

VICENTE, GIL. *Auto da Barca do Inferno,* ed. I. S. Révah. Lisbon: Centre d'Histoire du Théâtre Portugais, 1951. (=I. S. Révah, *Recherches sur les œuvres de Gil Vicente. I. Edition critique du premier "Auto das Barcas."*)

VICENTE, GIL. *Auto de Inês Pereira,* ed. I. S. Révah. Lisbon: Centre d'Histoire du Théâtre Portugais, 1955. (=I. S. Révah, *Recherches sur les œuvres de Gil Vicente. II. Edition critique de l' "Auto de Inês Pereira."*)

VICENTE, GIL. *Comédia de Rubena,* ed. Giuseppe Tavani. Rome: Edizioni dell'Ateneo, 1965.

VICENTE, GIL. *Copilaçam de Todalas Obras de Gil Vicente* (Lisbon, 1562), reprinted in facsimile as *Obras Completas de Gil Vicente.* Lisbon: Biblioteca Nacional, 1928.

VICENTE, GIL. *Obras Completas,* ed. Marques Braga. 6 volumes. Lisbon: Sá da Costa, 1958.

VICENTE, GIL. *Obras dramáticas castellanas,* ed. Thomas R. Hart. Madrid. Espasa Calpe, 1962.

VICENTE, GIL. *Poesía,* ed. Thomas R. Hart. Salamanca: Anaya, 1965.

VICENTE, GIL. *Quem Tem Farelos?,* ed. Ernesto de Campos de Andrada. Lisbon, 1938.

VICENTE, GIL. *Tragicomedia de Amadís de Gaula,* ed. T. P. Waldron. Manchester: Manchester University Press, 1959.

VICENTE, GIL. *Tragicomedia de Don Duardos,* ed. Dámaso Alonso. I. Madrid: Consejo Superior de Investigaciones Científicas, 1942.

VITERBO, FR. JOAQUIM DE SANTA ROSA DE. *Elucidário das Palavras, Termos e Frases que em Portugal Antigamente se Usaram e que Hoje Regularmente se Ignoram* . . . . Edição crítica baseada nos manuscritos e originais de Viterbo por Mário Fiúza. Porto: Livraria Civilização, 1962-1966.

WEBER DE KURLAT, FRIDA. "Latinismos arrusticados en el sayagués," *Nueva Revista de Filología Hispánica,* I (1947), 166-170.

WEDGWOOD, C. V. "The Last Masque," in her *Truth and Opinion. Historical Essays.* New York: Macmillan, 1960. Pp. 139-156.

WELSFORD, ENID. *The Court Masque. A Study in the Relationship between Poetry and the Revels.* New York: Russell and Russell, 1962.

WHINNOM, KEITH. "The Origin of the European-Based Creoles and Pidgins," *Orbis,* XIV (1965), 509-527.

WILLIAMS, EDWIN B. *From Latin to Portuguese. Historical Phonology and Morphology of the Portuguese Language.* Second edition. Philadelphia: University of Pennsylvania Press, 1962. (References are to paragraphs.)

WILLIAMS, EDWIN B. *Spanish and English Dictionary.* Revised edition. New York: Holt, Rinehart and Winston, 1962.

WIND, EDGAR. *Art and Anarchy.* New York: Alfred A. Knopf, 1964.

ZAMORA VICENTE, ALONSO. *Dialectología española.* Second edition. Madrid: Gredos, 1967.

Index to the Notes

The index is divided into two parts, one for Spanish and the other for Portuguese. If the note is primarily concerned with the meaning of the word, I have provided an approximate English equivalent; if the note is primarily concerned with its linguistic form, an equivalent in Modern Spanish or Modern Portuguese. A few words, mostly referring to customs or things no longer in use and hence lacking a readily intelligible modern equivalent, are not provided with a gloss. Forms found only in Moorish or Negro dialect are omitted. Proper names are included only when the note deals with their linguistic form. References are to line numbers. The titles of the plays are abbreviated as follows: *AI, Auto da Índia; CJ, Cortes de Júpiter; FA, Frágua de Amor; QTF, Quem Tem Farelos?; TI, Triunfo do Inverno.*

Spanish

a, omitted before infinitive introduced by a verb of motion: *FA,* 59-60
a, omitted before personal object: *AI,* 115
a según, 'según': *AI,* 99
adó, 'adónde': *FA,* 59
adónde, 'dónde': *FA,* 112
aína, 'soon': *FA,* 77
ál, 'something else': *FA,* 514
alto (imperative): *FA,* 520
amaro, 'amargo': *FA,* 149
Anibal, 'Aníbal': *FA,* 627
aosadas, 'certainly': *FA,* 539
apheresis: *FA,* 201
apregonar, 'pregonar': *FA,* 393
aquesto, 'esto': *AI,* 147
artellaría, 'artillería': *CJ,* 631
ascondido, 'escondido': *FA,* 394
assimilation of *-r* in infinitive followed by object pronoun beginning with *l-*: *FA,* 228

b for MSp. *v*: *AI,* 171
balisa, 'baliza': *TI,* 1076
bonança, 'good weather': *TI,* 413

cadaldía, 'every day': *TI,* 1276
caler, 'to be appropriate': *TI,* 1019
callentar, 'calentar': *TI,* 446
carillo, 'friend': *TI,* 441
carpazos, '?': *TI,* 602
casal, 'couple': *TI,* 1135
Cepiones, 'Escipiones': *QTF,* 103
cesto, 'stupid person': *QTF,* 93
comigo, 'conmigo': *TI,* 251
contino, 'continuamente': *FA,* 317
cosa, 'nothing': *FA,* 307
crer, 'creer': *FA,* 85
crieleisón, 'kirie eleisón': *FA,* 311
cubo, 'tower (of a fortress)': *FA,* 17
cuerpo de mí: *TI,* 433
¡Cuerpo de San!: *QTF,* 31
cuidar, 'to think, believe': *TI,* 337

chueca = Ptg. *choca*: *QTF,* 135

-d, omitted in nouns: *AI,* 309

-d, omitted in imperatives: *FA*, 557
dalle, 'a type of lance': *QTF*, 97
dambos a dos, 'ambos': *FA*, 178
de, introducing an infinitive: *FA*, 240
de dos en dos, 'in plenty': *TI*, 249
decender, 'descender': *FA*, 104
decir, 'to descend': *TI*, 715
definite article, preceding a possessive adjective: *TI*, 197
definite article, omitted after *todo*, preceding a numeral: *FA*, 19
dende, 'desde': *FA*, 626
derreñegar, 'derrenegar': *AI*, 161
desbarato, 'defeat': *AI*, 159
descrición, 'discreción': *FA*, 40
desestrado, 'desastrado': AI, 130
devino, 'divino': *AI*, 163
diabro, 'diablo': *TI*, 226
diçan, present subjunctive of *decir* 'to descend': *TI*, 715
diesa, 'diosa': *FA*, 93
diphthongization, lack of or incorrect: *AI*, 143
diz que, 'se dice': *FA*, 11

dónde, 'de dónde': *FA*, 637
e for pretonic *i*: *AI*, 163
-e, omitted in certain verb-forms: *FA*, 458
-e, omitted in future subjunctive: *FA*, 70
el, definite article before feminine noun beginning with unstressed *a-*: *TI*, 725
ell, 'el': *CJ*, 351
embiar, 'enviar': *AI*, 171
emendar, 'enmendar': *FA*, 398
en buen hora, 'en buena hora': *FA*, 561
enhadar, 'enfadar': *FA*, 695
enlevarse, 'to be contented': *QTF*, 120
enxalçamiento, 'ensalzamiento': *TI*, 945
(*de*) *espacio*, 'slowly': *QTF*, 116
estilar, 'destilar': *FA*, 153
estó, 'estoy': *FA*, 58

(*en*) *faldetas*, 'exposed to the cold' (?): *TI*, 360
flanco, 'franco': *QTF*, 89
fortuna, 'storm': *AI*, 112
fragüero, 'fraguador': *FA*, 238
fundarse, 'to declare, affirm': *AI*, 333

ge la, 'se la': *FA*, 175
genelosía, 'genealogía': *FA*, 20
genero, 'enero': *TI*, 1131
grumete, 'apprentice seaman': *TI*, 599

h for *f* in hypercorrect forms: *FA*, 242
ha hi, 'hay': *QTF*, 131
hablar en, 'hablar de': *AI*, 157

idade, 'edad': *FA*, 680
imbiar, 'enviar': *TI*, 511
imperative, apocopated forms of: *TI*, 795
infinitive, inflected: *AI*, 134
inorar, 'ignorar': *TI*, 601
ir + infinitive: *FA*, 59-60

la before feminine nouns beginning with *ha-*: *TI*, 416
lavor (m.): *FA*, 78
le, 'les': *TI*, 954
longo, 'luengo': *FA*, 402

ll for *l* before *ie*: *TI*, 446
lle for *le*: *TI*, 425

media blanca, 'a type of coin': *QTF*, 92
metathesis, of *l* and *d* in imperatives: *FA*, 244

metathesis, of *r* after initial consonant: *FA,* 43
momiento, 'momento': *AI,* 143
morió, 'murió': *TI,* 398
mucho, 'muy': *QTF,* 95

'n, 'en': *FA,* 201
nada, not preceded by a negative: *QTF,* 112
namorado, 'enamorado': *QTF,* 63
natureza, 'naturaleza': *FA,* 42
niegro, 'negro': *FA,* 307
nobrecido, 'ennoblecido': *FA,* 4
nos, 'nosotros': *FA,* 179

ñ for *n* before *ie*: *AI,* 161
ñ for *n* in *sayagués*: *TI,* 91

o for pretonic *u*: *AI,* 163
object pronoun, before verb in affirmative imperative: *FA,* 361
object pronoun, fused with imperative: *FA,* 244
object pronoun, fused with infinitive: *FA,* 228
ossos, 'huesos': *AI,* 322

parcera, 'companion': *FA,* 8
peco = Ptg. *peco,* 'stupid': *QTF,* 69
pecha, 'bribe': *FA,* 549
pedió, 'pidió': *FA,* 90
pelejo, 'pellejo': *FA,* 639
per, 'por': *FA,* 50
perguntalde, 'preguntadle': *CJ,* 672
per[h]echo, 'perfecto': *FA,* 16
perlongado, 'prolongado': *TI,* 235
petrecho, 'tool': *FA,* 27
pevidoso: *FA,* 643
planto, 'llanto': *TI,* 220
prefeción, 'perfección: *FA,* 43
preterite, for present perfect: *FA,* 61
priessa, 'prisa': *FA,* 94
pullas: *TI,* 251

qualquiera, 'cualquier': *FA,* 242

r, metathesis of: *FA,* 43
regelo, 'hielo': *TI,* 231
rehundir, 'refundir': *FA,* 242
reis, 'reyes': *FA,* 391
remocecer, 'remozar': *FA,* 409
resgar, 'rasgar': *TI,* 711
reverdear, 'reverdecer': *TI,* 1027
Roçasvalles, 'Roncesvalles': *QTF,* 103
roncas, 'halberds': *QTF,* 97
rosal, 'rosaleda': *TI,* 1023

sabedoría, 'sabiduría': *FA,* 23
saints, fantastic: *AI,* 304
sal, 'sale': *FA,* 458
saludad, 'soledad': *TI,* 1080
se, 'si': *QTF,* 99
ser + past participle, to express resultant state: *FA,* 9
ser + past participle, to form perfect tenses of intransitive verbs: *TI,* 1053
serena, 'sirena': *TI,* 707
sevandija, 'sabandija': *TI,* 428
si + future subjunctive, followed by present indicative: *FA,* 70
sino, 'signo': *FA,* 5
sinó, 'flaw': *FA,* 85-86
so, 'soy': *FA,* 58

terná, 'tendrá': *TI,* 431
tien, 'tiene': *TI,* 186
tódolas, 'todas las': *TI,* 375
trayo, 'traigo': *AI,* 164
trezientos, 'trescientos': *TI,* 203
tromento, 'tormento': *FA,* 164
turar, 'durar': *TI,* 1113

vos, 'os': *AI,* 313
vuesso, 'vuestro': *AI,* 127

Portuguese

acrecentodo: *QTF,* 329
acupar, 'ocupar': *QTF,* 337
adés, 'right now' (?): *TI,* 604
adjectives, used adverbially: *CJ,* 444
adversairo, 'adversário': *CJ,* 531
-airo, '-ário': *AI,* 90
al, 'something else': *AI,* 27
alcapetor, 'a kind of fish': *CJ,* 254
(*partes d'*) *além,* 'Portuguese possessions overseas': *CJ,* 550
alfenar, 'to dye (the hair) with *alfena*': *CJ,* 234
almotacé: *CJ,* 230
amarelo, as symbol of despair: *CJ,* 424
amorado, 'red': *CJ,* 375
antre, 'entre': *CJ,* 20
aosadas, 'certainly': *QTF,* 43
Apariço, 'Aparício': *QTF,* before line 1
apó-las, 'após as': *CJ,* 229
Aque del-Rei!: *TI,* 791
arrabil, 'rebec': *CJ,* 291
artelharia, 'artilheria': *CJ,* 536
árvore seca: *AI,* 467
assi, 'assim': *AI,* 64
atabaqueiro, 'drummer': *TI,* 8
(*d'*)*avantagem,* 'best': *CJ,* 389
aviar: *QTF,* 303
azevia, 'dab, flounder': *AI,* 269

bareja, 'vareja': *TI,* 275
baxo, 'baixo': *TI,* 618
bengò, 'benza-o': *TI,* 522
béspora, 'véspera': *FA,* 663
bo, 'bom': *QTF,* 77
bofá, 'a boa fé': *QTF,* 86
breviairo, 'breviário': *TI,* 1204
briguigão, 'berbigão': *AI,* 274

caçar, 'atar velas, cabos': *TI,* 624
çafado, 'safado': *AI,* 212
çafio, 'safio': *CJ,* 258
camilha: *QTF,* 336
camisa (*em*): *AI,* 449
canaval, 'canavial': *TI,* 578
capecete, 'head' (fig.): *TI,* 662
ceja (Spanish), for Portuguese *celha*: *QTF,* 494
cenreira, 'stubbornness': *QTF,* 520
charrua, 'a kind of warship': *QTF,* 258
cinquinho, 'a stye of coin': *AI,* 282
cirne, 'cisne': *CJ,* 296
çoçobrar, 'soçobrar': *TI,* 798
color, 'cor': *TI,* 1355
coma, 'como': *AI,* 71
comesta, past participle of *comer*: *QTF,* 307
concrusão, 'conclusão': *CJ,* 361
cranguejo, 'caranguejo': *TI,* 816
cremesim, 'carmesim': *CJ,* 389
crenchas, 'tresses (?); part in hair (?)': *CJ,* 488
curar, 'to care about, be interested in': *QTF,* 74

dé, 'dê' (present subjunctive of *dar*): *FA,* 654
debrũado, 'debruado': *CJ,* 493
deceplina, 'disciplina': *FA,* 666
definite article, omitted after *todo*: *QTF,* 12
definite article, omitted before possessive pronouns: *AI,* before line 1

deles . . . deles, 'some . . . others': *TI,* 1271-72
despois, 'depois': *TI,* 67
devação, 'devoção': *AI,* 469
dixeram, 'disseram': *AI,* 17
doairo, 'elegance; countenance': *QTF,* 372
dozena, 'twelfth': *CJ,* 75

e for pretonic *i*: *QTF,* 20
-ea, -eo, for MPtg. *-eia, -eio*: *AI,* 27
embicado, 'madly in love': *QTF,* 25
em bo-hora: *AI,* 122
emparar, 'amparar': *TI,* 830
entonces, 'então': *AI,* 188
enxarroco, 'a kind of fish': *CJ,* 255
eramá: *AI,* 9
-es for *-eis* in verb forms: *TI,* 498
-ês, rhyming with *-éis*: *QTF,* 30-31
escomungado, 'excomungado': *AI,* 387
escrença, 'excrescência': *QTF,* 371
escudeiro: *AI,* 211
escurana, 'darkness': *TI,* 863
espera, 'esfera': *CJ,* before line 1
espíritu, variant forms: *AI,* 452
esprital, 'hospital': *CJ,* 148
estar + present participle to form progressive tense: *AI,* before line 1
estremos: *CJ,* 190
estromento, 'instrumento': *QTF,* 208

facundo, 'marvelous (?)': *CJ,* 591
fantesia, 'presumption': *QTF,* 536
farnesia, 'frenesi': *CJ,* 85
farnétego, 'frenético': *TI,* 1168
fermosa, 'formoso': *AI,* 75
fidalgo afidalgado: *QTF,* 323
(*tomar*) *figas*: *QTF,* 424
fim (f.): *TI,* before line 1301
forioso, 'furioso': *CJ,* before line 85
frol, 'flor': *CJ,* 497

gamo, 'cuckold': *AI,* 8
g'eu, 'já eu': *TI,* 549
grão, 'grande': *CJ,* 457
grumete: *TI,* 599
guar-te, 'guarda-te': *QTF,* 451

há hi, 'há': *CJ,* 314
hi, 'there': *CJ,* 314
hi há, 'há': *CJ,* 314

i for pretonic *e*: *QTF,* 20
i, 'ide': *AI,* 348
imos, 'vamos': *TI,* 792
imperative, apocopated forms of: *QTF,* 451
imperative in *-de*: *AI,* 3
inda, 'ainda': *AI,* 216
ira má: *AI,* 9
isto, in expressions of time: *QTF,* 533

Jupiter, 'Júpiter': *CJ,* 116

lavrar, 'embroider': *QTF,* 505
leixar, 'deixar': *AI,* 10
lhe, 'lhes': *AI,* 292
los, las for *os, as,* after words ending in *-s*: *CJ,* 229
lũa, 'lua': *CJ,* 60

má (*doairo*): *QTF,* 372
maginar, 'imaginar': *CJ,* 595
má-hora: *AI,* 9
maíça, '?': *CJ,* 477
mau pesar: *AI,* 67
mei migo, 'meu amigo': *TI,* 802
Meoterrano, 'Medioterrâneo': *CJ,* 529
mercêa, 'mercê': *TI,* 622
mercolina: *TI,* 746
Meredião, 'the south': *CJ,* 58

messajaria, 'message': *CJ*, 88
mi, 'mim': *AI*, 357
micer, 'sir': *AI*, 303
milhor, 'melhor': *AI*, 82
moço de esporas: *QTF*, before line 1
(*a*) *molhos*, 'many': *QTF*, 312
moradia, 'royal pension': *QTF*, before line 1
muitieramá: *AI*, 9

não, after a negative expression: *QTF*, 32
nécio, 'néscio': *AI*, 89
nem, followed by *não*: QTF, 32
no for *o* after *não*: *QTF*, 68
nô-mais, 'não mais': *AI*, 184

o for pretonic *u*: *QTF*, 20
ò, 'ao': *AI*, 202
oaths, neutralized: *QTF*, 258
olhade, 'olhai': *AI*, 3

par Deus, 'por Deus': *QTF*, 125
partitive: *QTF*, 491
(*falar*) *passo*, '(to speak) softly': *AI*, 303
peitar, 'to pay': *FA*, 589
pendença, 'pendência': *QTF*, 172
per, 'por': *QTF*, 14
pera, 'para': *AI*, before line 1
pesar de Deus: *QTF*, 258
(*estar a*) *pique*: *AI*, 26
pluperfect for conditional: *QTF*, 188
poer, 'pôr': *QTF*, 491
pola, 'pela': *AI*, 76
polo meu, 'for my sake': *QTF*, 464
por ende, 'there': *CJ*, 290
prefia, 'porfia': *QTF*, 265
preminência, 'preeminência': *CJ*, 121
prez, 'determination; eloquence': *CJ*, 14
quant'eu, 'in my opinion': *AI*, 89
quási, 'quase': *QTF*, 35

r for *l* after consonant: *CJ*, 361
rascão, 'loafer': *AI*, 210
reboto, 'awkward, unskilled': *TI*, 684
(*de*) *recado*, 'prudent': *AI*, 423
refião, 'rufião': *AI*, 205
renegar, 'to curse': *QTF*, 530
retrogado, 'retrógrado': *CJ*, 168
rezão, 'razão': *AI*, 292
rosmear, 'resmungar': *AI*, 409
ruivo, 'a kind of fish': *CJ*, 205

sa, 'sua': *QTF*, 433
sam, 'sou': *QTF*, 27
senhos, 'one apiece': *QTF*, 216
si, 'sim': *AI*, 64
siquer, 'at least': *AI*, 61
spirito, 'espíritu': *AI*, 452
suidade, 'saudade': *TI*, 1098
tirte, 'tira-te': *TI*, 795
trama, 'calamity': *QTF*, 455
treçado, 'terçado': *CJ*, 587
tromenta, 'tormenta': *AI*, 441
trosquiar, 'tosquiar': *TI*, 1239

u for pretonic o: *QTF*, 20
u, 'where': *TI*, 793
ũa, 'uma': *AI*, before line 1

verão, 'spring': *TI*, 67
viço, 'pleasure, idleness': *QTF*, 196
vinagreiro: *AI*, 261
vinta nove, 'vinte e nove': *FA*, 642

$8.00

Gil Vicente
Farces and Festival Plays

Though three-quarters of Gil Vicente's plays are wholly or partly in Portuguese, most American students and teachers of Spanish know him only through his Castilian works. Vicente's Spanish plays, however, do not reveal the full measure of his achievement as a dramatist. They include none of his court entertainments, which belong to a rich international tradition with no other real counterpart in sixteenth-century Hispanic literature; nor do they include any of his farces, perhaps his most enduring contribution to the Hispanic theater. The present edition provides reliable texts of these two types of plays; the introduction and notes are designed to make them accessible to English-speaking students of Spanish who have had no previous acquaintance with the literature of Portugal.

Thomas R. Hart is professor of romance languages at the University of Oregon, and editor of *Comparative Literature.* Professor Hart received his B.A. and Ph.D. from Yale; before coming to Oregon, he taught at Amherst College, Harvard, Johns Hopkins, and Emory. His scholarly interests center in the medieval and renaissance literature of Spain and Portugal. In 1962, he published an edition of Vicente's Spanish plays in the *Clásicos castellanos* series; in 1965, an edition of his poems, both Spanish and Portuguese, in the *Biblioteca Anaya.* He has twice received Fulbright grants: in 1950-51, to study romance philology at the University of Montpellier, France, and in 1966-67 to work in Spain and Portugal on this edition of Gil Vicente.

poras a buscar farelos, & diz logo

Apariço.

¶ Quem tem farelos.
Ordo. Quien tiene farelos.
Apa. Ordonho Ordonho espera mi
oo fi de puta roim
çapatos tẽs amarelos
ja nam falas a ninguem.
Ordo. Como te va companhero
Apa. Seu moço cum escudeyro
como me pode a mi yr bem.

Ordonho.

¶ Quien es tu amo di hermano?
Apa. He o demo que me tome,
morremos ambos de fome
e de lazeyra todo anno.
Ordo. Con quien biue? Apa. q̃ sey eu
viue assi per hi pelado
coma podengo escaldado.
Ordo. De q̃ sirue? Apa. De sandeu
¶ Pentear e jejuar
todo dia sem comer
cantar e sempre tanger
sospirar e bocejar.
Sempre anda falando soo
faz hũas trouas tam frias
tam sem graça, tam vazias
que he cousa pera auer doo.
¶ E presume dembicado
que com isto rayno eu
tres annos ha que sam seu
e nunca lhe vi cruzado.
Mas segundo nos gastamos
hum tostam nos dura hum mes.
Ordo. Cuerpo de san que comeis?
Apa. Né de pam nam nos fartamos.

Ordonho.

¶ Y el cauallo? Apa. Estaa na pelle
que lhe faraa ja a ossada,
nam comemos quasi nada

e hungir mais desforçado
e todo o dia atirado
se lhe vay em se gabar.
¶ Est'outro dia ali num beco
deram lhe tantas pancadas
tantas tantas que coçadas.
Ord. Y con q̃? Apa. Cũ arrocho sec
Ordo. Hi hi hi hi hi hi.
Apa. Folguey tanto. Ord. Y el call
Apa. E elle calar e leuar,
assi assi ma ora assi.
¶ Tem alta noyte de andar
de dia sempre encerrado,
porque anda mal roupado
nam ousa de se mostrar.
Tem tam ledo seu cear
como se tiuesse que,
e eu nam tenho que lhe dar
nem elle tem que lhe eu de.
¶ Toma hum pedaço de pam
e hum rabam engelhado,
e chanta nelle bocado
coma cam.
Nam sey como se mantem
que nam estaa debelitado
Ordo. Basta le ser namorado
en demaas si le va bien

Aparico.

Comẽdo ho demo a molher
nen casada nen solteira
nenhũa negra tripeira
nam no quer
Ordo. Seraa escudero poco
o desdichado.
Apa. Mas a poder de pelado
da em seco.
¶ Todas querem que lhe dem
e nam curam de cantar
sabe que quem tem que dar
lhe vay bem.
querem mais hum bo preso